D1708991

NYSTCE ESOL (116) Study Guide

TEST PREP AND PRACTICE TEST QUESTIONS FOR THE ENGLISH TO SPEAKERS OF OTHER LANGUAGES EXAM

Table of Contents

Introduction

Congratulations on choosing to take the New York State Teacher Certification Examinations: English to Speakers of Other Languages (116) test! By purchasing this book, you've taken the first step toward becoming an ESOL teacher.

This guide will provide you with a detailed overview of the New York State Teacher Certification Examinations: English to Speakers of Other Languages (NYSTCE: ESOL) test, so you know exactly what to expect on test day. We'll take you through all the concepts covered on the test and give you the opportunity to test your knowledge with practice questions. Even if it's been a while since you last took a major test, don't worry; we'll make sure you're more than ready!

What Is the NYSTCE?

New York State Teacher Certification Examinations (NYSTCE) are part of a testing program that assesses an examinee's knowledge and skills in accordance with professionally accepted standards of teaching in New York State. The NYSTCE website, www.nystce.nesinc.com, contains information detailing the role of the NYSTCE tests in determining teaching certification and what scores are required.

What's on the ESOL CST?

The content in this guide will prepare you for the New York State Teacher Certification Examinations: English to Speakers of Other Languages test. This test assesses whether you possess the knowledge and skills necessary to become an ESOL teacher using both a multiple-choice section and a written section that includes one constructed-response essay question.

You have a maximum of three hours and fifteen minutes to complete the entire test. The test always has a total of ninety multiple-choice questions and one constructed-response question; however, the number of questions specific to each subject is approximate (see the table below). The test makers recommend allotting 135 minutes to the multiple-choice questions and one hour to the constructed-response question. Expect to write about 400 – 600 words for the constructed-response question.

NYSTCE: ESOL CST 116 Content

Domain	Approximate Number of Questions	Approximate Percentage of Test Score
Language and language learning	15 multiple choice	13%
Knowledge of English Language Learners	15 multiple choice	13%
ESOL instructional planning, practices, and assessment	15 multiple choice	13%
Instructing English Language Learners in English language arts	15 multiple choice	14%
Instructing English Language Learners in the content areas	15 multiple choice	14%
ESOL professional environments	15 multiple choice	13%
Analysis, synthesis, and application	1 constructed response	20%
Total	always 90	3 hours and 15 minutes

You will answer approximately fifteen questions (13 percent of the test) about language and language learning. You will be expected to understand the development of second-language acquisition (including the cognitive processes involved), the processes through which second languages are acquired from first languages, the nature of bilingualism, and the variations that can affect the process of language acquisition. You must also know the New York State Education Department's five levels of English language proficiency (entering, emerging, transitioning, expanding, and commanding). Finally, this section may test your knowledge of applied linguistics and English conventions and structure, such as grammar and syntax.

You will answer approximately fifteen questions (13 percent of the test) about knowledge of English Language Learners. This section tests your knowledge of diverse learners and ability to apply pedagogy in order to reach learners of different backgrounds and needs. You should understand the nature of culture and be familiar with the major theories and research related to it. Review your knowledge of the English Language Learner subpopulations as defined by New York State (Newcomers, Developing English Language Learners, Long-term English Language Learners, Students with Inconsistent/Interrupted Formal Education [SIFE], English Language Learners with Disabilities, and Former English Language Learners).

You will answer approximately fifteen questions (13 percent of the test) about ESOL instructional planning, practices, and assessment. You will be expected to demonstrate a knowledge of effective goal setting, English literacy instruction, relevant state and local learning standards like NYCCLS, the New York State Bilingual Common Core Initiative—New Language Arts Provisions and various state and national standards, and designing instruction aligned with these standards. The role of formal and informal assessment tools in ESOL programs as well as how those assessments can be used to plan and adjust classroom instruction will be covered in this section. Be aware of the shortcomings of assessment methods in evaluating English Language Learners. Review methods of promoting classroom engagement, varying learning materials, and maintaining a safe and respectful learning environment.

You will answer approximately fifteen questions (14 percent of the test) about instructing English Language Learners in English language arts. This section assesses your ability to promote communicative language and student literacy development in English with standards-based instruction in listening and speaking, reading, and writing in various situations, both formal and informal. Be aware of differentiated instructional methods for English Language Learners of varying proficiency according to the New York State Bilingual Common Core Initiative—New Language Arts Provisions and the importance of supporting English language arts learning for all ELLs, regardless of proficiency.

You will answer approximately fifteen questions (14 percent of the test) about instructing English Language Learners in the content areas. Prepare to demonstrate your understanding of your role in supporting ELLs' ability to achieve in general academics. This requires a knowledge of state academic learning standards, English language and literacy skills specific to certain academic disciplines, and the interdisciplinary nature of language learning and general education. Expect to encounter questions about promoting learning skills such as test-taking, research, note taking, and other learning strategies and the ESOL educator's role in promoting these among ELLs.

You will answer approximately fifteen questions (13 percent of the test) about ESOL professional environments. This section will assess your knowledge of the foundations of ESOL programming and its research methods. Be aware of key court cases, current research and development in the field, and the nature of professional development (including goal-setting, self-reflection, and addressing stakeholder feedback). Your role as an ESOL teacher also includes serving as an advocate and resource for learners, their families, and administration; demonstrate an understanding of collaboration with students and their families in the community.

In the constructed-response question, you should be able to evaluate student understanding and design instruction that will achieve specific learning goals. You will be tested on your ability to analyze information about a group of ELLs, identifying their strengths and designing appropriate activities or instructional strategies that enable them to achieve grade-specific New York State learning standards.

Expect to defend the efficacy of your strategy. You will also be expected to demonstrate your ability to tailor your attention and instruction toward a student with specific needs to help that student achieve the grade-level standard. Your constructed response must demonstrate your knowledge of pedagogy and application of pedagogical skills.

How Is the ESOL CST Scored?

On the ESOL CST, the number of correctly answered questions is used to create your scaled score. Scores are scaled to a number in the range of 100 – 300; a passing score is 220. The score shows your performance on the test as a whole and is scaled to allow comparison across various versions of the tests. The multiple-choice questions are equally weighted. The 90 multiple-choice questions consist of 80 percent of your overall score, while the constructed-response essay comprises the other 20 percent. There is no penalty for guessing on the ESOL CST, so be sure to eliminate answer choices and answer every question. If you still do not know the answer, guess; you may get it right!

Your score report will be available three to five weeks after testing. Score reports contain the overall scaled score and diagnostic information that indicates your performance on the domains of the test. You can use diagnostic information to better understand your strengths and weaknesses in the material. Scores are automatically added to your certification application file and reported to the New York State Education Department.

How Is the NYSTCE: ESOL CST Administered?

The NYSTCE ESOL CST is available at testing centers across the nation. To find a testing center near you, go to www.nystce.nesinc.com. This is a computer-administered test; the website allows you to take tutorials to acclimate yourself to the computerized format.

On the day of your test, be sure to arrive at least thirty minutes early and bring proof of registration and a valid photo ID. You are allowed no personal effects in the testing area and will be provided with a locker to store them. Tobacco products, weapons, and visitors (including friends, relatives, and children) are not permitted in the testing center at all, and bringing these may be cause for dismissal, forfeiture of your testing fees, and cancellation of your scores. For details on what to expect at your testing center, refer to the NYSTCE website.

ABOUT CIRRUS TEST PREP

Cirrus Test Prep study guides are designed by current and former educators and are tailored to meet your needs as an incoming educator. Our guides offer all of the resources necessary to help you pass teacher certification tests across the nation.

Cirrus clouds are graceful, wispy clouds characterized by their high altitude. Just like cirrus clouds, Cirrus Test Prep's goal is to help educators "aim high" when it comes to obtaining their teacher certification and entering the classroom.

ABOUT THIS GUIDE

This guide will help you master the most important test topics and also develop critical test-taking skills. We have built features into our books to prepare you for your tests and increase your score. Along with a detailed summary of the test's format, content, and scoring, we offer an in-depth overview of the content knowledge required to pass the test. Our sidebars provide interesting information, highlight key concepts, and review content so that you can solidify your understanding of the exam's concepts. Test your knowledge with sample questions and detailed answer explanations in the text that help you think through the problems on the exam and two full-length practice tests that reflect the content and format of the ESOL. We're pleased you've chosen Cirrus to be a part of your professional journey.

Part I: Review

Linguistics

L inguistics is the scientific study of language. Like any other scientific discipline, it is a complex field in which specialists use industry jargon, conduct rigorous studies, and publish significant findings in academic journals. While it is not necessary for a language teacher to be a linguist, a basic understanding of linguistic theory and its cultural implications is essential to understanding how students acquire language.

THEORY

Linguistic theorists seek to define and understand language by breaking it down into several components. **Phonetics** is the study of the production of sounds in speech, while the closely related field of **phonology** looks at the sounds and patterns of particular languages. **Intonation** is the way the voice rises and falls in speech, and **stress** is emphasis placed on syllables or words. The smallest unit of meaning in a language is a **morpheme**, and the study of how morphemes are combined to make words is called **morphology**. **Syntax**, similarly, examines how words are constructed into phrases or sentences. **Semantics**, on the other hand, is the study of meaning in language.

PHONETICS

In order to study and explain how humans produce sounds, linguists have developed a system of **transcription**, a way to visually represent sounds. Perhaps the best-known transcription system is the **International Phonetic Alphabet (IPA)**, seen in Figure 1.1 on the following page. It is not necessary for an ESOL teacher to know the IPA completely, but it helps to have an understanding of the transcriptions for the sounds used in American English.

THE INTERNATIONAL PHONETIC ALPHABET (revised to 2015)

CONSONANTS (PULMONIC)

© 2015 IPA

	Bilabial	Labiodental	Dental	Alveolar	Postalveolar	Retroflex	Palatal	Velar	Uvular	Pharyngeal	Glottal
Plosive	p b			t d		ʈ ɖ	c ɟ	k g	q ɢ		ʔ
Nasal	m	ɱ		n		ɳ	ɲ	ŋ	N		
Trill	ʙ			r					ʀ		
Tap or Flap		ⱱ		ɾ		ɽ					
Fricative	ɸ β	f v	θ ð	s z	ʃ ʒ	ʂ ʐ	ç ʝ	x ɣ	χ ʁ	ħ ʕ	h ɦ
Lateral fricative				ɬ ɮ							
Approximant		ʋ		ɹ		ɻ	j	ɰ			
Lateral approximant				l		ɭ	ʎ	ʟ			

Symbols to the right in a cell are voiced, to the left are voiceless. Shaded areas denote articulations judged impossible.

CONSONANTS (NON-PULMONIC)

Clicks	Voiced implosives	Ejectives
⊙ Bilabial	ɓ Bilabial	' Examples:
ǀ Dental	ɗ Dental/alveolar	p' Bilabial
ǃ (Post)alveolar	ʄ Palatal	t' Dental/alveolar
ǂ Palatoalveolar	ɠ Velar	k' Velar
ǁ Alveolar lateral	ʛ Uvular	s' Alveolar fricative

OTHER SYMBOLS

ʍ Voiceless labial-velar fricative

w Voiced labial-velar approximant

ɥ Voiced labial-palatal approximant

ʜ Voiceless epiglottal fricative

ʢ Voiced epiglottal fricative

ʡ Epiglottal plosive

ɕ ʑ Alveolo-palatal fricatives

ɺ Voiced alveolar lateral flap

ɧ Simultaneous ʃ and x

Affricates and double articulations can be represented by two symbols joined by a tie bar if necessary. t͡s k͡p

VOWELS

	Front	Central	Back
Close	i y	ɨ ʉ	ɯ u
	ɪ ʏ		ʊ
Close-mid	e ø	ɘ ɵ	ɤ o
		ə	
Open-mid	ɛ œ	ɜ ɞ	ʌ ɔ
	æ	ɐ	
Open	a ɶ		ɑ ɒ

Where symbols appear in pairs, the one to the right represents a rounded vowel.

SUPRASEGMENTALS

ˈ Primary stress

ˌ Secondary stress   ˌfoʊnəˈtɪʃən

ː Long   eː

ˑ Half-long   eˑ

˘ Extra-short   ĕ

| Minor (foot) group

‖ Major (intonation) group

. Syllable break   ɹi.ækt

‿ Linking (absence of a break)

TONES AND WORD ACCENTS

	LEVEL			CONTOUR	
e̋ or ˥	Extra high		ě or ˨˩˦	Rising	
é	˦ High		ê	Falling	
ē	˧ Mid		e᷄	High rising	
è	˨ Low		e᷅	Low rising	
ȅ	˩ Extra low		e᷈	Rising-falling	
ꜜ Downstep			↗ Global rise		
ꜛ Upstep			↘ Global fall		

DIACRITICS

Some diacritics may be placed above a symbol with a descender, e.g. ŋ̊

̥ Voiceless	n̥ d̥		̤ Breathy voiced	b̤ a̤		̪ Dental	t̪ d̪
̬ Voiced	s̬ t̬		̰ Creaky voiced	b̰ a̰		̺ Apical	t̺ d̺
ʰ Aspirated	tʰ dʰ		̼ Linguolabial	t̼ d̼		̻ Laminal	t̻ d̻
̹ More rounded	ɔ̹		ʷ Labialized	tʷ dʷ		̃ Nasalized	ẽ
̜ Less rounded	ɔ̜		ʲ Palatalized	tʲ dʲ		ⁿ Nasal release	dⁿ
̟ Advanced	u̟		ˠ Velarized	tˠ dˠ		ˡ Lateral release	dˡ
̠ Retracted	e̠		ˤ Pharyngealized	tˤ dˤ		̚ No audible release	d̚
̈ Centralized	ë		̴ Velarized or pharyngealized	ɫ			
̽ Mid-centralized	e̽		̝ Raised	e̝ (ɹ̝ = voiced alveolar fricative)			
̩ Syllabic	n̩		̞ Lowered	e̞ (β̞ = voiced bilabial approximant)			
̯ Non-syllabic	e̯		̘ Advanced Tongue Root	e̘			
˞ Rhoticity	ɚ a˞		̙ Retracted Tongue Root	e̙			

Figure 1.1. International Phonetic Alphabet (IPA) Chart

Available at http://www.internationalphoneticassociation.org/content/ipa-chart, available under a Creative Commons Attribution-Sharealike 3.0 Unported License. Copyright © 2015 International Phonetic Association.

To help ESOL students improve their pronunciation, it is important to understand some phonetic terms relevant to issues that ESOL students might encounter. In teaching ESOL, the concepts of **voiced** and **voiceless** are especially important, as a number of letter pairs in the English language have only this distinction: **voiced** sounds are made by vibrating the vocal chords, while **voiceless** sounds are made without vibrating the vocal chords. The /p/ and /b/ sounds, for example, are made at the same **place of articulation**, but the /b/ sound is voiced while the /p/ sound is not.

One can determine whether a consonant is voiced or voiceless by putting a hand to his or her throat while making the sound. If it is voiced, the throat will vibrate. For example, when someone makes an /s/ sound, his or her vocal chords should not vibrate; when making the /z/ sound, on the other hand, they should.

Place of articulation is the point where two speech organs come together to make a sound, as in the top and bottom lips coming together to produce the **labial** consonant sound of the letter –*m*. Some words in the English language require **nasalization**, in which air comes through the nose when making a sound such as /n/, while still others require **aspiration**, in which a sound is made with a burst of air out of the mouth as in the /h/ in *hope*. Together, voice, articulation, nasalization, and aspiration create the sounds that form words. In instruction for English learners, these concepts are helpful for being able to teach proper pronunciation.

> **TEACHING TIP**
>
> Words sound different in isolation than they do in the course of everyday speech. **Connected speech** occurs when speakers simplify sounds and run words together. ESOL students will likely need help in understanding the elements of connected speech and in trying to use it to sound more natural in their interactions.

English learners will still, however, encounter challenges when it comes to understanding and being understood. **Assimilation** occurs when a speech sound changes due to the influence of nearby sounds; thus English language learners must study not only the individual sounds but also the unique sounds that result from combinations of letters. A **diphthong**, for example, is the sound made when one vowel sound blends into another vowel sound in one syllable (as in the /ou/ sound in *loud*); diphthongs pose a challenge to nonnative speakers because they add to the list of vowel sounds that must be learned.

Consonant clusters, groups of two or more consonants (as in /pl/ in *place*, /nt/ in *bent*, and /sp/ in *whisper*), pose a similar challenge, as learners must know not only the sounds made by the individual letters but also the unique sounds formed by their pairs. Some learners may attempt to approach these pairs by pronouncing both letters and inserting a vowel sound in between them, saying "puh-lace" for *place*, for example. This is known as **epenthesis**, inserting an additional sound in the middle of a word.

Still other facets of pronunciation result from the casual nature of everyday speech: words and phrases are adjusted to make speech as easy and free-flowing as possible. **Voicing**, for example, occurs when a voiceless consonant changes to a voiced consonant because of nearby sounds. For example, the /f/ in *reefs* is unvoiced so the /s/ sound is also unvoiced; however, the /v/ in *leaves* is voiced, so the /s/ is also voiced. **Elision** occurs when sounds are omitted from the pronunciation of a word, usually because the omission makes the words easier to use in everyday speech. For example, *mac and cheese* is usually pronounced as *mac 'n' cheese*.

Metathesis occurs when sounds are rearranged in a word, as when *iron* is pronounced *iern*.

SAMPLE QUESTIONS

1) **Which of the following IPA symbols represents the sound of the consonant cluster /ng/ in the word *swing*?**

    A.   [θ]
    B.   [æ]
    C.   [ŋ]
    D.   [ʃ]

    Answers:

    A.   Incorrect. This symbol represents the /th/ sound in *there*.
    B.   Incorrect. This symbol represents the vowel sound /a/ as in *cat*.
    C.   Correct. This symbol represents the /ng/ sound.
    D.   Incorrect. This symbol represents the /sh/ sound in *ship*.

2) **Which of the following would most likely explain why a student is having problems being understood when she says the words *think, wreath, the,* and *ruthless*?**

    A.   She is not distinguishing between the voiced and unvoiced /th/ sounds.
    B.   She has problems making /r/ sounds.
    C.   She is not putting stress on the correct syllables.
    D.   She needs more instruction in semantics.

    Answers:

    A.   Correct. Because the /th/ sound is in all the words, both voiced and unvoiced, this is the best answer.
    B.   Incorrect. The /r/ sound does not occur in all of the words, so this is not the problem.
    C.   Incorrect. Three of the words only have one syllable, so stress is not an issue.
    D.   Incorrect. Semantics deals with meaning, which is not relevant to her pronunciation issue.

INTONATION AND STRESS

Though they are two separate notions, intonation and stress often go hand in hand in ESOL instruction. **Intonation** is the way the voice rises and falls in speech, and **stress** is the emphasis placed on particular syllables or words. Intonation is related to pitch, as in the way an English speaker's voice rises at the end of a question as opposed to a statement. Stress, on the other hand, can be seen as more rhythmic: stressed syllables or words are louder and longer than unstressed syllables or words and therefore receive emphasis by breaking the rhythm of the sentence.

Vowel reduction, the shortening or diminishing of a vowel sound, occurs with many unstressed vowels in English. The most common example of this kind of reduction is the replacement of a vowel with the schwa sound, ə, as in *hundred*, *again*, and *amazing*.

Native English speakers may find that intonation and stress come naturally to them; however, English learners may not hear or sense these things as easily. As such, ESOL teachers must explicitly instruct students in these concepts and provide ample opportunity for practice and observation.

SAMPLE QUESTION

3) **In which of the following would a speaker most likely have rising intonation?**

   A.   Please bring some bread.
   B.   I am afraid.
   C.   Frankie and Johnny are waiting outside.
   D.   Do you want to watch a movie?

Answers:

   A.   Incorrect. This sentence would likely end in falling intonation.
   B.   Incorrect. This sentence would likely end in falling intonation.
   C.   Incorrect. Rising intonation at the end of this sentence would change it to a question.
   D.   **Correct.** English speakers usually end a question with rising intonation.

MORPHOLOGY

Morphology is the study of word forms and their component parts. A word is considered the smallest unit of language that can stand on its own, while a **morpheme** is the smallest unit of meaning in a language. The word *player*, for example, is made up of two morphemes: *play* (which is also a word on its own) and /er/ (which cannot stand on its own).

Morphology breaks words down into morpheme types. A **bound morpheme** must be attached to a word to have meaning, such as /er/ in the previous example, whereas a **free morpheme** (like *play*) can stand on its own.

<table>
<tr><td>

DID YOU KNOW?

Inflectional morphemes can serve to make a word plural (girl/girls), indicate a comparative or superlative (fast/fast*er*), or change a verb's tense (climb/climb*ed*). Derivational morphemes change a word's meaning (run/*re*run) or its part of speech (drink/drink*able*).

</td></tr>
</table>

A **stem/root** is a base word, often a free morpheme, to which other morphemes can be added. An **affix** (either a prefix or a suffix) is a bound morpheme that can be added to a root word to change its meaning, grammatical function, tense, case, or gender. **Inflectional morphemes** are bound morphemes that do not greatly alter the meaning or part of speech of a word, whereas **derivational morphemes** create a word that has a new meaning or part of speech.

SAMPLE QUESTIONS

4)   The underlined part of the word *rebuilding* is

A.   a bound morpheme.

B.   an affix.

C.   a diphthong.

D.   a stem or root.

Answers:

A.   Incorrect. A bound morpheme must be attached to a word to have meaning.

B.   Incorrect. An affix is added to a root word to change its meaning, as *re–* and *–ing* do here.

C.   Incorrect. *Diphthong* is a phonetic term describing a type of vowel sound made up of two vowel sounds.

D.   Correct. *Build* is the root/stem of this word.

5)   Which of the following statements is/are true?

A.   A morpheme is the smallest unit of meaning in a language.

B.   All words are morphemes, but not all morphemes are words.

C.   An affix is a free morpheme.

D.   Both A and B are true statements.

Answers:

A.   Incorrect. This statement is true, but so is choice B.

B.   Incorrect. This statement is true, but so is choice A.

C.   Incorrect. An affix is a bound morpheme.

D.   **Correct.** Both A and B are true statements.

SYNTAX

Syntax examines how words are arranged into phrases and sentences. Of particular importance in the linguistic study of syntax are the writings of Noam Chomsky, whose theories of **transformational grammar** revolutionized the study of language by turning the focus away from semiotics and meaning, toward the system of rules that dictate proper sentence construction. Although it is not quite so simple, many people think of syntax simply as grammar, which can be a useful way to distinguish it from other linguistic terms. Grammar and parts of speech are looked at in more detail in the section "Grammar and Parts of Speech."

SAMPLE QUESTION

6)   **Syntax is concerned with which of the following?**

A.   how words are combined to convey meaning

B.   stages of second-language acquisition

C.   ensuring transfer of language skills from L1 to L2

D.   how words are formed into phrases or sentences

Answers:

A.   Incorrect. This is semantics.

B.   Incorrect. Syntax is a linguistic, not a language acquisition, term.

C.   Incorrect. Syntax is a linguistic, not a language acquisition, term.

D.   **Correct.** Syntax is closely aligned with grammar.

SEMANTICS

Semantics, or the study of meaning in language, looks at how words are put together to create meaning. **Connotation** is the emotional association of a word, while **denotation** is a word's actual dictionary definition. The difference between the two is especially important for teaching ESOL students, as they do not possess the connotative understanding of word meanings that native speakers often have without realizing it. For example, a native speaker may intuitively know the difference between *wise*, *crafty*, and *bright*, while an English language learner may recognize them only as synonyms for *smart*.

The most effective way for students to learn the connotative meanings of common words is to immerse themselves in the language. Reading books by English-speaking authors, watching English movies and television, and talking to native speakers will allow English language learners to begin building their connotative understandings.

It is also important to explicitly teach the use of idioms to ESOL students. An **idiom** is a group of words whose meaning cannot be deduced from the meanings of the individual words in the group; put together, the words take a new meaning. For example, *to feel under the weather* is an idiom meaning to feel ill, while *to jump on the bandwagon* means to follow another's example.

SAMPLE QUESTIONS

7) **Semantics could be applied to which aspect of everyday English?**
   A.   the use of quotation marks in quoted speech
   B.   the use of idioms
   C.   the pronunciation of vowels
   D.   the use of commas with conjunctions

   Answers:
   A.   Incorrect. The use of quotation marks is a matter of syntax.
   B.   **Correct.** An idiom's meaning is connotative and thus a matter of semantics.
   C.   Incorrect. Phonetics deals with the pronunciation of sounds.
   D.   Incorrect. Commas are also a matter of syntax.

8) **Which of the following statements, said while eating Cajun food for the first time at a friend's house, would suggest that an ESOL student has a good grasp of connotative understanding?**
   A.   This cuisine is delicious.
   B.   This slop is delicious.
   C.   This feed is delicious.
   D.   This stuff that people and animals eat is delicious.

   Answers:
   A.   **Correct.** The use of the word *cuisine* demonstrates an understanding of the positive connotations of the word.
   B.   Incorrect. *Slop* has a negative connotation and would not be appropriate.
   C.   Incorrect. *Feed* has a connotation associated with livestock and would not be appropriate.
   D.   Incorrect. This is a dictionary, or denotative, definition.

DIFFERENCES AMONG LANGUAGES

In ESOL instruction, it is important to know that there are differences in the phonology, morphology, semantics, and syntax among the thousands of languages spoken in the world. Therefore, language concepts that seem innately familiar to native English speakers may be unknown to a native Japanese speaker, for example. One important concept related to language differences is that of *interference*. *Interference*, or *negative transfer*, occurs when language learners incorrectly apply the rules of their native language to the rules of the language they are learning.

Table 1.1. Common Instances of Interference in Native Spanish Speakers

Incorrect	Correct	Explanation
I won one prize!	I won a prize!	The Spanish language does not distinguish between the indefinite article (*uno*/a) and the number one (*uno*/one).
I was exhausted after a long day in the sun; he was bright and hot today.	I was exhausted after a long day in the sun; it was bright and hot today.	In Spanish, nouns take genders, but in English they do not; *sun* in Spanish is a masculine noun, so the student incorrectly inserted a masculine pronoun.
Don't know.	I don't know.	The Spanish language allows speakers to drop subject pronouns when they are unnecessary; in English, this is less common and usually is not considered grammatically correct.
My mom made wonderfuls cookies for the bake sale.	My mom made wonderful cookies for the bake sale.	In Spanish, adjectives and articles must agree in number with the noun they are modifying; in English, plurality is implied only by the noun.
Have seen you my sunglasses?	Have you seen my sunglasses?	The construction of questions is different in Spanish and English; while the verb precedes the subject in Spanish, the reverse is usually true in English.

Of course, ESOL teachers cannot be expected to be familiar with the characteristics of every language in the world, but it is useful to have a basic understanding of differences between English and the native language(s) of ESOL students in the classroom. Teachers should listen for consistent mistakes among students from similar language groups to determine if these mistakes might be due to interference.

Furthermore, it helps to understand that languages are divided into families according to ancestral and structural similarities. For example, both English and Spanish are in the Indo-European language family because of their shared origins, but they are in different branches of that family (Germanic and Romance, respectively) based on their structures. However, it might surprise many Americans to learn that languages that come from similar parts of the world are not necessarily related. Mandarin Chinese and Japanese, for example, are from different language families. Similarly, several indigenous languages in Central and South America, many of which are spoken in conjunction with Spanish, are from different language families.

> **HELPFUL HINT**
>
> "False friend" cognates appear to be the same word but are not: *librería* in Spanish means *bookstore*, *affluence* in French means *a crowd of people*, and in German *gift* means *poison*.

SAMPLE QUESTION

9) A Spanish speaker who says, "I *have* fifteen years," when asked how old he is, is likely making a mistake because of

  A. morphemes.

  B. pronunciation.

  C. metathesis.

  D. interference.

Answers:

  A. Incorrect. The use of the word *have* is not related to morphemes.

  B. Incorrect. The use of the word *have* is not an issue of mispronunciation.

  C. Incorrect. Metathesis deals with switching sounds in a word.

  D. Correct. The student is mistakenly applying the word *have* to talk about age, a rule that applies in Spanish but not English.

LINGUISTICS AND CULTURE

To master the English language, nonnative speakers must learn much more than the basic rules of English grammar; indeed, they must have an understanding of the significant relationship between culture and language and the implications of culture on their interactions with other English speakers.

PRAGMATICS

The field of **pragmatics** goes beyond the concept of semantics to examine meaning in context. In pragmatics, study focuses on **utterances**, speech acts of one or more words that contain a single idea and are surrounded on both sides by silence. The context of the situation and the relationship between speaker and listener lend additional, significant meaning to the words and phrases. For example, when one friend shows up thirty minutes late for a lunch date and the waiting friend says, "Really?" it is understood by both that the question is not about the true existence or presence of the late friend, but about the untimely arrival.

SAMPLE QUESTION

10) **Pragmatics is concerned with**

    A.   the way the voice rises and falls in speech.

    B.   how humans produce sounds.

    C.   meaning in context.

    D.   how words are constructed into phrases or sentences.

Answers:

    A.   Incorrect. Intonation deals with the way the voice rises and falls in speech.

    B.   Incorrect. Phonetics deals with how humans produce sounds.

    C.   **Correct.** Pragmatics examines meaning in context.

    D.   Incorrect. Syntax deals with how words are constructed into phrases or sentences.

SOCIOLINGUISTICS

Sociolinguistics, the study of language and its relation to society and culture, is significant because of its influence on language policy. **Language policy** is the set of actions a government takes to regulate what language(s) is/are spoken in the given country. In a nation with a multilingual population, the actual or attempted exclusion of languages can cause social and political conflict. Indeed, language has played a crucial part in the regional separatist movements of many countries, namely, Quebec in Canada and the Basque in Spain.

Another important element in sociolinguistics is the study of regional and social dialects. **Regional and social dialects** are language variations that are common to the people in a certain region or social group. Most people notice dialects, which can thus carry the weight of sociocultural stereotypes and prejudice. For example, in the United States, the "Southern drawl" is well-liked but often associated with ignorance and backwardness in news, television, film, and literature.

When people of two or more language groups need to communicate, they might develop a **pidgin** language, a grammatically simplified mode of communicating that uses elements of both languages. A pidgin is not a language that is native to an area or group; rather, it is a language of necessity that allows speakers of different languages to communicate. The need for pidgin languages is most often associated with trade, such as occurred with the development of Chinese Pidgin English when the British began to trade heavily in China during the eighteenth century.

HELPFUL HINT

If a pidgin language becomes nativized (that is, people begin speaking it as a first language), it is then known as a **creole**. For example, the Gullah language spoken on the South Carolina coast is a creole derived from the influence of Central and West African languages on English during the transatlantic slave trade.

SAMPLE QUESTION

11) While her class is working on a science project, the teacher overhears a native English speaker and a Spanish-speaking ESOL student communicate using an impromptu simple language that seems to have both English and Spanish words. What would their "language" be called?

A. a pidgin

B. a social dialect

C. a regional dialect

D. Universal Grammar

Answers:

A. **Correct.** A pidgin is a grammatically simplified mode of communicating that may use elements of two or more languages.

B. Incorrect. A social dialect is a variety of a language that people in a certain social group speak.

C. Incorrect. A regional dialect is a variety of a language that people in a certain region speak.

D. Incorrect. Universal Grammar is a language-learning theory developed by Noam Chomsky.

WORLD ENGLISHES

Another area in which dialect plays a part is the study of **World Englishes**. Because of early colonialization efforts by England and the United States, many countries in the world have adopted English as a first or second language. Moreover, because of the prevalence of English as a lingua franca in business, entertainment, commerce, and academia throughout the world, many more people choose to learn English as a second language to engage with the world around them. As the globe continues to become more connected, both native English speakers and those speaking English as a second language must become accustomed to understanding the language in its many forms; thus, teachers should expose ESOL students to a variety of dialects in the classroom.

SAMPLE QUESTION

12) In an ESOL classroom, the teacher makes an effort to use authentic audio materials that feature English speakers from England, India, Australia, and the United States as well as nonnative English speakers from Europe and Africa. Which concept would explain why this is a good strategy?

   A.   interlanguage

   B.   Sheltered Instruction Observation Protocol (SIOP) model

   C.   Language Experience Approach (LEA)

   D.   World Englishes

Answers:

   A.   Incorrect. Interlanguage describes a phase of second-language acquisition.

   B.   Incorrect. SIOP is a program delivery model.

   C.   Incorrect. The LEA is a method for teaching reading and writing.

   D.   Correct. The concept that there are English speakers with various accents all over the world is part of World Englishes.

COMMUNICATIVE COMPETENCE

Communicative competence means being able to speak a language both appropriately in a social context as well as correctly in terms of rules and structure. Linguists break down communicative competence into four distinct areas. **Linguistic competence** refers to one's knowledge of the linguistic components of a language such as morphology, syntax, and semantics. **Sociolinguistic competence** involves using the language in a socially appropriate way and understanding **register:** degrees of formality, differences in setting, considerations of context, and so on. **Discourse competence** is the ability to effectively arrange smaller units of language like phrases and sentences into cohesive works like letters, speeches, conversations, and articles. Finally, **strategic competence** is the ability to recognize and repair breakdowns in communication through strategic planning and/or redirecting.

SAMPLE QUESTION

13) Which of the four components of communicative competence would involve understanding the appropriate way for a student to speak to the principal while visiting a class at school?

    A.   linguistic competence

    B.   sociolinguistic competence

    C.   discourse competence

    D.   strategic competence

Answers:

    A.   Incorrect. Linguistic competence deals with syntax, semantics, and so on.

    B.   **Correct.** Sociolinguistic competence deals with using language in a socially appropriate way.

    C.   Incorrect. Discourse competence deals with using language in longer forms such as letters and speeches.

    D.   Incorrect. Strategic competence deals with recognizing and repairing communication breakdowns.

SOCIAL AND ACADEMIC PROFICIENCY

ESOL students need a range of both social and academic English proficiencies to succeed in and out of the classroom, and teachers must be aware that proficiency in one does not necessarily mean proficiency in the other. To distinguish between the two areas, researcher Jim Cummins developed terms and descriptions for each.

Basic Interpersonal Communication Skills (BICS) are social skills students use in everyday life when socializing on the playground, in the cafeteria, and outside of school. Students may develop these skills quickly because they are context driven and do not rely heavily on formalized rules.

On the other hand, students usually take longer to develop **Cognitive Academic Language Proficiency (CALP)**, language needed for academic work and study. CALP includes understanding both the formal language of academics and the vocabulary of critical thinking and problem-solving: compare, classify, synthesize, evaluate, and infer. CALP relies less on context than does BICS and requires higher levels of cognition; thus, it is more difficult for students to acquire.

TEACHING TIP

A variety of activities in the ESOL classroom—from formal writing assignments to casual interactions with peers—is important to ensure students can excel in different environments.

SAMPLE QUESTION

14) Why are Basic Interpersonal Communication Skills (BICS) usually easier for ESOL students to acquire than Cognitive Academic Language Proficiency (CALP) skills?

   A.   Students can study BICS in textbooks at home.

   B.   Jim Cummins developed BICS to be easier than CALP.

   C.   ESOL teachers stress BICS over CALP.

   D.   BICS are most often context driven, whereas CALP requires more advanced knowledge and skills.

Answers:

   A.   Incorrect. BICS are not skills that can be studied in textbooks.

   B.   Incorrect. Cummins developed these theories to explain the concepts; he did not invent social and academic skills.

   C.   Incorrect. Most ESOL teachers stress the development of both kinds of skills.

   D.   **Correct.** BICS rely heavily on context, which makes them easier to develop.

GRAMMAR AND PARTS OF SPEECH

ESOL teachers need to have a clear understanding of English grammar so they can readily explain it to ESOL students. While it is necessary first to set an example of fluency, it is not enough for the teacher to speak correctly: ESOL students sometimes need explicit instruction in grammar, so teachers must understand the parts of speech and the rules governing them.

PARTS OF SPEECH

In English, eight parts of speech are commonly recognized: **nouns, pronouns, verbs, adjectives, adverbs, prepositions, conjunctions,** and **interjections.** Some grammarians also include a ninth, **determiners.** Words are classified into parts of speech according to the role they most commonly fill; however, many English words can fall into more than one category.

NOUNS AND PRONOUNS

A **noun** names a person, place, thing, or idea. Nouns can be **proper** or **improper.** A **proper noun** is the name of a specific person, place, or thing as in *Cheryl McGregor, Lake Seneca,* or *Jones Landing.* An **improper noun** is a general person, place, thing, or idea such as *writer, lake, dock,* or *fear.* A noun formed from more than one word is a compound noun (*fire truck*).

Pronouns take the place of nouns in order to minimize repetition. The noun a pronoun replaces is called the **antecedent**. For example, in the sentence *Jamal loves Sandra*, pronouns could be substituted for the nouns as in *He loves her*, where *Jamal* is the antecedent for *he* and *Sandra* the antecedent for *she*. There are three types of pronouns: subject (used as actors in a sentence), object (acted upon in a sentence), and possessive (substitutes for a noun phrase).

- subject pronouns: I, you (singular and plural), he, she, it, we, they
- object pronouns: me, you (singular and plural), him, her, it, us, them
- possessive pronouns: mine, yours (singular and plural), his, hers, its, ours, theirs

Relative pronouns begin dependent clauses. Like other pronouns, they may appear in subject or object case, depending on the clause.

In the sentence *Charlie, who made the clocks, works in the basement*, the relative pronoun *who* is substituted for Charlie, indicating that Charlie makes the clocks; *who* is in the subjective case because its antecedent is performing the action (*makes the clocks*).

In cases where a person is the object of a relative clause, the writer would use the relative pronoun whom. For example, in the sentence *My father, whom I care for, is sick*, *whom* is the object of the preposition *for*. Therefore, the pronoun appears in the objective case.

When a relative clause refers to a nonhuman, *that* or *which* is used. (*I live in Texas, which is a large state. I want the model that has the sunroof.*) The relative pronoun *whose* indicates possession. (*I don't know whose car that is.*)

Table 1.2. Relative Pronouns

Pronoun Type	Subject	Object
person	who	whom
thing	which, that	
possessive	whose	

Interrogative pronouns begin questions (*Who worked last evening?*). They request information about people, places, things, ideas, location, time, means, and purposes.

Table 1.3. Interrogative Pronouns

Interrogative Pronoun	Example
who	Who lives there?
whom	To whom shall I send the letter?

Interrogative Pronoun	Example
what	<u>What</u> is your favorite color?
where	<u>Where</u> do you go to school?
when	<u>When</u> will we meet for dinner?
which	<u>Which</u> movie would you like to see?
why	<u>Why</u> are you going to be late?
how	<u>How</u> did the ancient Egyptians build the pyramids?

Demonstrative pronouns point out or draw attention to something or someone. They can also indicate proximity or distance.

Table 1.4. Demonstrative Pronouns

Singular	Example	Plural	Example
this	<u>This</u> is my apartment—please come in!	these, those	<u>These</u> are flawless diamonds.
that	<u>That</u> is the Statue of Liberty.	those	<u>Those</u> mountains are called the Rockies.

Indefinite pronouns simply replace nouns to avoid unnecessary repetition. (*Several* came to the party to see *both*.)

Table 1.5. Common Indefinite Pronouns

Singular		Plural	Singular or Plural*
another	neither	both	some
anybody	no one	few	any
anyone	nobody	several	none
anything	nothing	many	all
each	one		most
either	somebody		more
everybody	someone		
everyone	something		
everything			

*These pronouns take their singularity or plurality from the object of the prepositions that follow: *Some of the pies were eaten.*

Some of the pie was eaten.

VERBS

Verbs express action (*run, jump, play*) or state of being (*is, seems*): the former are called action verbs, and the latter are linking verbs. Linking verbs join the subject of a sentence to its subject complement, which follows the verb and provides more information about the subject, as in the following sentence:

> *The dog is cute.*

The dog is the subject, *is* is the linking verb, and *cute* is the subject complement.

Verbs can stand alone or they can be accompanied by **helping verbs**, which are used to indicate tense (when the action occurred). The action may have occurred in the past, present, or future and may have been simple (occurring once) or continuous (ongoing). The perfect and perfect continuous tenses describe when actions occur in relation to other actions.

Table 1.6. Verb Tenses

Tense	Past	Present	Future
simple	I <u>answered</u> the question.	I <u>answer</u> your questions in class.	I <u>will answer</u> your question.
continuous	I <u>was answering</u> your question when you interrupted me.	I <u>am answering</u> your question; please listen.	I <u>will be answering</u> your question after the lecture.
perfect	I <u>had answered</u> all questions before class ended.	I <u>have answered</u> the questions already.	I <u>will have answered</u> every question before the class is over.
perfect continuous	I <u>had been answering</u> questions when the students started leaving.	I <u>have been answering</u> questions for thirty minutes and am getting tired.	I <u>will have been answering</u> students' questions for twenty years by the time I retire.

helping verbs: is/am/are/was/were, be/being/been, has/had/have, do/does/did, should, would, could, will

The process of changing the spelling of a verb and/or adding helping verbs is known as **conjugation**. In addition to being conjugated for tense, verbs are conjugated to indicate *person* (first, second, and third person) and *number* (whether they are singular or plural). The conjugation of the verb must agree with the subject of the sentence. A verb that has not be conjugated is called an infinitive and begins with *to* (*to swim, to be*).

Table 1.7. Verb Conjugation (Present Tense)

Person	Singular	Plural
first person	I answer	we answer
second person	you answer	you (all) answer
third person	he/she/it answers	they answer

Verbs may be regular, meaning they follow normal conjugation patterns, or irregular, meaning they do not follow a regular pattern.

Table 1.8. Regular and Irregular Verbs

	Simple Present	Present Participle	Simple Past	Past Participle
Regular	help	helping	helped	(have) helped
	jump	jumping	jumped	(have) jumped
	am	been	was	(have) been
	swim	swimming	swam	(have) swum
	sit	sitting	sat	(have) sat
Irregular	set	setting	set	(have) set
	lie	lying	lay	(have) lain
	lay	laying	laid	(have) laid
	rise	rising	rose	(have) risen
	raise	raising	raised	(have) raised

Verbs can be written in the active or passive voice. In the **active voice**, the subject of the sentence performs the main action of the sentence. In the following sentence, Alexis is performing the action:

Alexis played tennis.

In the passive voice, the subject of the sentence is receiving the action of the main verb. In the following sentence, the subject is *tennis*, which receives the action *played*:

Tennis was played.

In the passive voice, the action itself—and not the individual who performed the action—is emphasized. For this reason, passive voice is used when the subject is unknown or unimportant. For example, the passive voice is commonly used in scientific publications:

The experiment was performed three times.

At most other times, the active voice is considered more appropriate because it is more engaging.

Finally, verbs can be classified by whether or not they take a **direct object**, which is a noun that receives the action of the verb. **Transitive verbs** require a direct object. In the following sentence, the transitive verb *throw* has a direct object (ball):

> *The pitcher will throw the ball.*

Conversely, a noun that receives the direct object is the indirect object.

> *The pitcher will throw Antoine the ball.*

Intransitive verbs do not require a direct object. Verbs like *run*, *jump*, and *go* make sense without any object:

> *He will run.*
>
> *She jumped.*

Many sets of similar verbs include one transitive and one intransitive verb, which can cause confusion. These troublesome pairs include *lie/lay*, *rise/raise*, and *sit/set*.

Table 1.9. Intransitive and Transitive Verbs

Intransitive Verbs	Transitive Verbs
lie—to recline	lay—to put / lay something
rise—to go or get up	raise—to lift / raise something
sit—to be seated	set—to put / set something
Hint: These intransitive verbs have *i* as the second letter. *Intransitive* begins with *i*.	Hint: The word *transitive* begins with a *t*, and it *takes* an object.

ADJECTIVES AND ADVERBS

HELPFUL HINT

Adjectives typically answer the questions *What kind? Which one? How many? How much? Whose?*

Adjectives are words that describe or modify nouns and pronouns. An adjective can be a word, a phrase, or a clause, as in *green shirt*, *well-worn shirt*, or *the shirt, which is green and well worn*. Numbers can also serve as adjectives, as in *three green shirts*. Adjectives have comparative and superlative forms. The comparative form is used to compare two things and uses *–er*.

> *This shirt is greener than that one.*

The superlative form is used to compare three or more things and uses *–est*.

> *This shirt is the greenest of all.*

For adjectives that have three or more syllables, more and most are used to show comparison.

The final exam will be the most difficult test of the semester.

Adverbs are words that describe or modify verbs, adjectives, and other adverbs. They often tell how, when, where, or why something happened. Like adjectives, an adverb can be one word, a phrase, or a clause. Many one-word adverbs end in *–ly* as in *quickly*, but many do not as in *well*. Adverbs also have comparative and superlative forms. Most one-syllable adverbs use *–er* and *–est*:

> *He ran <u>fast</u>.*
>
> *He ran <u>faster</u>.*
>
> *He ran <u>fastest</u>.*

HELPFUL HINT
Adverbs typically answer the questions *Where? When? Why? How? How often? To what extent? Under what conditions?*

Most adverbs with two or more syllables use *more/most*:

> *She danced <u>gracefully</u>.*
>
> *She danced <u>more gracefully</u> than her partner.*
>
> *Out of the whole troupe, she danced <u>most gracefully</u>.*

An **adverb clause** is a dependent clause that modifies a verb, adjective, or adverb in the main or independent clause of a sentence:

> <u>*Because it was raining*</u>*, I decided to take my umbrella.*

In the previous sentence, *because it was raining* is an adverb clause modifying the past tense verb *decided*.

PREPOSITIONS

Prepositions set up relationships in time (*after the party*) or space (*under the cushions*) within a sentence. A preposition will always function as part of a prepositional phrase—the preposition along with the object of the preposition. If a word that usually acts as a preposition is standing alone in a sentence, the word is likely functioning as an adverb. (*She hid underneath.*)

The following is a list of common prepositions:

▸ along	▸ besides	▸ from
▸ among	▸ between	▸ in
▸ around	▸ beyond	▸ into
▸ at	▸ by	▸ near
▸ before	▸ despite	▸ of
▸ behind	▸ down	▸ off
▸ below	▸ during	▸ on
▸ beneath	▸ except	▸ onto
▸ beside	▸ for	▸ out

- outside
- over
- past
- since
- through
- till

- to
- toward
- under
- underneath
- out
- until

- up
- upon
- with
- within
- without

The following is a list of common compound prepositions:

- according to
- as of
- as well as
- aside from
- because of
- by means of

- in addition to
- in front of
- in place of
- in respect to
- in spite of

- instead of
- on account of
- out of
- prior to
- with regard to

CONJUNCTIONS

Conjunctions are short words that connect words, phrases, or sentences. The most commonly used conjunctions are the coordinating conjunctions: *and, but, or, so, for, nor,* and *yet.* In a phrase, a conjunction can be used to join two things as in *apples and oranges.* Two independent clauses can be joined with a comma plus a conjunction as in *We ate juicy apples, and we peeled a dozen oranges.* (For more on commas and conjunctions, see the *Usage* section.)

> **TEACHING TIP**
>
> Use the trusty acronym *FANBOYS* to help you remember the coordinating conjunctions: **F**or, **A**nd, **N**or, **B**ut, **O**r, **Y**et, **S**o.

Correlative conjunctions (*whether/or, either/or, neither/nor, both/and, not only/but also*) function similarly to coordinating conjunctions. That is, they join together words, phrases, or independent clauses.

Subordinating conjunctions join dependent clauses (typically adverbial clauses) to the independent clauses to which they are related. (*Because we love pizza, we treat ourselves during football season to several orders.*)

Table 1.10. Subordinating Conjunctions

Circumstances	Examples
time	after, as, as long as, as soon as, before, since, until, when, whenever, while
manner	as, as if, as though
cause	because

Circumstances	Examples
condition	although, as long as, even if, even though, if, provided that, though, unless, while
purpose	in order that, so that, that
comparison	as, than

INTERJECTIONS

Interjections are words that express emotion, such as *oh* and *wow*. They are often used on their own and are followed by an exclamation point (*Wow!*), but they can also be part of a sentence: *Oh, your costume is so scary!*

DETERMINERS

The articles *a*, *an*, and *the* are known as **determiners** and are used before nouns. *A* and *an* are indefinite articles because they are do not indicate a specific noun, while *the* is a definite article, indicating a specific noun: *I would like a pizza and an eggplant parmesan from the Italian place on the corner.*

SAMPLE QUESTIONS

15) **Which of the following sentences is/are correct?**

   A.   You and he should go to the store.

   B.   You and him should go to the store.

   C.   Stan and him should go to the store.

   D.   Both B and C are written correctly.

   Answers:

   A.   **Correct.** *You* and *he* are subject pronouns and thus are correct.

   B.   Incorrect. *Him* is an object pronoun and thus is not correctly used.

   C.   Incorrect. *Him* is an object pronoun and thus is not correctly used.

   D.   Incorrect. Neither B nor C is written correctly.

16) **A student writes the following sentence on the board:** *I am going to beach tomorrow.* **What is the sentence mistakenly missing?**

   A.   future verb tense

   B.   adverbs

   C.   determiners

   D.   a subject

   Answers:

   A.   Incorrect. The sentence uses the future verb tense correctly.

B.   Incorrect. The sentence does not need adverbs to be correct.

C.   **Correct.** A determiner is needed before the noun *beach*.

D.   Incorrect. The sentence has a subject.

USAGE

Along with understanding the basic parts of speech in the English language, instructors must understand the rules governing the usage of these elements.

NOUNS

Nouns can be either **singular** (one) or **plural** (more than one). Most nouns are made plural by adding –s.

> *writer/writers*
>
> *dock/docks*
>
> *lake/lakes*

Nouns that end in –s, –x, –z, –ch, and –sh add –es in their plural form.

> *dress/dresses*
>
> *affix/affixes*
>
> *dish/dishes*

In a noun ending in a consonant then –y, the –y changes to –i and –es is added to make the word plural.

> *mystery/mysteries*
>
> *spy/spies*
>
> *party/parties*

Some nouns do not change form to become plural.

> *fish/fish*
>
> *deer/deer*
>
> *aircraft/aircraft*

There are many irregular plural nouns as well.

> *woman/women*
>
> *life/lives*
>
> *thesis/theses*

Nouns are also divided into count and noncount. **Count nouns** are those nouns that can be put into plural form (e.g., *two books, seven sins, many people*). **Noncount nouns** are those that cannot be counted and thus cannot be changed into a plural form (e.g., *money, greed,* and *furniture*).

Gerunds are nouns that are formed by adding –*ing* to a verb (e.g., *fishing, cooking,* and *eating*).

PRONOUNS

To be used effectively, a **pronoun** must clearly refer to the noun it replaces. Clear **pronoun reference** prevents vagueness and confusion.

> vague: *Maria called Sylvia because she was sad.* (Who was sad, Maria or Sylvia?)
>
> clear: *Maria was sad, so she called Sylvia.*
>
> not in agreement: *The student left their books.*
>
> in agreement: *The students left their books.*

Personal, possessive, and reflexive pronouns must all agree with their antecedents in gender (male, female, or neutral), number (singular or plural), and person. **Person** refers to the point of view of the sentence. First person is the point of view of the speaker (I, me), second person is the person being addressed (you), and third person refers to a person outside the sentence (he, she, they).

Table 1.11. Pronoun Usage

Case	First Person		Second Person		Third Person	
	Singular	**Plural**	**Singular**	**Plural**	**Singular**	**Plural**
subject	I	we	you	you (all)	he, she, it,	they
object	me	us	you	you (all)	him, her, it	them
possessive	my	our	your	your	his, her, its	their
reflexive	myself	ourselves	yourself	yourselves	himself, herself, itself	themselves

VERBS

Though there are many verb tenses in English, six basic **verb tenses** are most common. Two of them, simple present and simple past, do not require the use of helping or auxiliary verbs (except in the negative and when forming questions); the others do.

The **simple present** is used to talk about habits and unchanging general truths and facts. It has two forms: singular and plural. The singular form is used with singular nouns and *he, she,* and *it.* It usually ends in *-s,* but some irregular forms do exist.

> *Roberto <u>eats</u> lunch at noon.*
>
> *He <u>eats</u> lunch at noon.*
>
> *Water <u>boils</u> at 212 degrees Fahrenheit.*

The plural form is used with plural nouns and *I, you, we,* and *they*; these words usually end without an *-s.*

Roberto and Sandra <u>eat</u> lunch at noon.

They <u>eat</u> lunch at noon.

Planets <u>revolve</u> around the sun.

Some simple present verbs in English have irregular forms. The *be* verb is the most common irregular verb.

I <u>am</u> short.

He/she/it <u>is</u> short.

You/we/they <u>are</u> short.

Latoya <u>is</u> short.

Latoya and Carla <u>are</u> short.

English uses the helping verbs *do* and *does* to form questions in the simple present tense and to make the simple present negative.

Do you have my clippers? No, I do not have your clippers.

The **simple past** is used to talk about things that happened, began and ended, at a certain point in the past. The regular forms end in *–d* or *–ed*. There is no subject-verb agreement; the verbs are the same for all subjects.

He <u>hoped</u> for a big win at the tournament in 2008.

Ming and Ana <u>listened</u> to the lecture.

Many **irregular past tense** verbs exist in English.

Mona <u>saw</u> the bike in the window.

They always <u>ate</u> lunch at noon when they lived at home.

Stefan <u>went</u> to the farm.

The **simple future** tense is used to talk about events in the future. It uses the helping verbs *will* + the simple form of a verb OR *be verb* + *going to* + the simple form of a verb.

We <u>will meet</u> them at 7:00 at the restaurant.

Tyrone <u>will graduate</u> next May.

She <u>is going to feel</u> so happy about the party.

Darryl <u>is going to be</u> there.

The **present perfect** tense is used to talk about events in the past that happened at an unspecified time. It is also used to talk about things that began in the past and continue to the present. The present perfect uses the helping verbs *has/have* + the past participle form of the verb.

We <u>have traveled</u> to Canada several times.

Ahmed <u>has been</u> in school for three years.

The **past perfect** tense is used to talk about an event in the past that happened before another event in the past. It uses the helping verb *had* + the past participle form of the verb.

> We *had finished* dinner when Susanna brought out the cake.
>
> He *had hoped* for a big win before he broke his leg.
>
> Ming and Ana *had listened* to the lecture, so they passed the quiz.

The **future perfect** tense is used to talk about something in the future that will be completed by a certain time or before another event. It usually uses the helping verbs *will have* + the past participle form of the verb.

> She *will have baked* the cake before dinner.
>
> I *will have arrived* by 5:00, so you can meet me after work.

SAMPLE QUESTION

17) **Which sentence uses the present perfect verb tense?**

    A.   He's been there a few times already.

    B.   Katrina thinks the present is perfect for her mother.

    C.   Juan is going to drive home tomorrow.

    D.   Sean leaves at 8:00 a.m. every day.

Answers:

A. **Correct.** *He's been* is in present perfect tense (*he has been*).

B.   Incorrect. This sentence uses the simple present tense (*thinks*).

C.   Incorrect. This sentence uses the future tense (*is going to drive*).

D.   Incorrect. This sentence uses the simple present tense (*leaves*).

PHRASES AND CLAUSES

Phrases and clauses are made up of either a subject, a predicate, or both. The **subject** is what the sentence is about. It includes the noun that is performing the main action of the sentence and the noun's modifiers. The **predicate** describes what the subject is doing or being; it contains the verb(s) and any modifiers or objects that accompany it/them.

A **phrase** is a group of words that communicates a partial idea and lacks either a subject or a predicate. Several phrases may be strung together, one after another, to add detail and interest to a sentence.

> The animals crossed *the large bridge to eat the fish on the wharf.*

Phrases are categorized based on the main word in the phrase. A **prepositional phrase** begins with a preposition and ends with an object of the preposition; a **verb phrase** is composed of the main verb along with its helping verbs; and a **noun phrase** consists of a noun and its modifiers.

Prepositional phrase: *The dog is hiding <u>under the porch</u>.*

Verb phrase: *The chef <u>would have created</u> another soufflé, but the staff protested.*

Noun phrase: *<u>The big, red barn</u> rests beside <u>the vacant chicken house.</u>*

An **appositive phrase** is a particular type of noun phrase that renames the word or group of words that precedes it. Appositive phrases usually follow the noun they describe and are set apart by commas.

My dad, <u>a clockmaker,</u> loved antiques.

Verbal phrases begin with a word that would normally act as a verb but is instead filling another role within the sentence. These phrases can act as nouns, adjectives, or adverbs. **Gerund phrases** begin with gerunds, which are verbs that end in *–ing* and act as nouns.

Gerund phrase: *<u>Writing numerous Christmas cards</u> occupies her aunt's time each year.*

The word *gerund* has an *n* in it, a helpful reminder that the gerund acts as a noun. Therefore, the gerund phrase might act as the subject, the direct object, or the object of the preposition just as another noun would.

A **participial phrase** is a verbal phrase that acts as an adjective. These phrases start with either present participles (which end in *–ing*) or past participles (which usually end in *-ed*). Participial phrases can be extracted from the sentence, and the sentence will still make sense because the participial phrase is playing only a modifying role:

<u>Enjoying the unobscured view of the night sky,</u> Dave lingered outside the cabin for quite a while.

Finally, an **infinitive phrase** is a verbal phrase that may act as a noun, an adjective, or an adverb. Infinitive phrases begin with the word *to*, followed by a simple form of a verb (*to eat, to jump, to skip, to laugh, to sing*).

<u>To visit Europe</u> had always been her dream.

Clauses contain both a subject and a predicate. They can be either independent or dependent. An **independent** (or main) **clause** can stand alone as its own sentence:

The dog ate her homework.

Dependent (or subordinate) clauses cannot stand alone as their own sentences. They start with subordinating conjunctions, relative pronouns, or relative adjectives, which make them incomplete:

<u>Because</u> the dog ate her homework

Table 1.12. Words That Begin Dependent Clauses

Subordinating Conjunctions	Relative Pronouns and Adjectives
after, before, once, since, until, when, whenever, while, as, because, in order that, so, so that, that, if, even if, provided that, unless, although, even though, though, whereas, where, wherever, than, whether	who, whoever, whom, whomever, whose, which, that, when, where, why, how

Sentences can be classified based on the number and types of clauses they contain. A **simple sentence** will have only one independent clause and no dependent clauses. The sentence may contain phrases, complements, and modifiers, but it will comprise only one independent clause, one complete idea:

The cat under the back porch jumped against the glass yesterday.

A **compound sentence** has two or more independent clauses and no dependent clauses:

The cat under the back porch jumped against the glass yesterday, and he scared my grandma.

A **complex sentence** has only one independent clause and one or more dependent clauses:

Because he saw my grandma's bird through the window, the cat under the back porch jumped against the glass yesterday.

A **compound-complex sentence** has two or more independent clauses and one or more dependent clause:

Because he saw my grandma's bird through the window, the cat under the back porch jumped against the glass yesterday; he scared my grandma.

Table 1.13. Sentence Structure and Clauses

Sentence Structure	Independent Clauses	Dependent Clauses
simple	1	0
compound	2 +	0
complex	1	1 +
compound-complex	2 +	1 +

Writers can diversify their use of phrases and clauses in order to introduce variety into their writing. Variety in **sentence structure** not only makes writing more interesting but also allows writers to emphasize that which deserves emphasis.

In a paragraph of complex sentences, a short, simple sentence can be a powerful way to draw attention to a major point.

SAMPLE QUESTIONS

18) **Identify the prepositional phrase in the following sentence:**

    Wrapping packages for the soldiers, the kind woman tightly rolled the T-shirts to see how much space remained for the homemade cookies.

    A.   wrapping packages for the soldiers

    B.   the kind woman

    C.   to see how much space

    D.   for the homemade cookies

    Answers:

    A.   Incorrect. This is a participial phrase that begins with the participle *wrapping*.

    B.   Incorrect. This is a noun phrase that contains the noun *woman* and modifiers.

    C.   Incorrect. This is an infinitive phrase that begins with the infinitive *to see*.

    D.   Correct. This phrase begins with the preposition *for*.

19) **Which sentence is correctly labelled according to its structure?**

    A.   The grandchildren and their cousins enjoyed their day at the beach. (compound)

    B.   Most of the grass has lost its deep color, despite the fall lasting into December. (simple)

    C.   The members who had served selflessly were cheering as the sequestration ended. (complex)

    D.   Do as you please. (complex)

    Answers:

    A.   Incorrect. This sentence is simple, with only one independent clause.

    B.   Incorrect. This sentence is complex, having only one independent clause and one dependent clause.

    C.   Incorrect. This sentence is simple, with only one independent clause and several phrases.

    D.   Correct. This sentence is complex because it has one independent clause (*Do*) and one dependent (*as you please*).

PUNCTUATION

English uses various forms of **punctuation**. The most common are end marks, commas, apostrophes, quotation marks, colons, and semicolons.

End marks are used at the ends of sentences. **Periods** are used to end imperative and declarative sentences, which constitute the majority of sentences. **Question marks** are used to end questions, and **exclamation points** are used at the end of interjections or exclamations.

> *It's time to go.*
>
> *Are you ready yet?*
>
> *Come on!*

Commas are used in several ways in English, some more common than others.

1. They are used when listing three or more things.

   I want mushrooms, olives, and onions on my pizza.

2. They are used to join independent clauses (clauses that could be sentences on their own) with conjunctions to form compound sentences.

   Marie went to pick up the pizza, but the restaurant was closed.

   She then went across town to the other pizzeria, and it was also closed.

3. Use commas after introductory words or phrases.

   Then, she went to a third pizzeria.

   In the morning, she realized she was out of gas.

4. Commas are also used to set apart extra clauses and phrases that are not necessary to make a complete sentence.

   The horse, now old and tired, was happy to spend her days grazing in the sun.

   Rogerio looked longingly at the car, a 1967 Camaro SS.

5. Use commas before a quotation.

   Kelsey said, "If you leave, lock the door behind you."

Apostrophes are perhaps the most misused type of punctuation. They are used correctly in only a couple ways. Apostrophes are used to show possession.

> *The cat's paw was over his eye while he slept.*
>
> *Is that Ruby's notebook?*

Apostrophes are also used to form contractions.

> *I'm tired, but I can't quit driving.*

Apostrophes are NOT used to form plurals.

> Incorrect: *We have swing's for sale.*

Correct: *We have swings for sale.*

Quotation marks are used to set apart the exact words being referenced (usually either from a conversation or from previously published works).

Rebecca asked, "What time is it?"

When I got there, he said, "Finally! We've been waiting all day."

Colons are used to let a reader know a list or explanation is upcoming in the sentence.

The restaurant called us for the following supplies: olive oil, cooking sherry, and white vinegar.

Semicolons are used to join two closely related sentences that could each stand on their own.

He broke his leg; he never went skating again.

Other marks of punctuation include:

- **en dash** (–): to indicate a range of dates
- **em dash** (—): to indicate an abrupt break in a sentence and emphasize the words within the em dashes
- **parentheses** ( ): to enclose insignificant information
- **brackets** [ ]: to enclose added words to a quotation and to add insignificant information within parentheses
- **slash** (/): to separate lines of poetry within a text or to indicate interchangeable terminology
- **ellipses** (...): to indicate information removed from a quotation, to indicate a missing line of poetry, or to create a reflective pause

SAMPLE QUESTION

20) **Which sentence, written by a student, contains a mistake in apostrophe usage?**

   A.   Stereos used to be a lot bigger.

   B.   I can't see the sign from here.

   C.   David's bag is still in the car.

   D.   Its' paw is hurt.

Answers:

   A.   Incorrect. No apostrophe is needed in this sentence.

   B.   Incorrect. The apostrophe is used correctly.

   C.   Incorrect. The apostrophe is used correctly.

   D.   Correct. No apostrophe is used with possessive *its*.

2

Language Learning and Acquisition

anguage learning is the process of procuring, comprehending, and utilizing language for communicative purposes. There are many important considerations to be made in second-language instruction. Teachers must not only have an understanding of the theoretical models that drive language instruction, but also be familiar with the ways that first languages can interfere with second-language acquisition and with ways to instruct and motivate students effectively. Further, they must understand the importance of literacy and its relationship to language acquisition. Each of these elements plays an integral role in the learning and acquisition of English.

Language learning comes through direct instruction. Students are conscious of the fact that they are learning and gaining knowledge; they are then able to speak about their new knowledge and explain where it comes from. **Language acquisition**, on the other hand, is a subconscious process in which language is internalized without deliberate intent. Despite the differences in their technical meanings, these two terms are often used interchangeably.

Still, understanding the distinctions between language learning and language acquisition can be helpful for establishing an effective language program that complements students' academic coursework and enhances their learning of English. In order to succeed in this endeavor, teachers must take a balanced approach that reflects an understanding of the fundamentals of English-language learning.

THEORETICAL MODELS OF SECOND-LANGUAGE LEARNING AND ACQUISITION

There are many research-based theories on second-language learning and acquisition. These theories have led to established models of instruction and practice that are used in classrooms across the country. As the interest in second-language acquisition has increased, so has the quality and quantity of research being done.

Researchers have begun to address a broader selection of topics, posing questions for further study and approaching old questions through new methodologies. However, all of these exciting findings are rooted in several well-established theories and models.

COGNITIVE

Jean Piaget, a developmental psychologist, established a cognitive theory of development that includes four stages, which have since become the foundation for many teaching practices. These stages describe the cognitive capabilities of children as they move through childhood and into adolescence, constructing their own knowledge about and understanding of the world. Piaget believed that these stages were universal and that no step could be skipped.

The first stage of Piaget's cognitive-developmental theory is the **sensorimotor** stage, which generally occurs from birth to two years of age. During the sensori motor stage, a child's knowledge is based upon physical interactions and experiences; the child learns about the world by trying and testing. Language, at this stage, is a purely physical skill, and babies begin to acquire language by experimenting with the various sounds their mouths can make. They learn to imitate familiar sounds and may even begin mimicking them in appropriate contexts. For example, a child may say his first word in response to repeated prompting using that word: a child whose father repeats the sound *dada* may eventually begin to speak the word when his father is near.

According to Piaget's theory, the second stage of cognitive development occurs from two to seven years of age; it is called the **preoperational** stage. During this stage, a child's intelligence is progressively demonstrated through his or her use of symbols. Children begin to talk constantly, but it may be with little purpose or meaning; much of their speech is essentially thinking aloud. Additionally, children at this stage show no awareness of others' viewpoints and display high levels of egocentrism. For example, a child may narrate only her own actions as she hosts an imaginary party.

The third of Piaget's stages is the **concrete operational** stage, which generally occurs from seven to eleven years of age. During this stage, children demonstrate increased intelligence through logical and organized methods of thinking. They are able to use inductive reasoning to apply specific examples to general principles and are less egocentric, becoming capable of recognizing others' perspectives. However, at this stage, Piaget believed, language is used to refer only to specific facts and concrete ideas, not abstract concepts. For example, a child may tell the story of a day at school, noting how a classmate responded to a joke or story that was told but may fail to recognize the thematic lesson of the story. Piaget postulated that some people may remain in this stage for the rest of their lives, never reaching the height of cognitive maturation.

The final stage of Piaget's theory, which begins at roughly eleven years of age and continues onward, is the **formal operational** stage of cognitive development.

Adolescents in this stage demonstrate intelligence through logical use of symbols and their relationship to abstract concepts. They are capable of using both inductive and deductive reasoning and have fully developed the capacity to use language for multiple purposes, including debating abstract theory, discussing philosophy, and using logic. For example, a young teenager may describe what he wants to be as an adult, including information on why it is something he is interested in and how it fits with his hopes for the future.

Though Piaget's theory of cognitive development has, like many other theories, been challenged by his contemporaries, some of the ideas therein continue to influence classrooms today. In particular, Piaget's work has been used to develop educational approaches that emphasize exploration and discovery.

DID YOU KNOW?

The phrase *Some Pigs Can Only Fly Occasionally* may be a helpful mnemonic device for remembering the order of Piaget's four stages.

Connectionist theory evolved in response to Piaget's work. This theory relies on several key ideas:

- Language usage is based upon a person's perception of language.
- Repeated linguistic input creates language patterns in learners.
- Language acquisition is the result of personal experiences.
- Neural mapping is essential to the acquisition of language.

Connectionism holds that language comprehension and production abilities develop through continual engagement with language. In particular, the theory emphasizes the importance of input in how language learners generate knowledge and extract meaning. When a language

QUICK REVIEW

Connectionism is unlike Piaget's stages of development. In what ways do these theories differ most?

learner experiences a form of lingual input, neural connections are created. These connections are then strengthened through repeated exposure to language stimuli. Eventually, as larger and larger groups of connections form, complex neural networks are created, reinforcing the learner's understanding of the language.

SAMPLE QUESTION

1) In which stage of Piaget's cognitive and linguistic development theory is a child most likely to narrate the process she is using to construct a fort with blocks?

   A. sensorimotor

   B. preoperational

   C. concrete operational

   D. formal operational

Answers:

A.   Incorrect. Children in the sensorimotor stage of development focus on the physical abilities of their mouths and grow into mimicking the familiar sounds around them.

B.   **Correct.** Children in the preoperational stage of development tend to do their thinking aloud, with little communicative intention.

C.   Incorrect. Children who have reached the concrete operational stage of development have moved beyond the egocentricism of younger children and are able to recognize the existence of multiple viewpoints.

D.   Incorrect. Children who have reached the formal operational stage of development have developed full lingual capacity. They understand and can discuss abstract ideas and concepts.

Behaviorist

Behavioral psychologist B. F. Skinner suggested that students' learning is based upon the presence of behavioral models and the use of rewards and repetition. **Behaviorist theory** suggests that repeated exposure to stimuli can create learning: the more frequently a behavior is performed, the more quickly it will become habit. This theory suggests that the same holds true with language: that is, the more frequently students are exposed to language, the more readily they will grasp and adopt it.

Behaviorists also hold that language development is partially contingent upon conditioning. In the case of language learning, rewards of praise, smiles, and excitement encourage the production of sounds by infants. As strings of familiar syllables are put together to create words, the rewards for baby become greater. They are encouraged to repeat their attempts, given corrected versions of their words, and spoken to directly. By about five or six years of age, children have internalized a **linguistic set**—a group of words and rules that compose an individual's working knowledge of a language—based upon their previously rewarded efforts, and much of their speech mirrors that of the adults around them.

During World War II, behaviorist theories came to prominence in the world of language acquisition. Traditional grammar instruction failed to equip America's servicemen to communicate effectively with foreign soldiers, so a new method of language instruction—the audio-lingual method—was created.

SAMPLE QUESTION

2)   **According to behaviorists, how are children encouraged to string together groups of syllables to form words?**

A.   by being provided with rewards and incentives for speech

B.   by being continuously corrected in their attempts at speech

C.   by being continuously spoken to by the adults around them

D.   by being provided with previously learned patterns of sounds

Answers:

A.   **Correct.** Children are encouraged to produce words by the responses they receive from those around them. Smiles, praises, and encouragement all motivate a child to make attempts at speech.

B.   Incorrect. While children are often corrected in their errors during their attempts at making words, repeated correction does not necessarily encourage their efforts.

C.   Incorrect. Though being spoken to by those around them does encourage children to speak, it does not provide direct encouragement for the formation of words; it simply provides them with additional exposure to the language.

D.   Incorrect. Children are exposed to patterns of speech through all of their interactions with adults but, according to behaviorists, exposure alone does not encourage speech production.

MONITOR MODEL

The **monitor model** is a set of five hypotheses developed by researcher Stephen Krashen. According to Krashen, there is no fundamental difference in the way that humans acquire first and subsequent languages. Our innate ability to learn languages comes just by listening conscientiously in order to create meaning, thereby relying on stimuli from outside sources.

According to the **acquisition-learning hypothesis** of the monitor model, the distinction between acquisition (the unconscious process of making meaning of language through repeated exposure) and learning (the conscious process of developing skills through formal instruction in grammar and syntax) is of the utmost importance. Krashen argues that *learning* the rules of a language will not allow users to produce output; memorization of grammatical and structural rules is not authentic and therefore will not allow learners to become better users of the language. In terms of production, only authentic *acquisition* will allow students to use their new language effectively.

Further, Krashen argues, the type of input students receive influences their ability to acquire the language. The **input hypothesis** of the monitor model states that **comprehensible input** is necessary for students who are in the process of acquiring a new language. Comprehensible input refers to language that is just slightly above the student's current grasp, thereby allowing him to utilize his current knowledge while simultaneously gaining exposure to new information. According to this theory, comprehensible input in itself is enough to lead to language acquisition.

Still, language learning has applications in the process of gaining proficiency. According to the **monitor hypothesis** of Krashen's model, knowledge that is gained through formal learning is useful in certain settings, such as in written work and in self-correcting when time permits. He argues that this practice allows students to solidify their understanding of their new language. However, he argues that monitoring one's own language output can also have drawbacks: conversation often leaves little time for this practice, and self-correcting can be very difficult, even when learners have a strong grasp of a language. Most importantly, focusing on one element of speech can distract learners from their main purpose—conveying meaning.

Krashen's final two theories address potential obstacles to language acquisition. The first, the **natural order hypothesis**, posits that language is attained in a foreseeable pattern by all learners. The order of acquisition does not rely on the grammatical features of the language and therefore cannot be altered through direct teaching methods. The learner must be ready to gain new knowledge of language in order to do so. Krashen states that a lot of the frustration experienced by language learners and their teachers results from students being presented with information that they are not yet prepared to learn.

Finally, Krashen's **affective-filter hypothesis** addresses the emotional risks inherent in learning a new language. He argues that language acquisition can only occur when comprehensible input reaches the processing facilities of the brain without being filtered; stressors such as low self-esteem, poor motivation, and anxiety may all inhibit this action. Thus, learners with lower filtering mechanisms are likely to be more efficient in comprehending input they receive. Additionally, because these learners are more likely to interact with others without fear of making mistakes, the input they receive will also increase.

Today, the application of Krashen's model of language learning and acquisition is varied. Educators should be aware that some of the hypotheses in this model have been disproven, namely, that formal grammar instruction is unnecessary. Contemporary research shows that the language acquisition capabilities of adolescents and adults are limited compared to those of a young child; thus, mere exposure is not sufficient, and formal grammar instruction should be integrated into ESOL classrooms.

On the other hand, some of Krashen's ideas continue to be relevant in today's classrooms. In particular, the concept of comprehensible input is applicable in nearly all classroom settings, as the integration of new and existing knowledge allows students to form connections and retain new information at a higher rate. In addition, the importance of emotional safety in the classroom continues to be of the utmost importance today. Though research suggests that low self-esteem, poor motivation, and anxiety are not actual filters in the brain, as Krashen suggested, they have been shown to have a clear impact on an individual's ability to learn and acquire new language.

3) **Which of Krashen's hypotheses from the monitor model stresses the importance of language as a series of patterns for learners to internalize?**

    A.   acquisition-learning hypothesis

    B.   affective-filter hypothesis

    C.   monitor hypothesis

    D.   natural order hypothesis

Answers:

    A.   Incorrect. The acquisition-learning hypothesis focuses on the differences between acquiring language and learning it. Krashen argues that learning language can only be useful after it has been acquired.

    B.   Incorrect. The affective-filter hypothesis focuses on the importance of a learner's emotional state during second-language acquisition. Learners with positive affects are likely to engage in participatory events, creating opportunities for increased input and thereby allowing for greater exposure to language. Those with higher affective filters are likely to fear making errors in front of others and therefore not engage with them, decreasing potential exposure to the language.

    C.   Incorrect. The monitor hypothesis states that we are able to use what we have learned about a language to self-correct our own output. This is difficult for many learners because they focus too much on a single element of their output rather than on the message they are trying to convey.

    D.   **Correct.** The natural order hypothesis states that language is acquired in a particular order by all language learners. Thus, a student must be ready to gain linguistic knowledge or no learning will occur.

UNIVERSAL GRAMMAR

American linguist Noam Chomsky shaped the theory of **Universal Grammar**. This theory states that children are born with the innate ability to understand the human voice and to distinguish between different parts of language. Specifically, they have the capacity to understand differences in phonemes, the smallest elements of sound that allow for distinguishing between words. Moreover, Chomsky argues that humans have an inherent capacity to acquire, create, and comprehend language despite differences in grammar and composition across languages. If grammar is viewed as the laws of language, Chomsky would argue, people are born with a tendency to follow these laws.

DID YOU KNOW?

The term *tabula rasa* is Latin for "blank slate." It is a commonly used term when discussing child development and psychology.

Prior to Chomsky, language learning theories primarily viewed children as blank slates; that is, they have no natural inclinations toward language but are, instead, entirely reliant on their experiences to build their language skills. Most behaviorists, for example, believed that children learned language by listening to people speak, practicing their own speech, and receiving rewards for their efforts. However, Chomsky believed that grammatical laws must be a constant in humans because of what he called the **poverty of stimulus**. The poverty of stimulus asserts that children are not born with enough exposure to their native languages to explain their ability to understand phonemes, and therefore this exposure cannot account for the sum of their learned language.

QUICK REVIEW

Chomsky argues that language learning and acquisition are partially genetic. What other theorists believed that the human capacity for language is innate?

Because of Chomsky's work, it is now commonly accepted that there is an innate genetic component to the human capacity to learn language. It is believed that the human brain is hardwired to develop language, whether or not one has been exposed to it as a baby.

SAMPLE QUESTION

4) **How does Noam Chomsky's theory of Universal Grammar differ from the behaviorist theories that existed before his?**

   A. It assumes an innate, genetic capacity to learn language.

   B. It explains how children are exposed to language prior to birth.

   C. It supports the hypothesis that children are born as blank slates.

   D. It is used to demonstrate how children learn to understand phonemes.

Answers:

   A. **Correct.** Chomsky's theory is the first to postulate that people are born with an inherent capacity to learn and understand language. He goes on to detail his notion that this ability is genetic.

   B. Incorrect. Chomsky's theory argues that children are not exposed to language prior to birth, and therefore their capacity for language acquisition cannot be based on exposure alone.

   C. Incorrect. Chomsky's theory works to disprove the notion that children are born as blank slates; he instead argues that they are born with a genetic capacity to learn and understand language.

   D. Incorrect. Chomsky's theory argues that children can understand phonemes without needing to learn them.

FIRST–LANGUAGE CONSIDERATIONS

When examining the impact of a first language on ESOL students, educators must consider many influences. Interference, transfer, accents, and code-switching all become significant factors in a student's ability to learn a second language.

A great deal of research has been done to understand the impact of first languages on the acquisition of second languages, and linguists are encouraging researchers to go even further in their studies of this significant relationship. Today, more and more new teachers are receiving training in first-language acquisition in order to improve their ability to teach students about their native languages and to strengthen their comprehension of the learning process that students undergo when taking on a second language.

FIRST–LANGUAGE ACQUISITION

The developmental sequence of first-language acquisition follows a pattern that is the same in nearly all cases. And while there is variation in the age at which children reach given milestones, each child's acquisition maintains the same gradual pace. Correct usage of the parts of speech emerges slowly, while full pattern recognition generally takes place over four stages of first-language acquisition.

In the **pre-speech stage**, infants learn to pay attention to speech, inflection, and rhythm before they begin to speak. In fact, research has revealed that they respond to speech more acutely than to other sounds; brain scans have shown speech to elicit electrical activity in the left side of the brain, where much of the language center is stored in a part of the brain called Wernicke's area. Infants' initial vocalizations may be expressions of discomfort, such as **crying** or fussing, or the by-product of involuntary actions such as sucking, swallowing, burping, and coughing. However, by two to four months, infants begin vocalizing expressions of comfort, usually in response to pleasurable interactions with a caregiver. These may be grunts or sighs, which later evolve into **cooing** sounds; laughter generally appears at about four months.

The **babbling stage** is unique to the human species. Infants usually play by controlling the **pitch** of their vocalizations to create squeals or growls; they change the **volume** of their sounds to create both quiet and loud sounds; finally, they learn to produce sounds based upon **friction** such as "snorts" or "raspberries." Toward the end of this stage, infants learn to create sequences of consonant-vowel sounds that they often repeat in lengthier spans as though they are speaking in sentences.

The **one-word stage** is characterized by a child's use of a single word to convey a full meaning. These utterances usually have one of three purposes: to identify an action, to convey an emotion, or to name something. Often a child's definition of a word is too narrow, called an **underextension**. For example, when a child refers only to a single stuffed animal as *toy*, he or she is underextending the definition of the word *toy*. The opposite holds true as well; children at this stage also frequently

overextend the definitions of words, as when a child refers to all animals with tails as *doggy*.

DID YOU KNOW?

Underextensions and overextensions occur with most children and vary from individual to individual. They change frequently over time until the correct definition of the word is learned.

The **two-word stage** usually occurs around the second year of a child's life. Vocabulary acquisition rates typically begin at one to three words per week, increasing to as high as ten words per week after about forty words have been learned. Word combinations also begin appearing, forming mini sentences in which simple semantic relationships are demonstrated. For example, a child might say, "Go bye-bye," with the intention of telling someone that he or she is ready to leave.

In the **early multiword stage**, also known as the **telegraphic stage**, children are mostly understood by their parents and caregivers. They begin using elements of grammar and repeating longer sentences, though they are still unable to create their own. Children at this stage also tend to leave out parts of speech such as pronouns, determiners, and modals; however, as they mature, children begin to alternate between childlike and adultlike speech, making fewer omissions and using more multiclause sentences.

By age five, children have generally reached the **later multiword stage**. They average four to six words per sentence and can experience vocabulary increases of as many as twenty words per day. By age eight, the average child knows approximately 28,300 words.

SAMPLE QUESTION

5) During which stage of first-language acquisition do children first begin using words with intentional meaning?

A. babbling stage

B. one-word stage

C. two-word stage

D. multiword stage

Answers:

A. Incorrect. Children are unable to utter complete words during the babbling stage. Instead, they make sounds to express basic emotions.

B. **Correct.** Children first use a single word to express complete ideas.

C. Incorrect. Children in this stage are able to use more than one word to express their meaning and often modify their intents with descriptors.

D. Incorrect. Children who have reached this stage are able to express themselves using complete sentences and no longer rely on basic communication to convey meaning.

FIRST-LANGUAGE INFLUENCE ON SECOND LANGUAGE

Students' native languages will always impact their learning of English. The influences will occur in all parts of language learning, from grammatical understanding to vocabulary acquisition to syntactical awareness. They are bound to transfer their understanding of their first language on to their studies of English in an effort to make sense of what they are learning.

Transfer is when one applies knowledge of a first language onto another; transfer can be both positive and negative. **Positive transfer** occurs when students find similarities between their native language and English and use those similarities to aid in their learning. For example, a Spanish-speaking student may recognize the English verb *to comprehend* because it looks very close to the Spanish verb *comprender* (to understand); visually similar words such as these are referred to as **cognates**. Words that appear similar but are different in meaning are referred to as **false cognates**; the Spanish verb *comprar*, for example, means "to buy," not "to compare." Students who are learning a new language should be made aware that both cognates and false cognates exist.

> **DID YOU KNOW?**
>
> Students' ability to recognize cognates and use them as a tool for understanding a second language is called *cognate awareness.*

Negative transfer, also referred to as **interference**, occurs when students incorrectly apply rules from their native language to their learning of English. For example, when a Spanish-speaking student is learning English, he or she may place an adjective after a noun (as in *the house red*) because of the noun-adjective structure in Spanish. However, in English the adjective comes before the noun, as in *the red house*.

Code-switching is another frequent occurrence with language learners. Students often mix words from their first language in with the language they are learning when they have forgotten a term or do not know how to express themselves in the second language. For example, if a Spanish-speaking student is looking for the bathroom but cannot remember how to ask in English, she might ask, "Where is the *baño*?" This type of linguistic back-and-forth is extremely common with bilingual and multilingual individuals.

Finally, students' **accents** will also have an impact on their learning and pronunciation of English. Often speakers will substitute the sounds of their first language for ones that they think are the same in English; for example, some Spanish speakers may pronounce the /v/ sound like the English *b*. Additionally, stresses and intonations of various words can be carried from first languages. Both of these speech patterns can cause changes in the meanings of words in English (for instance, as the meanings of the words *read* and *read* can change) leading to an unclear message in a student's speech.

SAMPLE QUESTIONS

6) Jamie has just moved to from Mexico to Texas, where his mother enrolled him in an ESOL class. A few weeks in, Jamie is still reluctant to speak because he mixes in words from his first language with the English he is learning. Which of the following linguistic behaviors is Jamie demonstrating?

A. code-switching

B. cognate awareness

C. difficulty with accent

D. language interference

Answers:

A. **Correct.** Code-switching is the process in which students mix words from their first language with their production of the second language.

B. Incorrect. Students who recognize similarities between words in first and second languages are demonstrating cognate awareness.

C. Incorrect. Students who struggle with accents are usually mixing sounds or tones from their first language with their second language.

D. Incorrect. Students who confuse the structure of first and second languages are said to be experiencing interference.

7) Mrs. Holly has noticed that Ana usually substitutes the /h/ sound each time the /j/ sound should be used in a word. What should she do in order to help Ana develop her pronunciation skills?

A. Teach Ana about code-switching.

B. Plan activities that focus on Ana's accent.

C. Create lessons that teach Ana about cognates.

D. Discuss Ana's trouble with transfer with a colleague.

Answers:

A. Incorrect. Code-switching occurs when students mix words from their first and second languages. Ana is not mixing words, only sounds.

B. **Correct.** Ana's accent is interfering with her pronunciation of English words. Mrs. Holly can help her with this by planning activities that allow Ana to identify when her accent is preventing clear communication.

C. Incorrect. Cognates are words that appear similar in different languages. Because Ana's trouble is with her pronunciation, learning about cognates will not necessarily help her advance.

D. Incorrect. Ana's primary difficulty is with her pronunciation of words due to her accent. While this may indicate struggle with transfer, Mrs. Holly should focus on teaching Ana specific pronunciation techniques to help her speak more clearly.

STAGES OF SECOND-LANGUAGE ACQUISITION

Much like first-language acquisition, second-language acquisition is made up of a series of stages that learners pass through as they strive for proficiency. The time spent in each stage is dependent upon the individual learner and will vary from student to student based on how frequently the student is exposed to the second language, how motivated he is to learn the second language, and how confident he feels in his own abilities.

SILENT PERIOD

Most second-language learners begin their language acquisition with a **silent period**. During this time, they are either unwilling or unable to communicate in their new language. They must be given time to listen to others speak and to digest what they hear before being asked to speak themselves. This will aid them in developing vocabulary and gaining familiarity with common phrases. Students in the silent period may comprehend what is being said and may simply be taking time to process what they are hearing.

Silent periods vary in length from learner to learner, with several factors acting as influences. First, a learner's personality plays an important part in acquisition. Students who tend to be more outgoing in their native languages, for example, are likely to feel greater comfort in making efforts in English. Culture also plays a role. In some cultures, women and girls are expected to be more passive. This cultural expectation can affect their willingness to speak in a mixed-gender second-language classroom.

Finally, the role of the teacher is very important for students in the silent period, as the teacher is responsible for creating a safe environment for learning. Though the silent period may last from a few days all the way up to a year, new learners should never be forced to speak if they are not ready to do so. They may be silent for many different reasons, and pushing for speech may cause discomfort or embarrassment for the learner, making him more resistant and less motivated to continue learning. Participation in hands-on activities and small-group interactions can provide a more comfortable, nurturing environment in which students feel more confident expressing themselves.

SAMPLE QUESTION

8)   **Mr. Swenson is trying to help Jacque work through his silent period and begin speaking more in class. What should he do to encourage Jacque's speech?**

   A.   Assign students in Jacque's class individual oral reports.

   B.   Take Jacque aside and work with him privately on speaking.

   C.   Tell Jacque that if he does not begin speaking in class he will fail.

   D.   Set up a rotation of small-group speaking activities for Jacque's class.

Answers:

A.   Incorrect. It is unnecessary to make all students complete an oral assignment to encourage one to speak. Additionally, learners in the silent period should not be forced to speak if they are not ready to do so.

B.   Incorrect. By taking Jacque aside, his teacher is encouraging him to speak only in front of one person. While Jacque may be more comfortable with this, it will not prepare him to participate in conversations with others.

C.   Incorrect. Learners in the silent period should never be forced to speak. This can cause frustration, embarrassment, and increased reticence.

D.   **Correct.** Providing learners with opportunities for small-group interactions can create a comfortable environment that encourages participation.

INTERLANGUAGE

As language learners progress through varying levels of study, they will usually develop an interlanguage to aid them in their progression. **Interlanguage** can be seen as the learner's present understanding of the language he or she is learning. It is a rule-based system that develops over time and that tends to blend aspects of the learner's first language with those of the second.

Interlanguage is often characterized by the learner's tendency to overgeneralize speaking and writing rules in the new language. For example, when learning that most English verbs in the past tense end in *–ed*, a student may apply this rule to all verbs. The learner then creates an interlanguage rule for himself by repeatedly neglecting to properly conjugate irregular verbs. Over time, these rules are adjusted and readjusted according to feedback, and the interlanguage evolves as the learner moves toward proficiency.

When language learners reach a point in which little progress is being made and the development of their interlanguage stops, their understanding can become fossilized. **Fossilization** refers to the point in second-language acquisition in which a learner's growth freezes in place and further linguistic development becomes highly unlikely.

SAMPLE QUESTION

9)   **Why do second-language learners develop an interlanguage?**

A.   to overcome first-language dominance

B.   to show proficiency in first and second languages

C.   to move past fossilization of second-language acquisition

D.   to help them move forward in their second-language learning

Answers:

A.   Incorrect. Interlanguage is a blend of first- and second-language rules and therefore cannot help students overcome first-language dominance.

B.   Incorrect. Because interlanguage is a blend of first and second languages, its use does not demonstrate proficiency in either language.

C.   Incorrect. Once a learner has reached fossilization, there is little chance that he will progress in acquiring the language beyond that point.

D.   **Correct.** An interlanguage is a set of rules that allows a learner to create a mental bridge between the language she knows and the language she is acquiring; it aids the learner in moving forward as she continuously gains new knowledge and revises her understanding of the new language.

MORPHEME ACQUISITION ORDER

Morphemes are the smallest unit of language that can convey meaning or play a part in the grammatical structure of a word. They can appear as affixes or as stand-alone words and are generally understood in the earliest **developmental stages** of language acquisition. For example, the word *cooked* is made up of the morphemes *cook* and *–ed*. Each plays a role in the meaning of the word, with *cook* playing a lexical role and *–ed* being the grammatical component that signifies the word is written in the past tense. **Morpheme acquisition order** is the pattern in which the knowledge of these elements is gained as people acquire language. Within first-language acquisition, the pattern remains consistently fixed for all learners.

> **QUICK REVIEW**
>
> Some linguists believe that morpheme acquisition order is an outdated concept. What might be some of the benefits and drawbacks of applying this theory in the classroom?

For English language learners, the pattern is less constant, and though it is unclear as to why it varies, there is some evidence to suggest that variances stem from cognitive or other nonlinguistic mental capacities. Additionally, differences in morpheme acquisition for second-language learners have been found to vary by first language.

Go on

Table 2.1. Example of a Commonly Recorded Morpheme Acquisition Order for English Language Learners

Morpheme Acquisition	Example	Morpheme Acquisition	Example
1. Plural –*s*	Boy*s* walk.	1. Definite and indefinite articles *the* and *a*	*The* boys walk.
2. Progressive –*ing*	Boys walk*ing*.	2. Irregular past tense	The boys *went*.
3. Copula (linking) forms of *be*	Boys *are* here.	3. Third person –*s*	The boy walk*s*.
4. Auxiliary (helping) forms of *be*	Boys *are* walking.	4. Possessive *'s*	The boy*'s* shoe.

SAMPLE QUESTION

10) **What are some of the factors that may lead to differences in morpheme acquisition order in English language learners?**

    A. gender and cognitive interference

    B. age and first-language interference

    C. cognitive and first-language interference

    D. nonlinguistic mental capacities and gender

Answers:

A. Incorrect. While there is evidence suggesting that cognitive interference can impact morpheme acquisition order, there is no evidence to suggest that gender plays a role.

B. Incorrect. While there is evidence suggesting that first-language interference can impact morpheme acquisition order, there is no evidence to suggest that age plays a role.

C. Correct. It has been noted that both cognitive and first-language interferences may play a role in determining morpheme acquisition order.

D. Incorrect. While there is evidence suggesting that students' nonlinguistic mental capacities can impact morpheme acquisition order, there is no evidence to suggest that gender plays a role.

FIVE STAGES OF SECOND-LANGUAGE ACQUISITION

Researchers agree that second-language acquisition occurs, much like first-language acquisition, through a series of stages. Learners must pass through each of the five stages on their way to proficiency, though the time spent in each stage varies from person to person.

The first stage—**preproduction**—is also known as the silent period. Though these learners may have upwards of 500 words in their receptive vocabulary, they refrain from speaking but will listen and may copy words down. They can respond to visual cues such as pictures and gestures, and they will communicate their comprehension. However, sometimes students will repeat back what they have heard in a process referred to as parroting. This can aid them in building their receptive vocabulary, but it should not be mistaken for producing language.

In the **early production** stage, learners achieve a 1,000-word receptive and active vocabulary. They can now produce single-word and two- to three-word phrases and can respond to questions and statements as such. Many learners in this stage enjoy engaging in musical games or word plays that help them to memorize language chunks (groups of related words and phrases) that they can use later.

English language learners have a vocabulary of about 3,000 words by the time they reach the **speech emergence** stage of second-language acquisition. They are able to chunk simple words and phrases into sentences that may or may not be grammatically correct. They respond to models of proper usage better than they do to explicit correction. At this stage, learners also are more likely to participate in conversations with native English speakers, as they are gaining confidence in their language skills. These learners can understand simple readings when reinforced by graphics or pictures and can complete some content work with support.

By the **intermediate fluency** stage, English language learners have acquired a vocabulary of about 6,000 words. They are able to speak in more complex sentences and to catch and correct many of their own errors. They are also willing to ask questions to clarify what they do not understand. Learners at this stage may be able to communicate fairly well, but they have large gaps in their vocabulary, as well as in their grammatical and syntactical understanding of the language. They are often comfortable speaking in group conversations as long as they do not require heavy academic language.

Second-language learners who reach **advanced fluency** have achieved cognitive language proficiency in their learned language. They demonstrate near-native ability and use complex, multiphrase and multiclause sentences to convey their ideas. Though accents are still detectable and idiomatic expressions are sometimes used incorrectly, the language learner has become essentially fluent.

Go on →

11) Lucia enjoys listening to songs in English. She memorizes the choruses and sings them to herself throughout the day, taking note of words that she does not recognize and integrating phrases from the songs into her everyday language practice. When asked about the songs she likes, Lucia can respond in single words and short phrases but still struggles to compose complete sentences. What stage of second-language acquisition might Lucia be in?

A.   preproduction

B.   early production

C.   speech emergence

D.   intermediate fluency

Answers:

A.   Incorrect. Though parroting can play a role in preproduction, Lucia is demonstrating an interest beyond mere repetition: she is using language chunking to retain phrases and groups of words more successfully. Language chunking does not occur in preproduction.

B.   Correct. Lucia is demonstrating an enjoyment of language chunking and is using song lyrics to aid her in building her vocabulary.

C.   Incorrect. Lucia has not yet reached this stage of second-language acquisition, as she is not able to create multiword responses to questions and statements.

D.   Incorrect. Lucia's discomfort in speaking about her song lyrics indicates that she has not yet reached this stage of second-language acquisition.

STUDENT MOTIVATION IN SECOND–LANGUAGE LEARNING

Motivation plays an important role in second-language learning. There are two types of motivation to consider when thinking about the best environment to create within a classroom. **Intrinsic motivation** is characterized by one's personal drive to succeed or learn, while **extrinsic motivation** relies more on external rewards for behaviors. Students with higher levels of intrinsic motivation will be more inclined to participate in discussions and to internalize feedback and error corrections, thereby increasing their success in language acquisition. Those who are less intrinsically motivated tend to have the opposite response to such interactions and may take longer to succeed in acquiring their second language.

The most successful educators know how to foster a sense of intrinsic motivation in learners. By getting to know the individuals in their classrooms, these teachers create lessons that take into account the unique preferences, interests, and strengths of their students, creating an environment of investment and ownership.

INTRINSIC MOTIVATION

Intrinsic motivation directly correlates with students' achievement in second-language acquisition. It is rooted in self-determination and a desire to take control of one's own learning. Students who demonstrate this kind of motivation are more inclined to set their own goals, monitor their own progress, and seek out opportunities to practice their linguistic skills. They seek challenges in order to continue developing their skills, and tend to show higher levels of participation in small-group and paired work, with less reliance on teacher-lead instruction.

SAMPLE QUESTION

12) Xiang is highly motivated in his English class. He strives for high grades, rarely misses an assignment, and asks thoughtful questions in class. How can Xiang's teacher continue to encourage his motivation?

- A.   by allowing him to skip an assessment
- B.   by having him complete easier assignments
- C.   by providing him with small-group opportunities
- D.   by giving him assignments to complete on his own

Answers:

- A.   Incorrect. Because Xiang shows intrinsic motivation, allowing him to skip an assessment would not motivate him because it does not enable him to progress in his learning.
- B.   Incorrect. Intrinsically motivated students like Xiang enjoy challenges and want to keep progressing in their language acquisition.
- C.   **Correct.** Xiang demonstrates intrinsic motivation, which is fostered by small-group interaction and activities in ESOL classrooms.
- D.   Incorrect. Independent work typically does not motivate learners like Xiang. Intrinsically motivated students thrive in collaborative environments, such as those that involve paired assignments or group work.

EXTRINSIC MOTIVATION

Students who are provided with continual positive feedback and encouragement by teachers, peers, and parents experience some motivation to develop their second-language skills. This outside praise is a form of extrinsic motivation that can serve to propel language learners to pursue their studies. Extrinsically motivated students work toward rewards for their efforts. These rewards can be tangible or intangible but, most importantly, must hold value for the students pursuing them. Studies have shown, however, that students who are driven by extrinsic motivation usually lose their drive to complete tasks and deem second-language acquisition "too difficult" for them. This research goes on to emphasize the importance of self-motivation in student learning and explains that teachers who value this trait over extrinsic rewards are likely to experience greater success with English language learners.

SAMPLE QUESTION

13) Anja has been in Ms. Becht's ESOL class for the past two years and has shown little interest in learning English. She does not participate in group activities and rarely has her assignments completed when she gets to class. Despite many attempts at rewarding Anja for participating and turning in her work, Ms. Becht has made little progress with her. What strategy could Ms. Becht try to motivate Anja?

A.   Allow Anja to create an assignment for herself to complete.

B.   Have Anja work in a small group in order to encourage her to speak.

C.   Provide Anja with a list of simple vocabulary words to memorize and recite.

D.   Design a contract in which Anja can earn homework passes for turning in her work.

Answers:

A.   **Correct.** By allowing Anja ownership of her assignment and permitting her to choose what she will work on, Ms. Becht is encouraging her to make a personal connection with the assignment. This can lead to genuine interest and increased intrinsic motivation from Anja.

B.   Incorrect. Anja has demonstrated that working in groups is not something she is willing to participate in, so a small-group setting is unlikely to foster intrinsic motivation.

C.   Incorrect. Anja is struggling with motivation. While her struggle may be content related, this assignment would only distance her from developing a desire to learn English because of its simplicity.

D.   Incorrect. Providing Anja with incentives will activate extrinsic motivation, which can temporarily motivate her but ultimately will not be sustainable.

LANGUAGE MODELING, COMPREHENSIBLE INPUT, AND SCAFFOLDING

Instructing second-language learners requires the use of many techniques within a classroom. Oftentimes these methods must be used simultaneously in order for students to grasp the material that is being taught. Language modeling, comprehensible input, and scaffolding can all aid learners in their efforts at second-language learning.

LANGUAGE MODELING

Language modeling refers to providing accurate examples of speech and language for language learners. In the classroom, language modeling occurs both formally and informally. In informal language modeling, teachers use age-appropriate, academic language as they conduct class, address behaviors, and teach lessons; this exposure increases the learners' familiarity with the language and sets the tone for the class.

A formal modeling exercise, on the other hand, typically takes a single, specific goal, referred to as a **target**, and involves learners in developing the skill through practice. These targets may be related to pronunciation, vocabulary, grammar, or any other element of linguistic development. Strong modeling requires a measured pace, and begins with the use of short sentences and targeted, appropriate vocabulary. It also calls for a great deal of repetition.

> **DID YOU KNOW?**
>
> Strong modeling encourages correct syllabic emphasis. For example, when teaching a child to say "please," it is important that models not overemphasize the /p/ sound, making it sound like "*puh*-lease."

SAMPLE QUESTION

14) **Mr. Horn has noticed that Miguel regularly ignores the *h* in many words. He would like to focus specifically on helping Miguel create the /h/ sound when speaking. What should Mr. Horn do to help Miguel with his /h/ sounds?**

    A. Speak more slowly when working with Miguel.

    B. Use only short sentences when speaking to Miguel.

    C. Create a list of *h* words that Miguel does not know and have him recite them.

    D. Pronounce familiar *h* words correctly and have Miguel repeat them.

Answers:

    A. Incorrect. While this approach focuses on the importance of slow and steady speech when modeling, it does not focus on Miguel's mispronunciation or provide him opportunity for practice.

    B. Incorrect. Using short sentences when modeling can be helpful to second-language learners, but in this case it does not target Miguel's problem.

    C. Incorrect. This method could cause Miguel to focus on the meaning of the words and not the pronunciation.

    D. Correct. Practicing the /h/ sound with words Miguel knows will help him to focus on his pronunciation without worrying about the definitions of the words.

COMPREHENSIBLE INPUT

Comprehensible input is new information that students are able to understand because it is introduced alongside information they already know. This integration of new information with existing knowledge helps create new learning: for example, an instructor may introduce the past tense by revisiting and editing a present-tense paragraph the class has already studied; because they are already familiar with the vocabulary, learners are free to focus on processing the new information. The blending of old and new makes the received input slightly more difficult, thereby extending students' learning without making it totally out of reach.

When used correctly, comprehensible input provides students with enough known language that they are able to use their knowledge to interpret the unknown. Students are able to understand most of what is being said, but must take cues from their prior knowledge in order to grasp the full meaning.

SAMPLE QUESTION

15) Which of the following is an example of using comprehensible input to increase student vocabulary?

    A.   Students are provided with a list of vocabulary words that focuses on a central theme.

    B.   Students generate a list of questions regarding vocabulary that they would like to know.

    C.   A teacher narrates what she is doing as she shows students how to work a math problem.

    D.   A teacher assigns a short reading paragraph that incorporates both familiar and unfamiliar words.

Answers:

    A.   Incorrect. The use of a common theme does not ensure that students are familiar with any part of the new material, and therefore does not constitute comprehensible input.

    B.   Incorrect. Material generated by students may not reflect prior knowledge; therefore there can be no guarantee of comprehensible input.

    C.   Incorrect. Unless students are familiar with some portion of the teacher's activities, there is not comprehensible input.

    D.   **Correct.** Comprehensible input refers to the use of the familiar material to aid in the comprehension of new material.

SCAFFOLDING

Scaffolding in a classroom is much like scaffolding on a construction site: it is in place to support students and to allow them to grasp what might otherwise be out of reach. Instructional scaffolding can come in many forms, including asking questions, offering contextual details, and providing visual cues and aids. Most importantly, scaffolding should provide a model of the thought process that students can use to answer the question or problem in front of them. For example, a teacher instructing his students in how to analyze a metaphor might ask English language learners first to define what a metaphor is, then to identify the things being compared in a particular metaphor, and finally to determine what these two things have in common; the students are then more likely to understand the comparison being made.

Because second-language learners are often learning content and language at the same time, this additional support can be extremely beneficial. As they complete assignments and coursework in areas outside of language learning, they are likely to encounter unfamiliar, academic words and sophisticated language usage that can reduce their comprehension. Thus, aiding them in understanding complex texts through scaffolding will allow second-language learners to overcome some of the hurdles in front of them as they delve into content and will prepare them to continue their progress without assistance once they are equipped to do so. As students develop new skills and increase their mastery, scaffolding is slowly removed.

SAMPLE QUESTION

16) Which of the following scaffolding techniques is *least* effective in presenting new content to students learning English?

    A.   using modified reading materials

    B.   previewing vocabulary prior to a lesson

    C.   providing students with an outline for notes

    D.   performing regular checks for understanding

Answers:

    A.   Incorrect. Modified reading materials can help second-language learners grasp the content they are learning by eliminating unfamiliar or overly difficult vocabulary.

    B.   Incorrect. Previewing vocabulary can be helpful for English language learners, as it allows them to anticipate challenging language in the text.

    C.   Incorrect. The use of outlines for notes can be helpful for second-language learners, as they may struggle to keep up with the progression of the lesson if they become lost or distracted by new vocabulary.

    D.   **Correct.** While checking on students' understanding and progress is important, this strategy provides students with no assistance in grasping content material; it only helps the teacher to evaluate where her students are in the learning process.

Literacy

Literacy no longer refers only to students' abilities to read and write; literacy now refers to students' abilities to read, write, think, speak, and understand a given language. As students are expected to meet higher standards and study more rigorous texts, focus on second-language learners' literacy skills becomes increasingly important. Teachers' understanding of literacy and their role in promoting it to students and their families is crucial, as many people do not recognize the significant impact literacy in one language can have on another.

Relationships between English Phonemes and Graphemes

Phonemes are the smallest units of sound that can be heard within a word. The term refers directly to the sound and not the letters that are used to represent it when writing. For example, the word *belt* has four phonemes (b-e-l-t), while the word *shell* has three phonemes (sh-e-l). Learners' abilities to identify and use various phonemes aid them in their understanding of spoken English, allowing them to see how these sounds work together to form words. These skills are generally referred to as **phonemic awareness**.

Graphemes are the symbols used to represent phonemes. They are single letters or groups of letters that represent a sound. For example, in the word *ramp* the grapheme *r* is used to represent the sound that the letter *r* makes in the word; in the word *wrap,* the grapheme *wr* represents the same sound. It is the use of varied graphemes in the English language that often causes English language learners to struggle with pronunciation and spelling.

The relationship between English spelling and pronunciation is a complicated one. There are twenty-six letters in the English alphabet, but nearly double that number of phonemes; further, there is nearly double the number of graphemes than there are phonemes. It's no wonder English language learners struggle with spelling and pronunciation. There are more exceptions to the rules than there are words that follow them! Because of this, spelling and pronunciation are two very different things in English, a fact of which students should be made explicitly aware. They will often need to learn words' pronunciations and spellings separately from one another to avoid confusion and to prevent them from making errors in either area.

DID YOU KNOW?

Mispronouncing a word based upon its spelling is called *spelling pronunciation*. Spelling a word incorrectly based upon its pronunciation is called *eye dialect*.

17) **Which classroom activity would best help students to understand phonemes?**

    A.   having students map out the syllables in sentences they create

    B.   asking students to sound out words they hear and write them down

    C.   asking students to write down all the ways the know to create the /f/ sound

    D.   having students break down the words of a story they hear into individual sounds

Answers:

    A.   Incorrect. This activity could help students understand what syllables are but would not impact their understanding of phonemes.

    B.   Incorrect. This activity will lead to spelling pronunciation errors and will not aid students in their understanding of phonemes.

    C.   Incorrect. This activity could help students understand the graphemes for assigned sounds, but it would not impact their understanding of phonemes.

    D.   **Correct.** This activity will help students in their understanding of phonemes by requiring them to break words up into their smallest sounds.

STANDARD CONVENTIONS OF WRITTEN ENGLISH

The **standard conventions of written English** are the grammar, usage, and mechanics rules that govern the proper production of the English language, particularly in written form. Second-language learners often study these rules as they begin writing in their classes.

Grammar is the set of rules that apply to properly structured sentences; it covers how words function within a sentence and how they are combined into various structures. As students become more proficient in English, their sentences move from simple to compound and reflect the increasingly complex thoughts they have in response to oral and written stimuli. **Usage** refers to the generally accepted ways in which words and phrases are used in different contexts. **Mechanics** are the rules of print that do not exist in spoken language. This term refers to spelling, capitalization, punctuation, and proper paragraphing of written work.

DID YOU KNOW?

Conventions differ between languages, and many students struggle to remember all of the rules when learning a second language. Before teaching a conventions-based lesson, instructors should consider and anticipate what exceptions might arise in the course of the lesson.

SAMPLE QUESTION

18) **Which assignment would allow students to practice applying the standard conventions of written English?**

   A.   editing a friend's history essay

   B.   reading a novel for a literature class

   C.   discussing how to write a lab report

   D.   writing a rough draft of a research paper

Answers:

   A.   **Correct.** This activity would help students understand standard conventions by requiring them to identify and correct errors in a paper.

   B.   Incorrect. This activity will expose students to standard conventions, but it does not allow them the opportunity to practice.

   C.   Incorrect. This activity will expose students to new genres of writing but will not provide much direct practice with standard conventions.

   D.   Incorrect. This activity allows students to practice their written English; however, students should be encouraged to focus on the development of their ideas—rather than the specific conventions—when writing a first draft.

RANGE OF GENRES IN WRITTEN ENGLISH

There are several **genres** in which students are expected to write. As they progress through grade levels, the assignments get more complex but the purposes of the various types of writing remain the same. The ability to successfully convey and analyze messages in several different genres is a key requirement for reaching second-language proficiency. Students are expected to master these skills as part of learning to communicate in their new language.

Students begin learning about **narrative** writing as early as preschool. They may begin by retelling familiar stories, eventually developing sequels, alternate endings, and updated versions of their favorite tales. As they learn to write, students tell about events in their own lives and the lives of those around them. Learners also begin creating original stories, taking into account plot, characters, and even figurative language.

Descriptive writing involves describing things so clearly that readers are able to form pictures in their minds of what is being written. It involves the use of details generated by all five senses, so writers must be very specific in what they choose to include. This type of writing can aid students in increasing their vocabulary and can help them to clarify their understanding of new content.

Expository writing is the genre that students will use most frequently. It is used to explain or inform. Works are written around a central topic and supported with facts and information that are relevant to the topic. These pieces begin with a thesis statement and are followed up by several body paragraphs and a conclusion, in which the material presented is summarized for a final time. When writing expository pieces, students are generally taught to assume that their readers have limited background knowledge on the topic, so they must be given as much information as the writing is able to provide.

In **argumentative** writing, students argue a position on something. They choose (or are assigned) a side, present their arguments, and then explain why their position is more logical, more correct, or otherwise stronger than that of the opposition.

Procedural writing provides readers with information about the necessary steps to accomplish a particular task. It is the kind of writing seen in how-to books and operating manuals. The structure for procedural writing includes a title for the process that is intended to be explained, followed by a purpose, in which writers specify what they want readers to be able to do when they finish reading. Necessary materials are indicated, and then the steps for completion of the procedure are laid out in detail.

> **DID YOU KNOW?**
>
> The ability to determine the author's purpose is essential for students in school and beyond. English language learners who are less attuned to the subtleties of their new language may struggle with this skill. Thus, teachers should prepare to provide scaffolding that helps students recognize important choices in diction and structure.

SAMPLE QUESTION

19) Ms. Worth has asked her students to write an updated version of their favorite Greek myth. What genre of writing should she review with them before students begin the task?

   A.   expository

   B.   descriptive

   C.   narrative

   D.   procedural

Answers:

   A.   Incorrect. Expository writing requires students to provide information about or explanations of a selected topic.

   B.   Incorrect. Descriptive writing is intended to provide details and information to adequately describe a given topic.

   C.   Correct. Narrative writing involves the telling of stories.

   D.   Incorrect. Procedural writing requires students to outline the necessary steps in completing a particular task or assignment.

RANGE OF RHETORICAL PATTERNS IN WRITTEN ENGLISH

A **rhetorical pattern** is the type of organization used in a written piece. There are many common rhetorical patterns in written English. From chronological order to problem and solution, students will be asked to write clearly and purposefully in many of them.

Table 2.2. Rhetorical Patterns in Written English

Pattern	Characteristics
listing	Generally considered a technique for brainstorming, listing is exactly as it sounds. The writer creates lists of possible topics and then breaks them down, creating subtopic lists of what could be said about each area.
chronological order	Chronological order is used to describe or explain events in the order in which they occur, either from first to last or from beginning to end.
cause and effect*	Cause-and-effect patterns show why something happened, the cause, and what the result of it was—the effect.
classification	The classification pattern is used to group information into predetermined categories. The information within each is explained in detail in order to support the writer's main idea.
compare/contrast	Compare/contrast patterns show both similarities (comparisons) and differences (contrasts) between two or more things.
problem and solution	In problem-and-solution patterns, a writer begins by presenting a problem and the causes that have led up to it. This is followed by a presentation of a solution to the problem in which the writer details how a problem can be, will be, or was solved.

*Students often understand *cause and effect* better when approached as *effect and cause* because the sequence of events is clearer: it is difficult to label something a cause without knowing what its effect will be.

20) Mylee is interested in doing extra credit for her science class. Her teacher tells her to write a report about the chemical reactions that occur between metals and acids. Which rhetorical pattern is Mylee being asked to write in?

   A.   argumentative

   B.   cause and effect

   C.   listing

   D.   problem and solution

Answers:

   A.   Incorrect. The report is not intended to present one side of an argument.

   B.   Correct. The report should contain information about what happened during the experiment and why it happened.

   C.   Incorrect. The report should have more details than are necessary in listing.

   D.   Incorrect. There is no indication that Mylee was presented with a problem to be solved.

APPROACHES TO LITERACY DEVELOPMENT

There are several approaches to literacy development that are popular among linguists today. The Whole Language, phonics/skills-based, and Language Experience approaches are used in schools around the country to aid students in strengthening their reading and writing skills.

Supporters of the **Whole Language** approach to literacy development believe that learners should start at the top and work their way down, meaning that language should be considered in its complete form prior to being broken down into smaller pieces. And because language is a social process that is intended for interaction, learners must be permitted to bring their unique backgrounds and experiences into their development and to learn in collaborative environments. Both of these elements are stepping stones for their developmental literacy skills. Students are encouraged to view the ability to communicate as a primary goal, while grammatical rules, spelling, and other functional elements follow. Conventions are taught primarily in response to learner questions.

The **phonics/skills-based approach** to literacy development focuses on transferring students' literacy skills independently. In this approach, specific skills in reading, writing, and speaking are targeted and practiced each day. Learners develop these skills through rehearsal and review, particularly of what is considered critical content. As students become more proficient at generating their own learning, the responsibility transfers over from teacher to student, and they are taught the importance of being accountable for their own literacy development.

The **Language Experience Approach** (LEA) uses learners' prior knowledge and experiences to generate specific lessons that are designed to enhance the learning of each individual student. The experiences are then written down, by either student or teacher, and the resulting text is used as reading material.

There is some contention as to whether teachers should correct student-generated writing. Some argue that students need the true language experience of their own words and therefore the work should not be altered; others feel that teachers should aid students in producing the text in order to ensure they are learning proper conventions. However, regardless of the approach, the material used to teach conventions must come from the student. This strategy capitalizes on learners' abilities to verbalize what they know and allows for a natural bridge between their spoken language skills and their literacy skills.

SAMPLE QUESTION

21) Mrs. Holtz has decided to try the Language Experience Approach (LEA) to developing literacy with her ESL class. She pulls students one by one to her desk and has them tell her a story about what they did over their weekend. As students tell the story, Mrs. Holtz writes down what each child says. She makes sure that her written words match the vocabulary that the student uses. She then has the children swap papers with classmates to read about what they have done over the weekend. As Mrs. Holtz walks around the room, she notices that the students are struggling to read each other's papers.

Where in her implementation of the LEA did Mrs. Holtz make a mistake?

A.   She has students tell her what they did over the weekend.

B.   She writes down what the students tell her about the events.

C.   She uses the same vocabulary in the writing as the students use in their speech.

D.   She has students swap papers to read about their classmates' weekends.

Answers:

A.   Incorrect. In LEA students generate their own stories based on their experiences.

B.   Incorrect. In order for students to have access to their own experiences, either the student or instructor must write it down.

C.   Incorrect. Students' written experiences should match their current spoken vocabulary in order to assist them in developing their reading and writing skills.

D.   **Correct.** Students should use their own written experiences to develop their literacy skills.

STAGES OF LITERACY DEVELOPMENT AND IMPORTANCE OF ORAL LANGUAGE SKILLS

The development of literacy skills for English language learners is unlike the development undergone by native speakers. These students are likely to have competencies in their first languages that they lack in English. Likewise, when instruction begins for these learners, teachers must recognize the potential for English language learners to struggle in areas where their peers may not, including speaking and listening. Addressing these discrepancies may require a special focus on oral language skills in an ESOL classroom.

Oral language plays a very significant role in the development of literacy skills in English language learners. Students' experiences talking and listening help to prepare them for reading and writing by exposing them to vocabulary, sentence structure, and grammar. **Phonemic awareness**, the knowledge that words are made of specific sounds, helps learners separate words into individual sounds, which then aids them in their ability to transfer those sounds to their corresponding printed letters. Exposure to different kinds of speech, including formal and informal settings, also helps students become familiar with the kinds of language that are used in various situations. This, in turn, aids them in using appropriate vocabulary and tone in both speaking and writing. The direct relationship between oral language skills and literacy development can be seen in each of the stages students pass through on their way to fluency.

The **emergent literacy** stage usually refers to the competencies that are developed in early childhood and preschool. In this stage, listening is a key component in making meaning of sounds. For second-language learners, these skills begin developing at the onset of their first experiences with the English language. They begin identifying letters and words and some basic linguistic patterns, such as consonant blends. It is not uncommon for language learners to begin writing before reading. The use of phonological awareness aids them in "sounding out" words as they transfer them to paper, helping them to make meaning of the alphabet.

The **early stage** of literacy development is characterized by the learner's use of multiple strategies to predict and understand words. Students pay close attention to visual cues and use the information gathered to aid them in making sense of language. They use their understanding of linguistic patterns to make meaning of what they are reading, and they benefit from discussions that allow them to explore the text further. Students also begin taking risks by using context to predict the meaning of unfamiliar words, often using background information and discussions about the work to assist them in their interpretations.

Students reach the transitional and fluent stages when they are able to read independently. The **transitional stage** is characterized by a steady reading pace and an understanding of multiple strategies that can be used to decode difficult texts. At this stage, students are able to provide oral summaries of what they are reading. Once they have mastered these skills and enter the **fluency stage**, students demonstrate the ability to maintain meaning throughout longer and more complex texts. They have an understanding of how different kinds of texts work and their purposes, and their discussions often reflect both summary and evaluation of a text.

SAMPLE QUESTION

22) **During which stage of literacy development are students likely to discuss what they are reading with others in order to make sense of the text?**

    A.   emergent

    B.   early

    C.   transitional

    D.   fluency

Answers:

    A.   Incorrect. Students in the emergent stage are generally focused on the sounds of language and how they combine to form words. They are not yet able to discuss texts.

    B.   **Correct.** Students in the early stage are beginning to make meaning of what they are reading and benefit from discussing it with others.

    C.   Incorrect. Students in the transitional phase are able to explain what they have read and discuss the meaning that they have found in it. Though discussion may help these students to further explore what they have read, it is not necessary to their understanding of it.

    D.   Incorrect. Students in the fluency stage are able to discuss what they have read and provide judgments and explanations for their opinions. They do not need to discuss readings in order to understand them.

INFLUENCES OF FIRST-LANGUAGE LITERACY

First-language literacy can play an integral role in students' learning of a second language. When learning a first language, students develop techniques and skills that assist them in decoding speaking, reading, and writing. These techniques can be applied to the acquisition of a second language and help students progress more quickly toward proficiency. For example, when learning new vocabulary, students can access the system of sounds they created when learning their first language.

Because they already possess some **phonological awareness**—the understanding that language is made up of sounds, syllables, rhythms, words, and patterns—students are able to then transfer this understanding to their second language. They recognize that words can rhyme, be broken into individual sounds, and be manipulated to make new words. For example, a teacher might dissect the word *snake* with a class, forming the /sn/ and /ake/ sounds. The teacher would then use the *sn* to create *snip* and the *ake* to create *bake*, discussing with students the new words created and the rhyming pattern found between *snake* and *bake*.

Research has shown that students with a firm grasp of phonological awareness in their first language are more likely to be successful in their acquisition of a second language because of the likelihood of their transferring skills from one language to the other. Students with deficits in this area can benefit from phonics instruction; however, they may have difficulty applying this information to reading and writing. It is best to review these skills in the context of content learning so that students can see the direct application of the skill.

Phonological awareness requires knowledge of phonemes. Thus, students who demonstrate overall phonological awareness usually demonstrate understanding of individual phonemes first; likewise, a student who struggles to identify individual phonemes will struggle with overall phonological awareness and, likely, pronunciation.

Across all languages, phonological awareness skills develop in a stable pattern. Students tend to learn from larger groups of phonemes, such as words, to the smallest groups, the phonemes themselves. And even if students are still developing these skills in their native languages, their learned abilities will transfer from their native language to their English learning. Of course, the closer the two phonologies are, the easier the transfer will be for the student.

SAMPLE QUESTION

23) **Why are students with strong phonological awareness of their native language more likely to succeed in learning to read English?**

   A. They have advanced reading levels in their native language.

   B. They have greater exposure to second-language vocabulary.

   C. They have a higher likelihood of knowledge transfer between languages.

   D. They have superior oral skills development in their native and second languages.

Answers:

   A. Incorrect. Having an advanced reading level in a native language does not indicate that one will succeed in reading in a second language.

   B. Incorrect. Phonological awareness in a native language does not indicate a student's exposure to vocabulary in a second language.

   C. Correct. Students who possess strong phonological awareness recognize that the patterns of language transfer.

   D. Incorrect. Phonological awareness does not directly impact a student's oral skill development in native or second languages.

3

Instruction

Effective ESOL instruction is comprised of several important elements. First, it must be grounded in one or more proven instructional theories, which guide how language teachers can shape their classrooms and lessons to help students continually acquire new language skills. In addition, effective instruction must take into account the school's or district's program model, which determines the kinds of additional supports—those outside the general education classrooms—that language learners will receive. Effective instructors must also apply purposeful teaching techniques, which shape how teachers interact with their students and each other to support learning. Classroom materials also play an essential role in effective instruction, as they provide a way for students to interact with the material in a meaningful way. Finally, effective instruction must be built on a foundation of strong classroom management skills, which allow teachers to build safe classroom environments in which students are engaged and motivated.

INSTRUCTIONAL THEORY

There are several significant theoretical approaches to teaching second-language classes. Each approach has specific goals as well as unique applications, strengths, and weaknesses in helping students achieve proficiency. Most students, therefore, benefit from the simultaneous use of several different instructional methods, each of which plays a key role in helping learners progress toward language proficiency.

DIRECT METHOD

The **direct method**, also called the **natural method**, of language instruction is based on the principle that second languages should be acquired in much the same way as first languages. Skills are slowly developed as students acquire targeted vocabulary through repeated exposure to authentic language usage, supported by pictures, objects, and pantomime. In direct method instruction, oral language skills are emphasized, but students are not required to speak; instead, teachers provide students with materials in the target language and permit them to take their time acclimating to the new language to create a stress-free learning environment. Proponents of this method believe that if students are not forced to speak and are provided with sufficient comprehensible input, they will produce comprehensible output when they are ready.

Teachers should remember that the terms *direct method* and *direct instruction* are not interchangeable. The direct method is a specific approach to language instruction in which students learn a second language through exposure and emersion; direct instruction is a general approach to instruction that involves explicitly teaching or demonstrating skills to students.

As students grasp new vocabulary, they build up a collection of sentences from which they can understand the grammatical structures of the language without being explicitly taught. According to this theory, students learn grammar through **induction**; that is, they figure out the rules of the language as they acquire speaking and listening skills, learning through a combined process of imitation and trial and error.

HELPFUL HINT

Though elements of the direct method are still used in classrooms today, a major weakness lies in this method's assumption that students can learn a second language the same way they learned their first: conditions for learning first and second languages are rarely the same, and many students require direct instruction in elements of English grammar to achieve proficiency in it.

Direct method instruction usually begins with exposure to simple questions aimed at eliciting simple responses in the target language. As students progress, the questions become more difficult, requiring multiword, and eventually sentence-length, responses. Still, the focus is never on grammatical structure; instead, the key objective is to create a wide vocabulary base with the understanding that grammar and syntax will be learned predominantly through induction and practice.

Culture—both that of the student and that which is associated with the target language—is also considered important to the natural method. Despite this, students' native languages are never used in the natural method, and translations are not provided. Therefore, learning material is often first presented with pictures, actions, or other visual cues to aid students in making connections between the target language and their prior knowledge.

SAMPLE QUESTIONS

1) **Which of the following activities uses the direct method of second-language instruction?**

    A. Students are paired together to write a short story.

    B. Students read a play together with each student taking a role.

    C. Students choose a topic from a teacher-provided list and have a discussion about it.

    D. Students give oral presentations on research they have done for their science classes.

    Answers:

    A. Incorrect. Authentic speaking and listening activities are the primary focus of the direct method; writing is not a primary focus of this type of instruction.

    B. Incorrect. While this activity would provide students practice speaking and reading aloud, it does not provide an opportunity for authentic engagement with the language.

    C. Correct. Students are provided with speaking and listening opportunities that revolve around authentic discussions in which they must actively engage and communicate.

    D. Incorrect. Though this activity focuses on oral presentation, it does not provide an opportunity for authentic engagement with relevant vocabulary.

2) **In order to ensure that she is using the natural method correctly, Mrs. Holmes must do which of the following?**

    A. provide specific targeted vocabulary

    B. require students to speak in the target language

    C. provide instruction in the students' first languages

    D. make specific corrections to grammatical errors

    Answers:

    A. Correct. Students are provided with materials in the target language to increase exposure and elicit communication.

    B. Incorrect. Teachers using the natural method must never require students to speak in any language as it may cause stress and anxiety.

    C. Incorrect. In order to provide students with maximum comprehensible input in the language they are learning, teachers using the natural method do not deliver instruction in the students' native languages.

    D. Incorrect. Proponents of the natural method place an emphasis on communication and vocabulary building over grammar and syntax because they argue that grammar and syntax will be learned inductively.

GRAMMAR-TRANSLATION METHOD

The **grammar-translation method** of language instruction was originally intended to assist students in reading and translating of foreign language literature. By teaching in students' native languages and concentrating on grammatical rules of a target language, instructors help students recognize similarities between their native and learned languages, aiding them in understanding grammatical rules and acquiring new vocabulary.

The grammar-translation method emphasizes translating between languages in activities that allow students to develop strengths in reading and writing, believed to aid students in achieving greater accuracy in their use of the target language. Additionally, proponents of the method believe that the development of reading skills increases students' vocabularies, allows for greater understanding of figures of speech and idiomatic expressions, enhances interpretation abilities, and allows students to produce strong written work in the target language.

QUICK REVIEW

Those who oppose the grammar-translation method frequently argue that students who learn this way develop only limited speaking skills. What other limitations might result from the application of this method?

SAMPLE QUESTION

3) Why do some language theorists and instructors OPPOSE the grammar-translation method of foreign language instruction?

   A. Students are taught in their native languages.

   B. Students do not learn to write in the target language.

   C. Students acquire vocabulary through reading exercises.

   D. Students are not required to speak in the target language.

Answers:

   A. Incorrect. Several methods of foreign language instruction allow for instruction to take place in students' native languages.

   B. Incorrect. This method calls for extensive writing and translation activities.

   C. Incorrect. All methods of foreign language instruction, at some stage of acquisition, require students to build their vocabularies through reading exercises.

   D. Correct. Opponents of the theory argue that students do not learn to speak and listen in the target language and therefore cannot gain proficiency.

AUDIO-LINGUAL METHOD

The **audio-lingual method** (ALM) is an oral-based approach to language instruction developed by linguists and behavioral psychologists. Originally intended for military use, the ALM started out as the Army Specialized Training Program, later known as the Army Method, and was funded by the United States government. The method was used to teach military personnel serving in World War II how to communicate with foreign soldiers and officers.

Much like the direct method, ALM teaches the target language through repetition. Students engage in repetitive exercises that emphasize grammatical structural patterns and vocabulary and focus on key phrases and significant dialogue that are considered most useful to the particular circumstances. (This element was a key component for WWII military personnel.)

ALM is based in behavioral theories of psychology. As learners work through drills, instructors reward them for correct responses, encouraging them to produce more of the same; incorrect responses are disregarded in hopes that they will be repressed. ALM proposes that through this series of purposeful rewards, students learn the necessary components of successful interaction. Instructors move on to new vocabulary and topics when they are confident students have grasped the previous material.

SAMPLE QUESTION

4) Mr. Hansen's students are learning new vocabulary that they might use in everyday conversation. They listen to a recording once, repeating each line after the speaker. As students recite back what they have heard, Mr. Hansen praises the pronunciation of some students while ignoring that of others.

What method of instruction is Mr. Hansen practicing?

A. audio-lingual

B. induction

C. direct method

D. grammar-translation

Answers:

A. **Correct.** The use of oral practice and behavioral conditioning indicates that this is the audio-lingual method of language instruction.

B. Incorrect. Induction is a key component of the direct method of instruction in which students are said to acquire second languages in the same way they acquired their first.

C. Incorrect. The use of rewards and emphasis on pronunciation indicates that it is not the direct method.

D. Incorrect. The focus of grammar-translation instruction is reading and writing, neither of which is present in this lesson.

COMMUNICATIVE APPROACH

The **communicative approach** to language learning, a combination of several methods of language instruction, is based on the notion that successful language acquisition comes from the need to communicate real meaning. To successfully acquire a new language, learners must be required to use real communication to engage their natural strategies for language acquisition.

One methodology housed under the communicative approach is **communicative language teaching** (CLT), which focuses on students' abilities to communicate through interactions in the target language. In CLT instruction, students use authentic texts and realistic scenarios to practice skills they would use outside the classroom. They are encouraged to consider personal experiences in an attempt to link their new learning to their prior knowledge, thus developing a greater understanding of the material. These practices aid learners in developing **communicative competence**—a person's knowledge of grammar and syntax, as well as his or her ability to interpret and execute appropriate social behaviors and conversational elements such as idiomatic expressions and cultural slang.

TEACHING TIP

Communicative language teaching focuses on elements of speaking and listening, so lessons become learner focused without an emphasis on language systems and conventions.

Task-based instruction (TBI) is another instructional method that falls under the umbrella of the communicative approach to language teaching. In TBI, lessons are designed around the completion of tasks that are either assigned by instructors or selected by students. It is important to note that tasks are usually defined as activities that are carried out by learners using their language knowledge and resources; these activities have real outcomes from which students are able to judge their performance on the task. Though this method does not call for direct instruction in grammar and syntax, it has been shown to produce favorable outcomes by mimicking first-language acquisition, allowing students' input in their own learning, and emphasizing the application of real-life skills.

SAMPLE QUESTIONS

5) Karla has been practicing interactions she will have with friends at her new school. She has been working to understand idiomatic expressions and rehearsing their use in casual conversation.

   What is Karla working to improve?

   A. communicative competence

   B. morpheme acquisition

   C. phonemic awareness

   D. rhetorical patterns

Answers:

A.   **Correct.** Karla is focusing on realistic interactions and the use of common expressions in her language learning.

B.   Incorrect. Morpheme acquisition refers to an individual's understanding of morphemes and their ability to convey meaning or play a part in the grammatical structure of a word.

C.   Incorrect. Phonemic awareness refers to an individual's knowledge that words are made of specific sounds, allowing learners to separate words into individual sounds.

D.   Incorrect. Rhetorical patterns refer to the types of organization used in written works.

6)   **Which of the following would be considered task-based instruction?**

A.   Students listen to songs on the radio, select a song, and rehearse the lyrics; they use the chorus of the song as a conversation starter.

B.   Students translate passages from their favorite short stories; they trade papers with a partner and read each other's papers.

C.   Students organize a classroom party using their target language; they create a detailed plan, distributing responsibility and mapping out activities.

D.   Students read aloud to one another from texts provided by the teacher; then they take turns asking one another questions about the text.

Answers:

A.   Incorrect. This example more closely resembles the audio-lingual method because students are being asked to repeat back what they have heard in order to memorize it.

B.   Incorrect. This example more closely resembles the grammar-translation method, as students are asked to focus on translation, reading, and writing.

C.   **Correct.** This is task-based instruction because students are given a specific task to execute and then must follow through to demonstrate their success.

D.   Incorrect. This example more closely resembles the direct method, as it has predetermined vocabulary in the text, provided by the teacher.

TOTAL PHYSICAL RESPONSE

Total physical response (TPR) is an instructional method that provides students, particularly beginning language learners, with the opportunity to acquire language skills by listening to and following spoken commands. Initially, instructors model commands and repeat them as students carry them out, using facial expressions and gestures to help students understand what they are supposed to do. Students are not required to speak, only to follow the commands. Continuous support and modeling aid in eliminating pressure and anxiety, allowing students to feel successful from the start of their language acquisition.

As students progress, commands become increasingly more complicated and eventually involve the use of props. Students begin to interact with the environment around them, expanding their vocabulary and comprehension. Additionally, this method can be used to reinforce vocabulary that students have previously learned, as a game to provide students with a break, or even as an assessment tool to provide teachers insight into student proficiency levels.

SAMPLE QUESTION

7) Mrs. Rose would like to try total physical response with one of her classes. Which class would this method MOST benefit?

   A.   students who are preparing to exit ESOL instruction

   B.   students who are in their first year of ESOL instruction

   C.   students who demonstrate advanced speaking and listening skills

   D.   students who demonstrate intermediate reading and writing skills

Answers:

   A.   Incorrect. Students who are preparing to exit ESOL may find that participation in TPR does not aid them in advancing their language skills because it is too simplistic.

   B.   Correct. TPR is most beneficial to students who are just entering ESOL programs.

   C.   Incorrect. Students with advanced speaking and listening skills may demonstrate strong vocabulary understanding and may not benefit from the use of TPR.

   D.   Incorrect. Students who demonstrate intermediate reading and writing skills may have a strong enough vocabulary that TPR is not beneficial to them. Its use is intended for beginning language learners.

THE SILENT WAY

The **Silent Way** is based on the idea that language learning should be much like problem-solving and discovery learning. Teachers are as silent as possible during lessons in order to promote student participation and experimentation and to concentrate on the learning over the teaching. Using gestures and minimal speech, teachers focus students on specific goals or activities and elicit responses that students are then encouraged to correct for themselves. Translation, repetition, and rote memorization are avoided, and students are encouraged to pay particular attention to their pronunciation. Additionally, teachers avoid using praise or criticism so that students develop a sense of self-reliance.

Manipulatives are a significant component of the Silent Way. Teachers frequently use tools such as **Cuisenaire rods**, Fidel charts, and sound-color charts to teach various elements of language pronunciation and speech. Cuisenaire rods are sets of colored rods of different lengths that can be manipulated to demonstrate prepositional relationships, make comparisons, represent objects, and even form models. Fidel charts are displays of English words, arranged according to their sounds. Students are encouraged to interact with these materials to produce comparisons and expand their knowledge of vocabulary, often through trial and error and experimentation. Many beginners start with sound-color charts, working with sounds that exist in their native languages in order to learn the sounds of English words. They then begin to practice sounds that are new to them as they progress through their learning. Eventually, these sound-color associations aid students in learning to read in their newly acquired language.

SAMPLE QUESTION

8) Which of the following manipulatives is NOT commonly found in a Silent Way classroom?

   A. Cuisenaire rods

   B. Fidel charts

   C. sound-color charts

   D. translation charts

Answers:

   A. Incorrect. Students use Cuisenaire rods to demonstrate prepositional relationships, as well as to create many other representations.

   B. Incorrect. Students use Fidel charts to build spelling and vocabulary skills.

   C. Incorrect. Students use sound-color charts to learn the sounds of the new language.

   D. Correct. Use of the Silent Way calls for minimal translation exercise, as the focus for students is vocabulary acquisition and pronunciation.

PROGRAM MODELS

Various ESOL program models are used in schools across the United States to meet the needs of a diverse population of learners. Most school districts have implemented one or two models, which work in conjunction to increase the effectiveness of students' second-language learning; it is the teachers' responsibility to work within the school's selected models to meet learners' unique needs.

Go on →

PUSH-IN

Push-in ESOL programs are intended to maximize the time English language learners spend in general education content classrooms. In this model, ESOL teachers travel to content classrooms, providing additional support and services to language learners. They may use one-on-one instruction, assign small-group work, or aid the content teacher in delivering whole-group instruction. The most effective ESOL instructors engage with content teachers in **co-planning** to create lessons, assessments, and activities that address the needs of all the students in the classroom.

Team-teaching is another effective way that ESOL teachers implement a push-in model. In team-teaching, each teacher plays an important role, and they take turns delivering lessons to the class: the classroom teacher is seen as the content expert, while the ESOL teacher is recognized as the expert in creating accommodations for language learners. Accordingly, the ESOL teacher leads the classroom teacher in scaffolding and differentiating for the language learners in the class. Team-teaching is considered one of the most effective models for pushing-in, as it provides both teachers the opportunity to actively contribute, creating an environment in which students receive plentiful support.

Small-group instruction is another type of push-in service. In this model, the ESOL teacher takes a group of language learners during independent work time and reinforces or reteaches skills that were covered in the content lesson. This type of support can also be used to provide instruction in other areas, such as grammar or communication skills, that language learners may require. In the push-in model, small-group lessons are intended to align with classroom content; however, they may be aligned to an ESOL objective-based plan as well. While this model is less effective for classes with many language learners, it can be beneficial when there is a small population of ESOL students.

When ESOL teachers work individually with language learners, they are practicing **one-on-one instruction**, an approach that is most often used to assess reading and writing skills and to address specific areas of challenge for individual learners. These one-on-one lessons, which usually occur during students' independent work time, should align with the content area goals and objectives to ensure that students are progressing simultaneously in their content and language learning. However, while these lessons can be beneficial when done sporadically, frequent one-on-one lessons can have a negative impact on learning, as students may not gain the confidence required to use their new language in group settings.

The effectiveness of the push-in model depends heavily on the relationship between the content teacher and the ESOL teacher. Unfortunately, ESOL specialists are sometimes limited in their contributions because content teachers are reluctant to engage them as equal contributors to the classroom environment. Thus, it is important for ESOL instructors to communicate early and often with content teachers about the roles they will each play and the specific kinds of support they will each provide. Effective collaboration allows ESOL and content teachers to provide the best instruction possible to the unique population of students in their classroom.

SAMPLE QUESTION

9)   Ms. Ortega is a new ESOL teacher, and she has been assigned to provide push-in instruction to students in an eighth grade English Language Arts class. Which of the following activities would NOT be a good use of Ms. Ortega's specialized training?

A.   helping her co-teacher grade multiple-choice quizzes from the language learners in her class

B.   creating differentiated materials for language learners in the classroom

C.   contributing to the co-teacher's lesson plan and helping her to execute it with the language learners in the classroom

D.   working with a small group of English language learners to understand a difficult passage in the novel the class is reading

Answers:

A.   **Correct.** ESOL specialists are not classroom assistants. Though they may occasionally help with grading, it should only be with the purpose of evaluating how language learners are progressing.

B.   Incorrect. ESOL specialists are trained in differentiating materials for students of varying proficiency levels, so designing appropriate materials is a good use a time.

C.   Incorrect. ESOL instruction is especially productive when specialists and content teachers cooperate to plan and execute lessons that can reach all learners.

D.   Incorrect. Small-group instruction within the content classroom is a primary responsibility of an ESOL instructor who is implementing a push-in model.

PULL-OUT

In **pull-out** programs, certified ESOL teachers take small groups of students from their content area classrooms for limited portions of the school day. During this time, English language learners receive specialized instruction, focusing not on content area work, but on intensive vocabulary and grammar objectives that will enable them access to academic content. These sessions generally last thirty to forty-five minutes and occur at different frequencies for each child depending on his or her needs. Common in elementary schools, pull-out programs are most effective in aiding students with low levels of English comprehension and those who need to develop basic skills very quickly.

Pull-out programs emphasize those English skills that will prepare students to participate in their content area classes. Because pull-out groups are usually determined by proficiency level, they provide a safe environment for English language learners to take academic risks, practice listening and speaking their new language, and participate in class without the fear or frustration. Small-group instruction allows ESOL specialists to observe student growth closely, providing continual support and feedback until the student reaches proficiency.

Opponents of the pull-out model cite time as the biggest challenge. States mandate a minimum period of time be devoted to pull-out programs; these minimums put a strain on limited resources and require students to miss a significant amount of content instruction. ESOL teachers are often overwhelmed by the schedules they must keep to meet all learners' needs, and student participants fall behind in content classes as a result of missing valuable instructional time.

SAMPLE QUESTION

10) **Pull-out ESOL instruction is most commonly found in which academic setting?**

A.   preschool level

B.   elementary school

C.   middle school

D.   high school

Answers:

A.   Incorrect. Students at the preschool level are not pulled from classes because their play is deemed an appropriate way to gain language skills.

B.   **Correct.** Pull-out programs are most frequently used in elementary schools because the small-group instruction allows for greater differentiation and closer observation; this structure provides beginning language learners the opportunity to develop basic, necessary skills as quickly as possible.

C.   Incorrect. Pull-out programs are less common at the middle school level, as students need to be in content classes for as much time as is possible.

D.   Incorrect. Pull-out programs are less common at the high school level, as students need to be in content classes for as much time as is possible.

SHELTERED

Sheltered instruction provides English language learners with access to appropriate, grade-level content while supporting their need for ongoing language instruction. Students in these programs do not attend classes with English-speaking students, but they do study the same curriculum: ESOL teachers use various methods in a self-contained classroom to teach students both English language skills and academic content.

The **Sheltered Instruction Observation Protocol (SIOP)** model is a research-based method of ESOL instruction that addresses the multiple needs of language learners. It was designed to increase the academic achievement of second-language learners by supporting their linguistic development and making grade-level academic content comprehensible. It is not the only model for sheltered instruction, but significant research supports its effectiveness. It consists of eight components:

1. **Lesson Preparation**—Teachers generate lessons that are purposeful, accessible, and relevant. Lessons are driven by clearly defined content and language objectives, which are appropriate to learners' ages and educational backgrounds. Teachers employ a variety of materials and methods to engage students in their learning, and content is adapted for all levels of language proficiency.

2. **Building Background**—Direct connections are made between students' prior learning and background experiences and the new material being covered. Key vocabulary is taught and emphasized prior to the lesson, when the new words are presented in the context of the larger learning objective.

3. **Comprehensible Input**—Teachers use language that is appropriate for their students, accounting for speed, pronunciation, and students' proficiency levels; teachers may also need to repeat things frequently, avoid the use of slang words and idioms, and pair spoken words with pictures and gestures. Teachers explain tasks step-by-step, pausing to check for student understanding, and they use a variety of support materials to ensure students clearly comprehend what is being communicated.

4. **Learning Strategies**—Teachers explicitly instruct students in higher-order thinking and metacognitive skills to encourage students' comprehension and retention of material. Purposeful and consistent scaffolding, which leads students through a clear thought process, allows continual growth and can be scaled back as students' language proficiencies increase. Lesson activities provide ample opportunity for students to rehearse their cognitive skills.

5. **Interaction**—Students are given ample time to interact with the teacher and with one another in order to fully engage with the material they are learning. Extended discussions allow students to gain deeper understanding of the concepts and to internalize new knowledge, sometimes by clarifying important information in their native languages. Interaction also allows students to practice both receptive and productive communication skills; thus, instructors carefully select

and continuously vary student groupings in order to support content and language development.

6. **Practice and Application**—Hands-on materials and manipulatives are used throughout lessons in order for students to practice and apply content knowledge to their language learning. Students participate in activities that integrate all aspects of language learning (reading, writing, speaking, and listening) in order to create connections between abstract concepts and concrete skills.

7. **Lesson Delivery**—Content and language objectives are clearly and continuously supported throughout lessons. Lessons are paced purposefully to match students' ability levels and keep them engaged in learning as much as possible. Engagement is achieved through discussions in which students are able to talk about lesson concepts and ideas and through hands-on activities that reinforce student learning.

8. **Review and Assessment**—Review, assessments, and feedback are incorporated into daily activities. Teachers review concepts and vocabulary throughout, as well as at the conclusion of each lesson, to reinforce material and improve student retention. In addition, teachers provide constructive feedback regularly based on ongoing formal and informal assessments, the results of which guide future instructional decisions and design.

SAMPLE QUESTIONS

11) **What is unique about the SIOP model of instruction?**

   A. Students are in a classroom with their peers for only some of their content studies.

   B. Students are in a self-contained classroom in which they learn both content and language skills.

   C. Teachers work in pairs to provide students with content and linguistic instruction in a single classroom setting.

   D. Teachers travel with language learners from class to class and work with them in their content classrooms.

   Answers:

   A. Incorrect. This description is of the pull-out model, in which students are pulled from their grade-level content classes for blocks of time to receive specialized language instruction.

   B. **Correct.** SIOP students work in a self-contained classroom where they learn both content and linguistic skills.

   C. Incorrect. This model of team-teaching is common in push-in programs but not in sheltered instruction programs.

   D. Incorrect. This model of push-in teaching is not common in the SIOP model.

12) **According to the SIOP model, how frequently should students' learning be assessed?**

A. daily

B. weekly

C. monthly

D. biannually

Answers:

A. **Correct.** Students' learning should be assessed daily to inform teachers' instructional plans.

B. Incorrect. Weekly assessments would not provide enough data to accurately inform teachers' daily lesson plans.

C. Incorrect. Monthly assessments would not provide enough data to accurately inform teachers' daily lesson plans.

D. Incorrect. Biannual assessments would not provide enough data to accurately inform teachers' daily lesson plans.

TEACHING TECHNIQUES

There are a variety of teaching techniques that encourage students' learning and foster the development skills in English language learners. Successful instructors seek to expose themselves to a plethora of techniques, implementing and evaluating them in the context of their own classrooms. Over time, educators can begin to use their experience to prepare and deliver lessons that are effective, meaningful, and engaging for their unique populations of students.

ORGANIZING AND COLLABORATING

Organizing instruction around specific content and language objectives is one way that teachers can ensure that their students are receiving effective, purposeful instruction. Clearly defined content and language objectives are guided by **academic standards**, which define the knowledge and skills that students must attain at each grade level.

Content area standards identify what students are supposed to learn throughout a given time period in a specific subject area; they are intended to guide instruction and clearly define achievement goals so that all students learn the same material and gain the same skills. Each content area has its own set of standards, the most significant of which are tested annually, such as those included in the Common Core curriculum; standardized state exams are based on and aligned with these standards. Schools, content teams, and individual teachers might also define a set of standards for specific semesters or units to ensure they are planning appropriately for students to meet all standards by the end of the school year.

Content objectives identify what students should be able to do at the end of a content area lesson. These objectives are usually the same for all students in the classroom because they are aligned with content area standards for which nearly all students are responsible. Classroom content objectives should be clearly stated so that students can understand them without explanation and should have measurable goals that are achievable in the available time. One example of a well-written content objective is "Students will explain three contributions made by George Washington that improved the lives of people living in the United States." This objective clearly states what students should be able to do at the end of the lesson and can be measured in a number of ways.

Language objectives describe how ESOL students will demonstrate their mastery of language materials by reading, writing, speaking, or listening. Effective language objectives meet several criteria:

1. They are formed using the tasks of the content area lesson.
2. They emphasize the communicative skills of speaking and writing without neglecting the importance of listening and reading.
3. They use active verbs to name targeted functions.
4. They specify targeted language knowledge or skills that students will need to complete the task.
5. They focus on language that is suitable for students' use in other contexts.

A well-written language objective provides a precise look at the expectations for ESOL students' learning. For example, the objective "Students will make predictions about the events in the short story using future tense and conditional verbs" states what students will be expected to do and what kind of language they will be expected to use. Each element of the objective is clear and measurable.

To ensure that both content and language objectives are appropriate for students, ESOL and content area teachers should collaborate to define them. Doing so will make both teachers aware of all expectations for students and will make students' learning more meaningful because their content area learning and their language learning will be connected.

SAMPLE QUESTION

13) **Which of the following statements is a clearly written language objective?**

A. Students will learn about the Battle of Antietam.

B. Students will write a summary of their science lab.

C. Students will identify and define the adjectives used in a character description.

D. Students will listen to two pianists' interpretations of Beethoven's Fifth Symphony.

Answers:

A.   Incorrect. This objective is not measurable and does not indicate targeted language skills.

B.   Incorrect. This objective is not measurable and does not indicate targeted language skills.

C.   Correct. This objective is clear, measurable, and transferable to other contexts, and it indicates targeted language skills.

D.   Incorrect. This objective is not focused on communicative linguistic skills.

PROMOTING MENTAL DEVELOPMENT OF STUDENTS

While students naturally develop many mental skills on their own, teachers can promote cognitive development through lessons and activities that are aimed at increasing students' understanding of cognitive and metacognitive strategies. Specific learning strategies—which are not intuitive—should be integrated into lessons so that students have the opportunity to learn and practice applying valuable thinking skills.

Cognitive strategies help students retain and organize the knowledge they gain; thus, deliberate instruction in these strategies can help all students become more successful in their learning. For example, effective readers skim titles, headings, and pictures for information before reading a new text. Because this is not an intuitive behavior (most students simply start at the top), teachers must explicitly teach children this skill as they are learning to read so that it becomes a habitual process. Eventually, skimming becomes an ingrained behavior, assisting students in anticipating what they are about to read and aiding them in making predictions, without even realizing they are doing so.

Six types of strategies aid students in their learning:

1.   **Comprehension strategies** help students process and retain content. These strategies are usually broken into the subcategories of monitoring, using text structures, summarizing, elaborating, and explaining. When explicitly taught to use these strategies, students can retain and comprehend new information more easily.

2.   **Writing strategies** help students complete unstructured tasks by emphasizing the importance of planning in order to conceive and organize ideas. Students should be taught explicit planning and brainstorming strategies, as well as processes for completing a complex assignment: after they have planned their work, students should be taught to produce an initial draft, to make revisions to their content, and to implement minor edits before presenting final products. Students who purposefully employ writing strategies are more likely to create comprehensive, well-composed pieces.

3. **Problem-solving strategies** help students see ways in which they can achieve a specific goal. There are several effective problem-solving strategies, but the most important skills equip students to understand a problem and then develop a plan for solving it. Additionally, students benefit from reflecting on their own problem-solving processes, looking back to see what can be learned from their processes and their solutions.

4. **Reasoning strategies** help students determine what they believe to be true or false, correct or incorrect. Successful reasoning involves the creation of arguments and counterarguments, the fair evaluation of evidence, and the careful consideration of source materials.

5. **Self-regulation strategies** help students monitor their behaviors. Students who master self-regulation are capable of successful self-monitoring and evaluation, time management, and goal setting. These skills aid them in their learning endeavors by contributing to their metacognitive processes and focus.

6. **Metacognitive strategies** are those that involve thinking about thinking: they require reflection on one's own thinking processes and knowledge. Metacognition is not an intuitive process; therefore, students must be taught how to analyze their knowledge in order to successfully plan, monitor, evaluate, and revise their thinking to meet various learning goals. Most importantly, metacognitive strategies allow students to identify their prior knowledge on a topic, recognize what they do not know, and determine what they still need to learn.

Direct instruction in a variety of metacognitive strategies can lead to increases in student learning:

1. **Identify what is known and what is not.** Students need to recognize their prior learning and then move forward in determining what they do not know, what they need clarification on, and what knowledge has stuck with them.

2. **Plan.** Estimating the amount of time that a task will take, organizing materials, scheduling group or individual work time, and determining procedures for completing the task all require planning. Students should be taught how to complete these components of planning in order to become more self-directed.

3. **Keep a thought journal.** Logging their thoughts and ideas can help students reflect upon their thinking and understanding of a topic. It can also help them to recognize any difficulties they are experiencing as they work through a problem or process.

4. **Talk about thinking.** This process must be modeled for students. Teachers should think aloud during problem-solving and planning activities to show students what this process looks like. This will enable

them to understand what it means to talk about their thinking and will demonstrate the benefits of the practice.

5. **Self-evaluate.** Students should be shown through modeling what it means to self-evaluate. Providing them with checklists or one-on-one conferences can help them to develop the skills necessary for evaluating their own success. As students come to recognize how they can implement strategies and where the strategies are most useful, they will develop the ability to evaluate not only their success on the task at hand but also their effectiveness at applying specific cognitive processes.

6. **Debrief.** Activities that focus on closure help students develop awareness of the strategies they implemented, as well as where their successes and areas of improvement lie. Taking time to discuss and debrief also helps them to recognize the cross-curricular uses of the strategies they have applied.

Activating students' prior knowledge can help them make connections between what they already know and what they are going to learn. Teachers can implement several strategies to activate students' prior knowledge:

1. **Introduce vocabulary before content.** Learning new words prior to being expected to apply them allows students to gain comfort and familiarity with the new vocabulary in a low-stress context. By reviewing relevant, familiar vocabulary alongside new words, teachers allow students to demonstrate mastery and activate prior knowledge.

2. **Use graphic organizers, outlines, and diagrams.** Helping students visualize content can aid them in recall. By creating a visual aid to organize information, students can make new connections as they recall prior learning.

3. **Brainstorm ideas about the topic or content.** When beginning with a brainstorming activity, students can share ideas and knowledge with one another, making connections between what they are learning and what they already know.

4. **Ask questions about the content or topic and things related to it.** This kind of free association exercise can help students use vocabulary they already know and prepare them to use their new knowledge in authentic, communicative ways.

Additionally, activating prior knowledge can aid students in the transfer of language skills from their first language to their second. Recognizing linguistic similarities in phonology, spelling, and word meaning allows students to retain new language learning more effectively by connecting it to existing knowledge.

The ability to transfer linguistic understanding from one language to another presents ESOL students with unique advantages and disadvantages. Students who have strong phonological processing and reading skills in their first language may transfer some of those skills to their second-language learning, so reading in their second language appears to come more easily. Additionally, knowing the rules of syntax and grammar in a first language can lend itself to structurally similar second languages. The sharing of common rules between languages allows for positive transfer of understanding.

QUICK REVIEW

Recall that negative transfer of information causes students to incorrectly apply rules from their first language to their second.

On the other hand, differences between first and second languages can cause negative transfer for English language learners. For example, a Spanish-speaking student may say "I no like it" instead of "I do not like it" because the use of the word *no* in Spanish indicates the negative. In this example, the student has incorrectly transferred knowledge of his first language into his use of English.

SAMPLE QUESTIONS

14) Mr. Carson wants to conduct a classroom experiment to see how many students are able to get an inflated balloon from one side of the room to the other without using their arms, legs, or mouths. He has set some obstacles in the room for students to get around, including a large blue tarp on the floor that he has labeled *quicksand*. Any student who touches the quicksand is automatically out.

What kind of cognitive strategy should Mr. Carson model for students before allowing them to attempt the activity?

A.   comprehension strategy

B.   problem-solving strategy

C.   reasoning strategy

D.   writing strategy

Answers:

A.   Incorrect. Students conducting this experiment do not need to recall content information.

B.   Correct. Students conducting this experiment need to work out how to solve the problem presented using a series of logical steps.

C.   Incorrect. Students conducting this experiment do not need to draw conclusions about what is true or false, logical or illogical.

D.   Incorrect. Students conducting this experiment are not working on an unstructured writing task.

15) **Which of the following strategies is NOT intended to aid students in activating prior knowledge?**

    A.   asking questions about the content

    B.   introducing vocabulary before content

    C.   using graphic organizers, diagrams, and outlines

    D.   listening to an expert speaker discuss the content

Answers:

    A.   Incorrect. Asking questions allows students to recall and process, through discussion, information they already learned.

    B.   Incorrect. Previewing vocabulary allows students to gain familiarity with new materials and may allow them to make connections between what they are going to learn and what they already know.

    C.   Incorrect. The use of graphic organizers allows students to create visual representations of what they have learned, enabling them to add and make connections to their prior knowledge in an organized way.

    D.   **Correct.** Listening to an expert speaker discuss a topic may be beneficial to students' understanding of the material, but it will not activate their prior knowledge.

STRATEGIES FOR INSTRUCTION

Successful ESOL instructors employ a combination of instructional strategies to support student learning in the classroom, all of which are aimed at helping students develop important skill sets.

Some strategies in the classroom focus on helping students develop **discrete language skills**, those aspects of language that are governed by rules such as phonics, grammar, and syntax. These skills are most often taught through direct instruction, with teachers providing explicit instruction in particular areas of language. ESOL students learn these specific language skills through focused exercises alongside their developing conversational capabilities.

More common in today's classrooms are activities that help students develop **integrated language skills**, those capabilities that allow students to practice and apply their knowledge of different elements of language simultaneously. Two different approaches are common in classrooms that seek to support integrated language learning: content-based language instruction and task-based instruction. **Content-based language instruction** involves the use of subject matter material (such as math, science, or social studies) as the basis for practicing communicative skills. Within this approach, learners are motivated to engage in stimulating activities that introduce them to new subject matter concepts while offering them the opportunity to be continuously exposed to the English language.

The second approach, **task-based instruction**, calls for students to participate in communicative acts in order to complete a particular task. These activities require students to comprehend, produce, manipulate, and interact with the English language while focusing on meaning and conveying ideas using proper grammar and syntax. However, the focus is not on the language practice itself; rather, students simply use language as a tool. Tasks are designed to be active, engaging, and relatable for students, who are able to evaluate their own effectiveness upon completion of the task.

ESOL teachers can promote students' productive and receptive language skills in both academic and social settings. By creating assignments that require integrated language skills in the classroom, teachers necessitate their practice and foster students' linguistic development; engaging in small-group activities, creating written works to share with other students, and participating in class discussions all allow students to develop their skills in the context of an academic setting. To promote social development, teachers can encourage students to hang out with friends outside of school, attend movies and watch popular television shows, and become involved in organizations; students who are continuously surrounded by English usage, both in and outside the classroom, substantially increase their likelihood of success in learning their new language.

When teachers provide students low-pressure opportunities to interact in the new language, they are helping students develop basic interpersonal communication skills. **Basic interpersonal communication skills**, or **BICS**, are applied when students use contextual support to aid in language learning and delivery. Face-to-face interactions provide nonverbal cues that support students' understanding and aid in their ability to interpret meaning. These supports also allow students to develop greater confidence in their interactions because they do not feel that their interpretations are guesses about meaning, but rather that they come from solving the clues that are provided to them. Because casual conversations occur with great frequency, BICS are acquired quickly: students can become fluent in as little as a year, although it can take longer.

Becoming successful students, though, requires more than a mastery of interpersonal communication skills; in addition, students must learn and become comfortable with academic language. **Cognitive academic language proficiency**, or **CALP**, is the learning and understanding of academic language. When receiving this type of language input, students have few contextual and social supports to aid their understanding: academic discourse does not offer the opportunity for gestures and facial expressions the way casual conversation does, so students are left to rely solely on their language skills. CALP calls for greater use of higher-order thinking skills such as analysis, synthesis, and evaluation due to the reduction in context. Tasks that require students to manipulate academic language are frequently more difficult, thus causing this learning process to take more time than learning basic interpersonal communication skills; still, direct instruction in and regular exposure to academic language can help students develop the skills necessary to succeed in English-speaking classrooms.

To help students achieve proficiency in all areas of language development, many teachers today employ the **multisensory strategy**: that is, they use learning materials that integrate multiple senses. Teachers provide instruction that targets visual, auditory, and kinesthetic pathways to enhance students' memory and learning. Materials are logically ordered by linguistic skill level, from the most basic elements to advanced content, and concepts are taught directly with constant interaction between the student and teacher, allowing for continual assessment of the student's needs and mastery of content. Additionally, this strategy often calls for part-to-whole instruction in which teachers provide students with a foundational understanding of parts of language and then show them how the parts work together to form a whole. These parts may include phonology, morphology, semantics, syntax, and sound-symbol associations.

SAMPLE QUESTIONS

16) **Ms. Perry is teaching a lesson on the grammatical structure of compound-complex sentences to one of her intermediate ESOL classes. What linguistic area is she focusing on?**

   A. content-based instruction

   B. discrete language skills

   C. integrated language skills

   D. task-based instruction

   Answers:

   A. Incorrect. The lesson is not connected to a content area lesson, so it is not content based.

   B. Correct. The lesson is given through direct instruction and is based on language that is governed by rules.

   C. Incorrect. The lesson does not call for the integration of linguistic abilities in reading, writing, speaking, and listening.

   D. Incorrect. The lesson is not based upon the completion of a task, so it is not task based.

17) **Why are students usually slower to gain cognitive academic language proficiency (CALP) than they are to learn basic interpersonal communication skills (BICS)?**

   A. Students are provided vocabulary words to study while they are learning BICS.

   B. Students are not provided with any interpersonal context to assist them in developing CALP.

   C. BICS relies entirely on facial cues, which students are familiar with because of their first language.

D.   CALP calls for a greater use of higher-order thinking skills because of a reduction in contextual clues.

Answers:

A.   Incorrect. While learning BICS, students base their acquisition and learning on the context around them.

B.   Incorrect. Students receive assistance from teachers when learning cognitive academic language, but the lack of social context makes interpretation more challenging.

C.   Incorrect. While BICS does involve facial cues, it also relies on context and prior learning for students to create new meaning for themselves.

D.   **Correct.** CALP has fewer contextual clues to aid students in interpreting meaning; therefore, it requires more analysis, synthesis, and evaluation than basic interpersonal communication skills.

AUTHENTIC LANGUAGE MATERIALS

Authentic materials in language learning are intended for use by native language speakers and not second-language learners. Most everyday objects, including signs, menus, pamphlets, commercials, and television broadcasts, are considered authentic materials. The use of these materials can make lessons in the target language seem more relevant to students, allowing them a deeper understanding of how the material applies to their own lives on a daily basis.

Using authentic materials allows students to build confidence in their ability to comprehend and interpret real-life experiences. Through authentic engagement with their new language, students encounter words and phrases that their academic texts are unlikely to use, giving them the opportunity to learn about abbreviations, slang, and other cultural elements of communication. Additionally, the use of authentic materials has been proven to increase students' motivation and better meet the needs of diverse groups of learners.

A multitude of activities can be generated from authentic materials. Students can ask and answer questions about products, role-play in true-to-life scenarios, or analyze elements of audiovisual pieces such as commercials and television shows. The array of assignments is contingent only upon the proficiency of the students and the imagination of the teacher.

Semi-authentic materials are created by native or nonnative speakers and based on original materials; however, they have been adapted to fit the lesson objectives and the needs of students. These kinds of materials can be very useful when looking to close the gap between students' understanding of material and the reality of its use; thus, semi-authentic materials are most popular with lower level learners. They enable students to access relevant content without being overwhelmed by new grammar and vocabulary.

Semi-authentic materials do not possess many of the characteristics of authentic materials. For example, though semi-authentic materials seek to mimic the language found in authentic materials, they are not exactly the same: they are specifically designed to match students' proficiency levels. Though they often seek to include realistic language, the focus lies on reinforcing previous learning and achieving new language goals.

In order to experience meaningful interactions in English, second-language learners must be provided with situations that are as authentic as possible. They must be allowed to ask and answer questions and must be given sufficient time to process what they are discussing. Additionally, interactions have greater meaning when the topics and content are student selected, as this quality allows learners ownership over their learning and their classroom environment, leading to increased investment.

TEACHING TIP

Activities and lessons that involve the use of semi-authentic materials mimic those that call for authentic materials. Students can be asked to complete the same kinds of tasks and activities while relying on content- and lesson-oriented materials.

SAMPLE QUESTION

18) Which of the following activities involves the use of semi-authentic materials?

  A. Students watch several television commercials and compare the products being advertised.

  B. Students read a newspaper article and create a list of questions that they would ask the reporter.

  C. Students watch an adapted version of *Taming of the Shrew* and discuss the plot and characters in the play.

  D. Students read a series of ad campaigns for local politicians and discuss which mayoral candidate they think would be best for the city.

Answers:

  A. Incorrect. This lesson involves authentic materials.

  B. Incorrect. This lesson involves authentic materials.

  C. Correct. The lesson calls for the use of adapted materials and therefore involves semi-authentic materials.

  D. Incorrect. The lesson involves authentic materials.

BEST PRACTICES FOR TEACHING ENGLISH LITERACY

Students who are literate in their native language have a distinct advantage over those who are not: they possess phonological awareness, which allows them to transfer much of their understanding of language and its component parts. Recall that phonological awareness is the understanding that language is made up of sounds, syllables, rhythms, words, and patterns.

When working with literate ESOL students, teachers employ a number of best practices, which aid them in creating environments and planning instruction that help students develop English language proficiency with confidence. Effective ESOL instructors:

1. have a language-rich environment that encourages students to interact with English in multiple ways
2. teach students strategies to aid them in their language learning
3. use students' native languages to support their English development
4. use instructional strategies and approaches that bridge language and content learning
5. correlate language standards and assessments with content area standards and assessments whenever possible
6. know the unique linguistic and academic needs of all ESOL students

The needs and experiences of preliterate and nonliterate ESOL students differ substantially from those of literate students. Preliterate and nonliterate students frequently have little or no classroom or formal educational experience and may be unfamiliar with the learning process and general classroom expectations. To help these students grow, teachers must implement measures to meet their specific needs, beyond the best practices used for literate students. Teachers of preliterate and nonliterate students must:

1. recognize and evaluate the oral skills that each learner possesses
2. remember that everything is new to these students—the lines on the page, the letters before them, the page numbers, and even the expectation that they are able to write their names
3. expect student progress to be much slower than that of literate learners
4. celebrate small achievements to make the learning process less intimidating
5. repeat things slowly and frequently to aid students in retaining new information
6. sequence materials from most concrete to most abstract to help students build upon their knowledge
7. teach students how to be students, guiding them in classroom expectations, rules, and learning practices

SAMPLE QUESTION

19) **Which of the following is considered a best practice for working with ESOL students?**

    A.   Provide students with written instructions.

    B.   Avoid the use of students' native languages in instruction.

    C.   Correlate academic and linguistic standards whenever possible.

    D.   Speak at a conversational pace to help students acclimate to conversation.

Answers:

    A.   Incorrect. Students should be provided with both written and oral instructions to ensure that their learning preference is met.

    B.   Incorrect. Students' native languages can be used as an aid for student learning if the ESOL teacher is familiar with the language.

    C.   **Correct.** Academic and language standards should be correlated whenever possible.

    D.   Incorrect. Students in the early stages of literacy may need speech to be delivered more slowly in order to understand what is being said.

MATERIALS

Materials used in ESOL classrooms serve multiple purposes. Not only do they aid students in learning English, but they also must engage students, help them with content area learning, and provide opportunities for authentic communication. The selection, modification, and creation of materials, then, is an extremely important element in ESOL instruction.

MATERIALS GEARED TOWARD STUDENT NEEDS

Many theories exist to explain differences in student learning. In recent decades, theories involving learning styles and multiple intelligences have become more prominent, making their way into classrooms across the country. While many theories are controversial, educational researchers agree that some important ideas can be taken from existing research: most importantly, they generally agree that all students learn differently and that they tend to be most successful when teachers present information in ways that are varied and appropriate to their needs.

Students' learning styles play an important role in their learning processes. When instruction and materials are matched to students' learning styles, learners are more likely to grasp and retain new information; thus, it is important for teachers to know the learning styles and preferences of the students in their classes so that they can select materials that will reach all learners. Students usually have more than one learning style that suits them. Therefore, designing lessons, activities, and assessments to suit multiple learning styles can help teachers effectively reach a greater number of students.

There are generally considered to be six different learning styles.

Visual learners learn best by seeing things. Inspecting pictures and written words can aid them in memory and comprehension. Classrooms filled with colorful posters and other visual aids ensure these students have helpful materials. Teachers can ensure they are reaching visual learners by using flashcards, texts with illustrations, charts or graphs, and visual resources such as computer graphics and videos.

Auditory learners learn best by listening. Spoken instructions are easiest for them to comprehend, and hearing stories or songs can help them retain information. These students tend to tune into sounds, so adding speaking and listening activities to lessons provides opportunities for these learners to interact with content in ways they understand best. Having these students create songs or short stories that use target words can help them to process and recall meaning, as well as keep them engaged in classroom activities. Additionally, auditory learners tend to excel in pronunciation exercises. They are able to pick up on details of sound and can often reproduce them with ease.

Tactile learners learn by touching and manipulating objects. Using sensory activities that allow students to work with manipulatives helps them to internalize new information. Even something as simple as passing around flashcards and allowing these learners to touch and trace the words can help them to retain material. Creating models, playing board games, gesturing, and using props such as puppets, toys, and blocks can all help tactile learners succeed in learning a second language. The more these students are able to interact with manipulatives, the more likely they are to create new knowledge for themselves.

Kinesthetic learners learn through physical movement. They enjoy playing games that require whole-body movement, setting up experiments and following instructions to do or make things, and participating in activities that involve gesturing and motion. Students who learn kinesthetically do not respond well to sitting, watching, and listening for extended periods of time. However, allowing these students to act out elements of a lesson can keep them engaged and allow them to process their learning. Incorporating action and motion are the keys to successfully teaching kinesthetic learners.

Analytic learners learn by focusing on details. This can often mean concentrating on grammar and syntax rules and dissecting words and sentences. These students require structured lessons in which information is provided logically and directions are delivered sequentially. Clear objectives provide these students with goals to work toward and can help keep them focused. These students tend to thrive when completing activities that require analytical thought. Completing activities where letters or words are missing, working puzzles, and engaging in concentration games can help these students interact with content in ways that are meaningful to them.

Global learners focus on the big picture and tend to show little interest in specific details. These students respond well to interactive lessons in which they are able to engage with classmates in group activities and conversations. Imaginative exercises such as writing stories and making up games also keep these learners actively involved with material. Providing these students with vocabulary in the target language and then allowing them to write a story or skit or to carry on a conversation without restrictions can help global learners create meaning for themselves. It is important to note that correcting global learners in mid-conversation can be very frustrating for them; it is best to wait until they are done speaking to explain errors to them, allowing them time to process the mistakes they made without stopping their thinking process as they speak.

Teachers should select materials and design lessons to accommodate as many learning styles as possible. While it can be overwhelming to attempt to incorporate them all, there are elements of each that overlap. Additionally, many students learn well in more than one style. For example, many kinesthetic learners can also benefit from tactile lessons. Though it may not be possible to incorporate physical activity into every lesson, these students can be assisted with the use of manipulatives, which are tangible objects that students can use to support their learning. Thus, incorporating strategies for engaging multiple learning styles in each lesson can end up being easier than it may seem.

> **QUICK REVIEW**
>
> The overlaps between learning styles are important when planning lessons. Besides the potential for tactile/kinesthetic overlap, what kinds of commonalities exist between learning styles?

In addition to students' learning styles, teachers must also consider level, age, and cultural appropriateness of materials for the classroom. When selecting **level-appropriate materials**, teachers should consider not only the length of what is to be used, but also the task that students are being asked to perform. For example, lengthy texts with many unfamiliar words are unlikely to motivate students and can inhibit their desire to learn. Instead, selecting a text with some familiar vocabulary or a recognizable organizational pattern can engage students by providing them with an opportunity to apply what they already know, thus building confidence and encouraging them to make connections to existing knowledge. Materials should be slightly more difficult than the students' current level of English proficiency to challenge them to learn new vocabulary and grammatical and syntactical structures.

Age appropriateness must also be considered when selecting materials for the classroom. Students may show levels of proficiency that allow them to access materials that are beyond the appropriate scope for their age; likewise, students may struggle to grasp suitable content if it is presented at levels beyond their understanding. **Age-appropriate materials** can be created by modifying various classroom activities and resources to fit students' needs, ages, and levels. There are also multiple internet sources with suggestions for age-appropriate content and instructional strategies. By ensuring that students have access to age-appropriate materials, teachers are better able to keep students engaged in their learning and allow them to progress to higher levels of proficiency.

A final area for consideration when selecting classroom materials is whether resources are culturally appropriate. **Culturally appropriate materials** take into account students' backgrounds, experiences, and interests. It is important to be aware of any political, religious, and/or social topics that may make students uncomfortable or are considered inappropriate conversation for school. Steering clear of these subjects can ensure that all learners are comfortable in the classroom.

It is also important for students to find classroom materials and instruction relatable and relevant. Teachers should first determine if the content they are teaching is relevant to those students who are learning about the culture of their second language; they might try asking themselves if this is something that students would encounter in a conversation throughout the school day or out in the real world. Teachers should also examine whether the topic has relevance to the students' native culture by evaluating whether it is something that students might talk about with their families at home. If neither of these is true for the student, the content may not be culturally appropriate and a more relevant area for study should be found.

SAMPLE QUESTION

20) Melvil tries to participate in his ESOL classes each day. However, he finds it difficult to focus when there is no movement involved in the lesson. What kind of learner is Melvil likely to be considered?

A.   auditory learner

B.   kinesthetic learner

C.   tactile learner

D.   visual learner

Answers:

A.   Incorrect. Auditory learners learn best by hearing and speaking.

B.   Correct. Kinesthetic learners need movement to best process information.

C.   Incorrect. Tactile learners need to touch and manipulate materials to process information.

D.   Incorrect. Visual learners learn best by seeing the materials they are learning.

MULTIMEDIA RESOURCES FOR ESOL AND CONTENT INSTRUCTION

Many resources are available for ESOL students and their teachers to make linguistic and content instruction accessible and relevant. From technology-based computer programs and devices to traditional manipulatives, the more resources ESOL teachers bring to students, the more likely students are to learn English.

One example of multimedia that can be greatly beneficial to students is **internet websites**. Language-learning websites offer opportunities for students to hone their skills through games, activities, web quests—lessons in which students explore and evaluate information taken from a variety of websites on a given topic—and other online lessons. The Internet has a tremendous number of resources for teachers as well. While students are able to practice skills on various websites, teachers can find lessons, activities, and materials for classroom use by working with simple search tools.

Computer software programs can help students hone their English skills as well. These programs are often able to grasp students' attention and engage them in lessons that can be geared toward learners' specific needs. For example, many ESOL software programs consist of games that allow students to develop and practice specific skills, such as applying proper pronouns or choosing correct conjunctions, which may not be a necessary topic of review for all students in the class. Carefully chosen software programs can provide individualized instruction and practice opportunities for each student in ways that are meaningful and fun.

The use of **realia**, objects and materials from everyday life, helps to create authentic learning experiences for students: learners are able to generate connections between what they are learning and their own lives by engaging with items and objects they are likely to encounter outside the classroom. For example, students who are studying a unit on food might take turns bringing in different examples of fruits, vegetables, beverages, or snacks. Students will make connections with the items in front of them and create new knowledge based on this interaction.

Audiovisual aids are also a necessity for any ESOL classroom. These include any items that stimulate students' sight and/or hearing. The use of music, television and movie clips, theater productions, photographs, and any other items that can promote visual or auditory learning has been proven to have a significant impact on learners' retention and understanding of their second languages.

21) Mr. Osborne is working on a banking and finance unit with his students. He is hoping to create some hands-on activities that will simulate real financial transactions. What might Mr. Osborne use in his lessons to make students' experiences feel more authentic?

   A.   internet websites that discuss banking procedures

   B.   audio recordings of a person's interaction with a bank teller

   C.   realia such as deposit slips and account statements

   D.   a computer software program that simulates what bank accounts look like

Answers:

   A.   Incorrect. While internet resources can help students in understanding content material, they are not always successful in creating authentic, engaging experiences.

   B.   Incorrect. Audio recordings of a banking interaction would help students to understand what they might hear at a bank, but they would not generate authentic experiences.

   C.   **Correct.** Realia such as deposit slips and account statements would create more authentic learning opportunities because they are used during real-life interactions.

   D.   Incorrect. Computer software programs can be beneficial in simulating experiences, but they would not create the most authentic experience because students cannot actively engage with the materials.

CLASSROOM MANAGEMENT

Teachers should keep in mind the many factors that may be influencing their students' learning on a daily basis. ESOL students in particular may face some challenges that other students do not encounter. Considering these influences can have a huge impact on lesson planning and relationship building.

FACTORS AFFECTING STUDENT PERFORMANCE

Second-language acquisition is affected significantly by the age of the learner. Research has shown that it is easiest to learn a second language between the ages of two and twelve, before puberty, when the brain undergoes **lateralization**, during which the hemispheres of the brain begin to function as distinct halves. This research has led to the development of the critical period hypothesis.

Typically, children who have some level of literacy in their native language have the easiest time acquiring a second language; children eight to twelve years of age who have had some formal education are the most likely to succeed in second-language acquisition. Adults who learn new languages often maintain their native accents and do not develop total fluency, though they can still be very successful in acquiring language skills.

In addition to age, the length and consistency of formal education that students have had will influence their second-language acquisition. Students who have had formal schooling in their first language tend to acquire proficiency faster than those who have not because proficiency in their first language aids them in transferring knowledge of linguistic skills to their second language, providing them with a stronger foundation for language acquisition than students without the same background.

> **HELPFUL HINT**
>
> The *critical period hypothesis* states that language acquisition after puberty is more challenging because of the firm localization of language processing to the left hemisphere of the brain.

Students who have little or no exposure to formal education must work harder to achieve language proficiency. This is also true for students with interrupted formal education (SIFE). These students are unlikely to have developed the language and literacy skills that many of their peers possess and can fall several academic years behind them because of these deficits. Despite these issues, all ESOL students will be expected to develop higher-order thinking skills in English. In order to assist them in this endeavor, teachers can see to it that their ESOL programs follow several important guidelines:

> **QUICK REVIEW**
>
> How might these differences influence teaching practices in a classroom where both populations are represented?

1. Students must be permitted to learn at their own pace.
2. Thematic and linguistic content should align for students.
3. ESOL and content area teachers should plan lessons together to ensure continuity.
4. Class sizes should be kept small to provide individual attention to students.
5. ESOL students and teachers should meet on a regular basis, with the knowledge that frequency and duration of the meetings are key elements to students' success.
6. Language lessons should involve a focus on communicative skills first.

These guidelines can aid all ESOL learners, both native literate and non-literate, in their efforts to learn English. Research has shown that students make greater gains in small classes that meet regularly and that focus on building communication skills through aligned content and language objectives.

SAMPLE QUESTION

22) **Mikko is motivated by his grandson's enthusiasm and enjoyment of his English lessons. He has decided to take lessons as well. What is likely to be the outcome of Mikko's lessons?**

   A.   He will become fluent in English if he persists in practicing.

   B.   He will learn to read and write in English but is unlikely to speak the language.

   C.   He will learn to speak and understand English but is unlikely to read or write it.

   D.   He will gain proficiency in English with practice but will not become completely fluent.

Answers:

   A.   Incorrect. Second-language learners are unlikely to achieve fluency if they begin learning past the onset of puberty.

   B.   Incorrect. The areas of language that Mikko excels in will be greatly influenced by what he chooses to practice most.

   C.   Incorrect. The areas of language that Mikko excels in will be greatly influenced by what he chooses to practice most.

   D.   Correct. Mikko could develop proficiency in English with practice, but because of his age he is unlikely to develop fluency.

ENGAGING, GUIDING, AND MOTIVATING STUDENTS

Engaging students in material, guiding their learning, and keeping them motivated are all significant elements of successful teaching. Teachers must be aware of how to do each of these things effectively to ensure students' success.

Teachers should keep in mind the significance of the affective domain when working with ESOL students. The **affective domain** defines how people deal with emotional things such as feelings, motivations, and attitudes. Students' feelings about learning will be influenced by their daily experiences, so teachers must be aware of their self-esteem, motivation, and inhibitions in order to keep them positively engaged.

To improve learning outcomes, teachers should seek to create comfortable, positive classroom environments that help students avoid feeling embarrassed, anxious, or frustrated. Setting clear, realistic expectations and objectives can help students feel prepared and confident, enabling them to avoid the anxiety and frustration that are often experienced by ESOL students who feel as though they do not know what is going on or why they are not progressing as quickly as they would like to.

Ensuring that a classroom is a **level-appropriate environment** is important as well. Classroom décor should represent multiple levels of ability, with students' work samples displayed to encourage their efforts and keep them motivated. Teachers who work with students of different proficiency levels should ensure that all students' levels are represented and supported within the classroom.

Language-rich environments can also help engage students and guide them in their learning. This kind of environment is one in which students feel surrounded by language—written, spoken, or both. Typically, a language-rich classroom engages students in communication and conversation on a daily basis. These classrooms also have word walls for vocabulary, an extensive classroom library, and posters displaying different language concepts on the walls. **Anchor charts** can be particularly useful, as they are specific representations of students' learning in the classroom and can cover any topic or material that the teacher sees fit for display. Anchor charts are posters made by members of the class, either the teacher or students, that outline, describe, or explain a topic that was covered in class. Examples include posters depicting the steps to the scientific method, the process for solving a math equation, or the definition of various plot elements. The content of the anchor chart depends entirely on the content being learned in class.

Feedback is another important factor in student growth. Learners need to understand both the strengths and weaknesses of their efforts to move forward in their learning. To foster a positive, successful relationship with students, teachers must always make sure that they are giving **constructive feedback**, which will ensure that students do not lose confidence in what they are doing, but instead recognize and implement ways to improve their skills. In delivering feedback, teachers should carefully select their words so that the feedback is objective, specific, and relevant to the lesson at hand. Effective constructive feedback allows students to take ownership of their learning and improve their efforts while maintaining a positive attitude.

Finally, teachers can help students feel good about their learning by building strong independent learning skills. **Independent learning skills** allow students to make progress in their learning without direct assistance from a teacher, enabling students to personalize what they are studying and take ownership of their skill development. Successful independent learning relies on strong relationships between teachers and students, a productive environment in which students feel motivated to seek knowledge, and an emphasis on self-monitoring that equips students to evaluate their own efforts on an ongoing basis.

> **QUICK REVIEW**
>
> The development of independent learning skills has multiple benefits for students. What are some of the effects that students might experience by learning these skills?

In order to foster students' independent learning skills, teachers must take an active role in ensuring students' involvement in their learning. Several strategies can be used to do this:

1. Scaffolding provides students with supportive aids that allow the gradual transfer of responsibility for learning from the teacher to the student. By remaining flexible in their level of involvement with students' learning, teachers are able to provide more or less assistance according to what individuals in the classroom require.

2. Teaching students self-monitoring skills helps them develop a system of feedback that allows them to determine if what they are doing is successful. Teachers should model the kinds of questions students should ask of themselves during this process, and then demonstrate how to answer those questions.

3. Modeling behaviors helps students see what independent learning looks like. Teachers should show students not what to study but how to do so by providing them with learning strategies that they can successfully execute.

4. Maintaining open communication that focuses on students' learning and achievements allows them to celebrate the progress they are making through their own efforts. It also helps students to recognize the steps they are taking in comprehending and retaining new knowledge, helping them to develop stronger metacognitive skills.

5. Providing open feedback on students' progress helps them to see where they are making gains and where they may need to extend greater focus. Framing these discussions with positive achievements can help students maintain their motivation and take pride in the progress they have made.

SAMPLE QUESTION

23) **How does the affective domain influence language learning?**

    A. It controls students' emotional responses to learning experiences.

    B. It controls students' physical capacities to produce speech and writing.

    C. It controls students' reasoning capacity to understand and transfer linguistic knowledge.

    D. It controls students' conceptual ability to comprehend how elements of language work together.

Answers:

    A. **Correct.** The affective domain controls people's feelings and emotions.

    B. Incorrect. The psychomotor domain controls manual functioning.

    C. Incorrect. The cognitive domain controls knowledge and mental skills.

    D. Incorrect. The cognitive domain controls knowledge and mental skills.

4

Assessment

ssessment informs instruction by providing a measure of students' skill levels and progress. It is both the means by which educators gather information about what students know and the guide for how curriculum can be designed to meet educational needs most effectively. Assessment results are often used to identify student strengths and weaknesses; to inform teachers, parents, and other stakeholders about student progress; and to measure student achievement against national data sets.

In the case of English language learners, assessment serves two critical purposes—to determine language proficiency and to determine content knowledge—with the ultimate goal of ensuring that these learners receive classroom instruction that is appropriate to their academic ability levels and effective at developing their English language proficiency. Assessment in the primary language demonstrates content area knowledge, while assessment in the second language illustrates proficiency level; combined, these measures can inform instructional design such that content area knowledge continues to strengthen in tandem with English proficiency.

TESTS AND STANDARDS

It is of critical importance that assessments for English language learners are appropriate and well developed. The use of high-quality assessment materials ensures that the academic and language proficiency progress of English learners is measured and that instruction can be adjusted to serve their educational needs. For this reason, tests should be evaluated prior to use for three key qualities: validity, reliability, and practicality.

A test demonstrates **reliability** if data show that the test produces the same predictable results under different conditions and in different settings. A test that is reliable produces consistent outcomes much like how a tape measure consistently reports the same measurement of a table regardless of how many times the table is measured: an assessment is said to be reliable, for example, if the same group of individuals receives the same results if given the test multiple times, in different places, under varying conditions. Still, a test can be reliable without being valid.

A test demonstrates **validity** if data show that the test measures what it purports to measure in a specific context. An assessment should be evaluated for three different types of validity: content validity, construct validity, and criterion-related validity.

Content validity is demonstrated when items on a test are shown to measure the content knowledge they purport to measure. In assessment design, content validity is often referred to as **alignment**, as the goal is to ensure that the test items are aligned with the subject matter being tested. For example, a literature test that is supposed to cover figurative language is considered to have content validity if the test items require knowledge of similes, metaphors, hyperbole, and personification; the test would be considered invalid if it included questions that covered grammar or text structures.

Construct validity is demonstrated when items on a test are shown to adhere to an underlying **construct** (concept, theory, or hypothesis) that represents the guiding purpose for the assessment. For example, a mathematics test is valid if it can be demonstrated to measure mathematics ability only, separate from other abilities such as reading proficiency or vocabulary comprehension. If the test is designed in such a way that success is dependent on skill sets other than mathematics ability (like the ability to read complex instructions), the final score is invalid because the test actually evaluates a conglomeration of interdependent abilities from which an area of strength or weakness cannot be pinpointed and addressed: the results do not present an accurate measure of the targeted ability.

Criterion-related validity is demonstrated when items on a test are shown to measure specific **criteria**, or predetermined standards, as confirmed by participant outcomes or scores. If the results of an assessment align as expected with other tests that measure similar criteria, the assessment can be said to demonstrate **concurrent** criterion-related validity. If the results of an assessment align as expected with future independent measures of the test takers, such as GPA, the assessment can be said to demonstrate **predictive** criterion-related validity because participant scores reasonably predict future outcomes.

Practicality refers to the relative ease of accessing, administering, and scoring an assessment or test. A test demonstrates practicality if the expense, time considerations, and usage are not prohibitive as a result of being too costly, too time-consuming, or too unmanageable for the community it is meant to serve. For instance, an assessment that is expected to take students five hours to complete is not considered practical for a two-hour final exam block.

Perhaps the most common type of assessment English language learners will undergo is the proficiency test. Proficiency tests are used to measure the English language abilities of students whose primary languages are not English. These tests typically measure English language proficiency in four or more **language domains**, most commonly listening, speaking, reading, and writing. Based on the results of proficiency tests, English learners are provided with instructional programs and services to support English language development in the context of subject matter curriculum.

SAMPLE QUESTION

1) After administration in different settings and under different conditions, an assessment has been shown to produce consistent outcomes.

   What quality does this assessment demonstrate?

   A. practicality

   B. construct validity

   C. reliability

   D. content validity

   Answers:

   A. Incorrect. An assessment demonstrates practicality when it is reasonably easy to obtain, use, and score.

   B. Incorrect. An assessment demonstrates construct validity when it can be shown to adhere to an underlying construct.

   C. Correct. An assessment that produces consistent outcomes in different settings and under different conditions demonstrates reliability.

   D. Incorrect. An assessment demonstrates content validity when it can be shown to measure the subject matter it purports to measure.

LITERACY ASSESSMENT

There are a number of specific assessments that have been developed to measure the English proficiency of English language learners. These assessments—which include both individual and group assessments—help school districts place English learners in instructional programs that are appropriate to their language proficiency and content area needs. **Individual literacy assessments** are administered one-to-one between examiner and student; **group literacy assessments** are administered by one examiner to a group of students. The following assessments are statistically supported to demonstrate validity and reliability in measuring language proficiency skills within one or more language domains.

Basic Inventory of Natural Language (BINL): The BINL is used to measure oral-language proficiency in one of thirty-two different languages by asking students to describe a set of images. The test, which must be administered individually, measures proficiency based on fluency, level of language complexity, and average sentence length of student responses. It can be used with students in grades K – 12.

Language Assessment Scales (LAS): There are various forms of the LAS, which are designed to measure the oral proficiency and reading and writing abilities of K – 12 students. The oral measure, which covers both speaking and listening, must be individually administered, but the reading and writing tests can be administered in small groups. LAS measure content such as vocabulary, listening comprehension, and story retelling and are available in both English and Spanish.

Bilingual Syntax Measure (BSM) I and II: The BSM I is used with students in grades K – 2; the BSM II is used with students in grades 3 – 12. Both assessments measure oral proficiency in English and/or Spanish and must be administered individually. Student scores are based on the grammatical structures of their oral responses.

Idea Proficiency Tests (IPT): There are various forms of the IPT, which are designed to measure the oral proficiency and reading and writing abilities of K – 12 students. The oral measure must be individually administered, but the reading and writing measures can be administered in small groups. In general, IPT measure content such as vocabulary, syntax, and reading for understanding and are available in both English and Spanish.

Woodcock-Muñoz Language Survey: This is an individually administered assessment that measures cognitive aspects of language proficiency in the form of vocabulary usage, verbal analogies, and letter-word identification. This assessment is available in both English and Spanish.

Both group and individual literacy assessments are also administered in the classroom to monitor student progress and verify that skill advancement is taking place. These assessments can be either formal or informal. Formal, individual literacy assessments include one-on-one interviews or observations using checklists or rating scales; formal, group literacy assessments include tests or writing assignments given to all students at the same time. Formal literacy assessments provide educators with a means by which to evaluate student performance against a particular standard or set of standards. Informal assessments, which include qualitative observation notes and reflections, provide an ongoing way for educators to ensure that the true abilities and potentials of English learners continue to be addressed in the context of instruction.

SAMPLE QUESTION

2) Which of the following assessments can be used to measure language proficiency in all four common language domains?

A. BSM II and BINL

B. BINL and LAS

C. LAS and IPT

D. IPT and BSM II

Answers:

A. Incorrect. The BSM II and BINL are used to measure only oral language proficiency.

B. Incorrect. While the LAS can be used to measure language proficiency in all four common language domains, the BINL is only used as a measure of oral language proficiency.

C. **Correct.** Both the LAS and the IPT provide measures of language proficiency in all four common language domains: listening, speaking, reading, and writing.

D. Incorrect. While the IPT can be used to measure language proficiency in all four common language domains, the BSM II is only used as a measure of oral language proficiency.

NATIONAL REQUIREMENTS FOR ENGLISH LANGUAGE LEARNERS AND ASSESSMENT

Under federal law, and in many cases state law, school districts are required to properly identify English language learners so that these students can receive effective instruction that meets both language proficiency and subject matter competency needs.

The federal **Elementary and Secondary Education Act (ESEA)**, a national education law, was passed by the US Congress in 1965 with the goal of establishing equal educational opportunity for all students. The law gives states the authority to provide programs for students who face obstacles to optimal learning.

DID YOU KNOW?

The ESEA was enacted as a part of President Lyndon B. Johnson's "War on Poverty."

In 2001, ESEA was reauthorized as the **No Child Left Behind Act (NCLB)**. This reauthorization provides federal funding for language instruction programs for English learners on the condition that identified students meet the same content and achievement standards as all general education students, regardless of language barriers. A key component of the NCLB Act is **accountability**—holding districts, schools, and educators accountable for student performance. Under No Child Left Behind, each state must submit an accountability plan to the US Department of Education.

In 2015, ESEA was reauthorized by President Barack Obama as the **Every Student Succeeds Act (ESSA)**, which continues government efforts to provide equal educational opportunity for all students without some of the more inflexible and punitive conditions of NCLB. Accountability remains a significant

DID YOU KNOW?

All provisions of the Every Student Succeeds Act are scheduled to be in place by the beginning of the 2017 – 2018 school year.

cornerstone of ESSA, but states have more authority to determine accountability criteria based on the specific challenges and needs of their student populations.

Many states have enacted laws that provide guidelines for the identification and redesignation of English learners. As students enter school, they are evaluated to determine if English language development (ELD) programs or services are needed. Home surveys are the primary method used to identify students whose primary languages are not English. School districts are legally required to administer placement tests to these students. These assessments are used to determine English learners' levels of English proficiency so that they can be assigned to the instructional programs that will best meet their language and academic needs. After placement, English learners must be periodically reevaluated to ensure that their instructional programs continue to meet their learning needs in the most effective and appropriate ways.

HELPFUL HINT

Each state has unique laws in place to uphold its responsibilities to English language learners. ESOL teachers should conduct, at least, a cursory review of these policies in order to familiarize themselves with the specific experiences of their student populations.

Most states use a combination of measures to determine appropriate services and support for English learners. These include but are not limited to proficiency tests in both English and the primary language, English literacy tests, prior educational records, and parent and teacher input. Instruction for English language learners is guided by curriculum aligned to **English Language Proficiency (ELP)** standards. Many states have developed ELP standards divided into levels or stages of proficiency that range from beginning to intermediate to advanced.

ELP standards identify the target language development skills an English learner is expected to meet in the context of instruction that is appropriately scaffolded for optimal learning. Ideally, placement tests correlate directly to ELP standards, which, in turn, correlate directly to effective ELP standards-based instruction that facilitates English learners' progress through the language-acquisition stages. When a sufficient level of proficiency is reached, English learners may be reclassified from Limited English Proficient (LEP) to Fluent English Proficient (FEP). School districts are required to have designated **reclassification** criteria, which are used to determine when English learners have achieved the language skills necessary to succeed in English-only classrooms. Specific scores on state-selected language and achievement tests are designated as **cutoff points** that determine when English learners no longer require English language programs and services.

SAMPLE QUESTIONS

3) **Which is the key purpose of the Elementary and Secondary Education Act of 1965?**

    A. to establish equal educational opportunity for all students

    B. to hold schools accountable for student performance

    C. to legally require school districts to administer language placement tests

    D. to identify students whose primary language is not English

    Answers:

    A. **Correct.** The Elementary and Secondary Education Act was enacted to address unequal access to quality education due to societal and environmental obstacles faced by many students across the nation.

    B. Incorrect. Accountability was one element of the No Child Left Behind Act of 2001, a reauthorization of the original Elementary and Secondary Education Act of 1965, which was enacted to establish equal educational opportunity for all students.

    C. Incorrect. This is one of several outcomes of the No Child Left Behind Act of 2001, a reauthorization of the original Elementary and Secondary Education Act of 1965, which was enacted to establish equal educational opportunity for all students.

    D. Incorrect. This is the key purpose of home language surveys.

4) **Which is one way that the Every Student Succeeds Act (ESSA) differs from the No Child Left Behind Act (NCLB)?**

    A. The federal government will take the lead in establishing accountability guidelines and measures that are compulsory for all states.

    B. States are provided with the authority to designate and provide programs for students who face societal or environmental obstacles to optimal learning.

    C. The federal government will no longer require states to demonstrate accountability in relation to student achievement due to new laws passed by Congress.

    D. States are provided more authority to establish accountability guidelines and measures appropriate to the specific educational needs of their student populations.

    Answers:

    A. Incorrect. The ESSA provides states with more control over how accountability is measured, not less.

    B. Incorrect. Both the ESSA and NCLB support the original underlying construct of the Elementary and Secondary Education Act of 1965.

    C. Incorrect. Under ESSA, states are still required to demonstrate accountability; however, they have more authority to determine how this can best be done with respect to the specific needs of the student populations in each state.

D. **Correct.** The ESSA provides states with more control over how accountability for student achievement will be mandated.

FORMAL AND INFORMAL METHODS OF ASSESSING LANGUAGE SKILLS AND PROGRESS

The language skills of English learners are divided into two categories: receptive and productive. **Receptive language skills** are abilities related to understanding language that is received from an external source, such as oral directions and commentary, visuals, sounds, and written words; thus, assessments of receptive language skills measure listening and reading abilities. **Productive language skills** are abilities related to producing comprehensible language from within, such as in writing and speaking tasks; thus, assessments of productive language skills measure writing and speaking abilities. Productive language skills are also referred to as expressive language skills.

The receptive and productive language skills of English learners are assessed using standardized and performance-based assessment methods, both formal and informal. **Standardized assessments** are those that use a standard means of scoring individuals who are responding to the same set of instructions and/or questions. They measure individual ability in relation to predetermined and established scoring criteria correlated to particular **constructs**, or areas of content knowledge. Examples of standardized assessments for classroom use include unit tests, quizzes, checklists, rating scales, and questionnaires.

Large-scale standardized tests are used to assess student language proficiency or academic achievement across a range of state and/or national educational standards. They are given to large populations of students under uniform conditions and are designed to measure their performance in broad terms against state and/or national norms for their grade levels and/or age ranges. In order to prepare students and to produce evidence of student progress toward mastering the criteria set forth, many educators plan and implement curriculum derived directly from the standards being tested.

QUICK REVIEW

Which large-scale state-mandated standardized tests are used to assess student language proficiency and/or academic achievement in your state?

In the classroom, standardized assessment is balanced with **performance-based assessment** in order to provide a more holistic perspective of individual student strengths, weaknesses, abilities, and learning styles. Performance-based assessment uses open-ended scoring based on teacher observation, measuring student ability in a wider context that incorporates creativity, innovation, insight, collaboration, and other abilities that do not lend themselves well to quantitative measures. Examples of open-ended assessments include portfolios, performances, project exhibitions, and classroom participation.

Portfolio assessment is a performance-based means of measuring student progress over time through work samples, observational notes, and student-teacher reflection. Portfolios provide concrete, visual markers that clearly demonstrate student academic growth, learning style, and language ability along the continuum of the school year. It is important that the work samples include teacher notes and student reflections related to the work accomplished and the processes used and observed (for example, notes about the student's organization, time management, collaboration, and research). Ideally, portfolio assessments provide evidence of student learning while also allowing students and teachers to periodically take stock of progress and address any areas of concern or strength along the way through goal setting or individualized assignments.

> **HELPFUL HINT**
>
> Portfolios can include a range of student work samples, including writing assignments, long-term projects, and visual art pieces, as well as evidence of student involvement in the learning process in the form of photographs and videos.

SAMPLE QUESTIONS

5) Mr. Williams has presented a student with four pictures of a cat and asked the student to point to the picture that shows the cat sleeping.

Which best explains the language skills Mr. Williams is assessing?

A. receptive language skills

B. productive language skills

C. social language skills

D. expressive language skills

Answers:

A. **Correct.** Mr. Williams is assessing the student's ability to respond accurately to oral language (listening) by using a nonverbal signal.

B. Incorrect. In this example, the student is responding to language, not producing language, so receptive language skills are being assessed.

C. Incorrect. Social language skills are used to communicate personal thoughts, ideas, and feelings and are best observed in group interactions.

D. Incorrect. In this example, the student is responding to language, not expressing language, so receptive language skills are being assessed.

Go on →

6) **Which of the following choices states the main purpose of a standardized test?**

    A.   to provide a holistic measure of student progress along the continuum of the school year

    B.   to provide a formal measure of student achievement using predetermined and established scoring criteria

    C.   to provide an informal measure of student ability based on observations of student progress

    D.   to provide a measure of student achievement in a context that incorporates creativity, innovation, insight, and collaboration

Answers:

    A.   Incorrect. A portfolio provides the best holistic measure of a student's progress over time.

    B.   **Correct.** Standardized tests demonstrate student achievement in relation to specific academic criteria or expectations.

    C.   Incorrect. A standardized test provides a formal measure of student ability.

    D.   Incorrect. The presentation of a final project incorporating a set of integrated skills provides the best measure of student achievement demonstrating creativity, innovation, insight, and collaboration.

DIAGNOSTIC ASSESSMENT

Home language surveys are short forms that are sent home as part of school enrollment packets, used by school districts to determine the primary languages spoken in the homes of students. This information is collected in order to identify students who need to be assessed for English language proficiency. State and federal mandates require school districts to administer placement tests to these students. These assessments are diagnostic in that they are administered prior to instruction in order to determine the language skills and/or concepts a student has already mastered.

Diagnostic assessments provide detailed information about a student's current levels of performance and help determine the curriculum and instructional methods most appropriate for that student's needs. This type of assessment provides a guideline that helps the instructor determine the specific skills and areas of language development that should be emphasized in order to increase student success levels.

> **HELPFUL HINT**
>
> Many of the literacy assessments listed earlier in the chapter are used to assist school districts in the placement process.

7) Which best states the purpose of a diagnostic assessment?

    A. to screen a student for language assessment

    B. to measure student achievement

    C. to provide an informal measure of student ability

    D. to determine the instructional needs of a student

Answers:

    A. Incorrect. The purpose of a home survey is to screen a student for language assessment.

    B. Incorrect. A diagnostic assessment is used to determine student placement in an instructional program, not measure student achievement resulting from instruction.

    C. Incorrect. Diagnostic assessments provide formal measures of students' current levels of understanding and ability.

    D. Correct. Diagnostic assessments are used to determine the instructional needs of a student so that the student can be appropriately placed in an instructional program.

MEASURING PROGRESS TOWARD STANDARDS

Once a student has been identified as an English learner and an instructional plan has been established based on diagnostic measures, assessment goals move from determining what the student already knows to how well the student is progressing toward meeting instructional objectives. Progress-monitoring assessments are administered on a regular basis to document and monitor a student's language proficiency and academic growth. Both formal and informal types of assessments are administered to gauge student progress. These assessments allow educators to determine which types of instructional methods and strategies contribute to student progress and which do not. They can be used to determine if different approaches to instruction or additional interventions need to be put in place to most effectively meet a student's needs.

One large-scale progress-monitoring assessment, **ACCESS** (Accessing Comprehension and Communication in English State-to-State), is provided by the **WIDA Consortium** to its state members. The WIDA Consortium has identified standards for student achievement in five content areas: social and instructional language (SI), English language arts (LA), math (MA), science (SC), and social studies (SS). It also identifies six English language proficiency levels: entering (1), beginning (2), developing (3), expanding (4), bridging (5), and reaching (6). The assessment is given annually to students identified as English learners with the purpose of measuring progress in English language proficiency.

The WIDA Consortium also provides **MODEL**, which stands for Measure of Developing English Language. MODEL is a series of assessments that can be used by educators anywhere in the world, regardless of membership. These assessments can be used to identify and place English learners as well as to monitor their progress toward instructional goals. The WIDA Consortium also provides educators with the **W-APT**, which is a diagnostic assessment, not a progress-monitoring assessment. It can be used to screen English learners for proper instructional programs and placements.

> **DID YOU KNOW?**
>
> The WIDA Consortium is composed of thirty-eight state education agencies and several research organizations

A second, separate consortium of states identifies as **ELPA21**, or **English Language Proficiency Assessment for the 21st Century**. Its goals are aligned to the English Language Proficiency standards developed by the Council of Chief State School Officers (CCSSO), which determines the states' college- and career-ready (CCR) standards for English language arts, mathematics, and science. In 2014, experts in the assessment field developed 2,600 items for an ELPA21 summative assessment item pool. After undergoing a series of content and bias reviews, these items were administered to students in a 2015 field test. After a review and analysis of the information collected from the field test, the first operational ELPA21 summative assessment was administered in the spring of 2016. In addition, ELPA21 has implemented plans to continue to develop and field-test additional assessments for the placement, progress monitoring, and reclassification of English learners. Thus, member states are in the process of transitioning their English learner populations to these new assessment models.

> **DID YOU KNOW?**
>
> State members of ELPA21 include Arkansas, Iowa, Kansas, Louisiana, Oregon, Nebraska, Ohio, South Carolina, Washington, and West Virginia. Florida and California left ELPA21 in 2014 and 2013, respectively; Florida went on to join the WIDA Consortium.

SAMPLE QUESTION

8) Which best states the purpose of the ACCESS assessment?

    A. to measure student progress in English language proficiency

    B. to place students in English language instructional programs

    C. to assess English learner achievement in core academic areas

    D. to identify students who are English language learners

    Answers:

    A. Correct. The ACCESS assessment is administered annually to measure student progress in English language proficiency.

B.   Incorrect. The ACCESS assessment is a progress-monitoring assessment, not a diagnostic assessment.

C.   Incorrect. The ACCESS assessment is used to measure progress in English language proficiency, not achievement in core academic areas.

D.   Incorrect. The ACCESS assessment is administered to students who have already been identified as English language learners.

ASSESSING CONTENT–AREA LEARNING

Assessment that takes place in the classroom combines formal, standards-based assessments and informal, performance-based assessments to gain in-depth, accurate, and holistic information about English learners' academic progress and language development. Several methods of assessment are used to gain the best overall perspective of students' abilities and needs.

STANDARDIZED CLASSROOM ASSESSMENTS

▶ **Observational or interview checklists**: Educators check off skills demonstrated according to specific criteria while observing or interviewing an individual student.

▶ **Observational or interview rating scales**: Educators rate student performance on a predeveloped scale while observing or interviewing an individual student. The scale provides levels of proficiency aligned to specific **constructs**, or concepts.

▶ **Grades**: Educators grade student work according to predetermined criteria and assign percentages or points based on how well a student has met the criteria of an assignment.

▶ **Standardized tests and/or quizzes**: Educators administer unit tests and/or quizzes that measure student understanding of taught concepts. Students receive points for accurate responses to questions, designed to ascertain how well they have comprehended the skills and knowledge covered in instruction.

PERFORMANCE–BASED CLASSROOM ASSESSMENTS

▶ **Observational notes**: Educators keep brief notes of student behaviors, actions, questions, and responses from class discussions, one-on-one discussions, and collaborative projects.

▶ **Work samples**: Educators keep samples of written or visual work that represent new understandings or language proficiencies in **portfolios** that illustrate progress over time.

▶ **Guided, shared, or interactive reading**: Educators listen and note repetitions, substitutions, insertions, omissions, or self-corrections as a student reads aloud. The student can read directly to the teacher or participate in paired reading or group reading exercises while the teacher focuses on his or her language usage and choices.

▶ **Retelling and/or paraphrasing**: Educators ask a student to retell a story or paraphrase a concept in his or her own words to determine how well that student has comprehended the meaning or underlying idea of written or spoken material.

▶ **Audio and video taping**: Educators record students engaged in learning activities or presentations in order to illustrate their ability to use a set of skills collectively and/or to highlight strengths or weaknesses that can be discussed at a later date.

▶ **Journals or logs**: Educators have students keep reading logs, writing folders, and/or science journals to respond to learning experiences or materials. These written records of student responses to new information provide comprehension indicators to teachers and show where concepts may require reteaching.

▶ **Student-conferences**: Educators meet with students to review work and ask questions to evaluate comprehension. One-on-one discussions related to reading materials, written work, and project goals are invaluable for gaining insight into how well a student comprehends classroom materials and assignments. Any misunderstandings can be corrected using language modifications, visuals, examples, and additional explanations.

SAMPLE QUESTION

9) **Which is an example of a performance-based classroom assessment?**

   A.   a teacher gives all students a test related to a geography unit

   B.   a teacher uses a rating scale during a student report on whales

   C.   a teacher photographs students solving problems with manipulatives

   D.   a teacher assigns a rubric-based grade to a student's expository essay

   Answers:

   A.   Incorrect. A unit test is an example of a standardized classroom assessment.

   B.   Incorrect. A rating scale is an example of a standardized classroom assessment.

   C.   Correct. Photographs of students at work are performance-based assessments that provide concrete evidence of student learning.

   D.   Incorrect. A grade is an example of a standardized classroom assessment.

SELF- AND PEER-ASSESSMENT

When students are active participants in monitoring and taking responsibility for their academic growth, they become agents of their own learning and are empowered to self-reflect and to make decisions that will help them gain mastery of concepts. This is why it is important to engage English learners in the assessment process using self- and peer-assessment techniques. These techniques include goal setting, guided practice using assessment tools, and portfolios. The teacher's role in self- and peer-assessment is to model and explain best practices for effective assessment, such as how to provide constructive feedback and how to accurately identify and apply criteria.

GOAL SETTING

Students reflect on their academic strengths and weaknesses and determine learning goals that they would like to achieve. These goals are reviewed with the teacher in order to ensure that they can be realistically reached within the set period of time. They are incorporated into assignments as individual focus areas of student effort. In this way, students become aware of their own progress as they self-monitor attainment of self-determined skills and abilities.

SELF- AND PEER-ASSESSMENT TOOLS

Students learn how to use checklists, rubrics, and reflection logs to assess their own work and the work of peers.

- **Checklists:** Checklists provide an inventory of criteria that must be met for the optimal completion of an assignment. They can include editing guidelines, project specifications, and any other type of criteria useful for evaluating a learning task. The teacher explains each item on the checklist and the requirements for meeting each one.

- **Rubrics:** Rubrics are organized as charts that provide a rationale for an assignment and focus on a small number of specific learning objectives (usually three to five). The criteria for each learning objective is described and assigned a numerical quality standard (usually one to five), which delineates the extent to which criteria are met. Rubrics allow students to review assignments along a continuum of mastery, according to a specific set of objectives. They provide more detail than checklists with respect to how well a student has met the criteria of an assignment.

- **Reflection Logs:** Reflection logs allow students to think about their assignments in terms of their own goals and growth process. It gives them the opportunity to identify next steps, recognize areas for improvement, and determine questions that need to be asked.

PORTFOLIOS

Portfolios provide students with concrete evidence of their progress toward learning goals. By reviewing work that has developed along a continuum of increasing mastery of skills and abilities, students can see their own growth over time along with evidence of the knowledge they have acquired.

SAMPLE QUESTION

10) Which best describes the fundamental purpose of student self-assessment tools?

   A.   Students take an active role in their learning outcomes.

   B.   Students correct mistakes before grading.

   C.   Students are better equipped to take standardized tests.

   D.   Students learn to value assessment scores.

Answers:

   A.   **Correct.** Self-assessment transforms the assessment process for students from one in which they are passive recipients to one in which they actively participate.

   B.   Incorrect. Self-assessment tools do allow students to discover and correct mistakes before turning in assignments, but this is not their fundamental purpose.

   C.   Incorrect. This is not the fundamental purpose of self-assessment tools, which is to actively engage students in the assessment process.

   D.   Incorrect. This is not the fundamental purpose of self-assessment tools, which is to actively engage students in the assessment process.

APPROPRIATE USE OF TESTS

REFERRALS TO SPECIAL/GIFTED PROGRAMS AND ACCOMMODATIONS FOR ENGLISH LANGUAGE LEARNERS

Three pieces of federal legislation exist to protect the civil rights of individuals with disabilities, including the right to a just and beneficial education: Section 504 of the 1973 Rehabilitation Act (504), the Americans with Disabilities Act (ADA), and the Individuals with Disabilities Education Act (IDEA). **Section 504 of the 1973 Rehabilitation Act** prohibits discrimination on the basis of disability in public and private programs that receive federal money. The **Americans with Disabilities Act** prevents discrimination in employment, public services, and accommodations based solely on an individual's disability. The **Individuals with Disabilities Education Act** mandates that all children with disabilities receive the highest standard of public education free from discrimination and tailored to their unique learning needs. It provides federal assistance to state and local educational agencies to guarantee that students with disabilities receive appropriate educational services. Student eligibility is determined by a multidisciplinary team that includes the student's counselor(s), teacher(s), and parent(s).

Learning disabilities (LD) are specific kinds of processing problems that can cause a person to have trouble learning and using certain skills such as reading, writing, listening, speaking, reasoning, and doing math. Students with learning difficulties are usually quite capable learners whose brains simply process information differently than those of the general population. IDEA ensures that students with disabilities are provided with the supports necessary to effectively facilitate their participation in general education curriculum. Once a student is iden-

> **HELPFUL HINT**
>
> Disability categories for students include autism, deafness, deaf-blindness, hearing impairment, mental retardation, orthopedic impairment, serious emotional disturbance, specific learning disabilities, speech or language impairment, traumatic brain injury, and visual impairment.

tified as having a disability, he or she receives an **Individualized Education Program** (IEP) that specifies the educational goals for the student and the services the school will supply to help the student achieve those goals.

IDEA also stipulates that children whose educational achievement is low due to challenges associated with learning a second language may not be mislabeled as having a learning disability. For these reasons, English learners can end up being both overrepresented and underrepresented in special education: difficulty due to linguistic or cultural factors can be misinterpreted as

> **HELPFUL HINT**
>
> Dyslexia (difficulty in reading), dysgraphia (difficulty in writing), and dyscalcula (difficulty in math) are identified as specific learning disabilities.

a disability, while a genuine disability can be overlooked if it is assumed that a student's difficulty relates to limited second-language proficiency.

In order to properly refer an English learner for special education services, educators must demonstrate that a significant difficulty remains consistent even when language barriers are removed and that over time the student has not kept pace with other English learners who entered school at comparable times with comparable levels of language proficiency. Thus, the classification of an English learner as learning disabled requires a thorough and methodical process that includes the participation of school administrators, teachers, and parents who have access to the services of an interpreter if needed. Any special education assessment should be preceded by documentation that shows (a) no progress or change resulting from the use of various instructional approaches and/or strategies, (b) staff agreement that the student's performance differs significantly from that of culturally and linguistically similar peers, and (c) parent input and feedback.

Assessment for potential learning disabilities must be **comprehensive** in that multiple sources of data are evaluated by a multidisciplinary team. For English learners, these data sources should demonstrate results both in the student's first language and in English. Enough evidence must be presented to clearly demonstrate that an English learner's learning difficulties are represented in both languages, and that he or she has not adequately progressed despite receiving qualified instruction.

> **HELPFUL HINT**
>
> Sources of assessment data include standardized tests, informal measures, observations, student self-reports, parent reports, and progress monitoring data.

The level of complexity surrounding the identification of learning disabilities in English language learners is matched by the level of complexity surrounding the identification of giftedness in the same population. English learners tend to be underrepresented in gifted programs due to a restricted ability to communicate knowledge and ideas in the second language. For this reason, teachers must be proactive in assessing the authentic skills and abilities of the English learners in their classrooms. This can be done by observing how these students approach, negotiate, and resolve problems in creative and insightful ways as well as by providing opportunities for them to demonstrate subject area expertise in the primary language.

ASSESSMENT-RELATED ISSUES

When selecting assessment tools for English learners, teachers need to be mindful of cultural and linguistic biases that may impact an assessment's reliability and validity for a particular group of learners. Typically, assessment **bias**—qualities that provide advantages or disadvantages to particular groups of students—results in scores that vary significantly from group to group according to gender, race, primary language, or ethnicity. **Language bias** occurs when a test that was originally developed for use in one language, for example, English, is translated to and administered in another language. This alters the original conditions under which the assessment was shown to have reliability, thus nullifying any resulting scores. **Cultural bias** occurs when a test offends or penalizes a test taker due to items related to socioeconomic status, gender, or ethnicity. For example, an assessment item may reference an experience or object that is undefined and unfamiliar for test takers who are not of the same cultural background as the item developer. This can cause items on an assessment to be more vague and difficult to answer for one group of students than another in spite of equivalent ability levels.

Many language assessments include both literal and inferential items related to reading comprehension. **Literal items** refer directly back to the content of reading material where the answer is defined word by word; **inferential items**, on the other hand, require the test taker to read between the lines in order to determine what an author is implying. Items that require inference may demonstrate cultural bias when a test taker makes a reasonable inference based on his or her cultural background that is subsequently scored as incorrect because it is not the expected answer as determined by the norms of the dominant culture.

For these reasons, it is important that the academic abilities of English learners are assessed in a variety of ways to eliminate assessment outcomes in which bias may play a role. In addition, educators must investigate the population samples, or **norms**, used to determine the reliability and validity of an assessment in order to ensure that the initial comparison groups included significant representation of linguistically, culturally, and socioeconomically diverse students.

SAMPLE QUESTION

11) **Which best illustrates assessment bias in an essay writing item?**

   A.   The topic is Halloween.

   B.   The topic is to describe a day at school.

   C.   The topic is to describe a favorite smell.

   D.   The topic is friendship.

Answers:

   A.   **Correct.** Halloween is a holiday recognized in some cultures but not others. In addition, some cultures choose not to celebrate some or all holidays. For these reasons, this assessment item could penalize some students because it conflicts with their values or background knowledge.

   B.   Incorrect. The topic of a day at school is open to each student's interpretation and experience of being at school, which limits potential bias.

   C.   Incorrect. The topic of a favorite smell is broad enough and familiar enough to people from different cultural groups to limit potential bias.

   D.   Incorrect. The topic of friendship is applicable to different cultural groups and has a positive connotation, which limits potential bias.

NORM-REFERENCED AND CRITERION-REFERENCED ASSESSMENTS

Assessments can be either criterion referenced or norm referenced. **Criterion-referenced assessments** measure test takers' results according to a pre-established criterion, or performance standard related to a specific content domain. These results provide information regarding a student's mastery of the measured skills. Each skill is expressed as an instructional objective, and scores are typically expressed in percentages. English learners are often required to pass criterion-leveled tests in order to progress from one level of an ELD program to the next. The focus is on student achievement in relation to the material, not other students or a normative sample. For this reason, criterion-referenced assessments are used to measure the achievement or progress of students in relation to specific instructional objectives.

Many large-scale standardized achievement and placement tests for English learners are norm referenced. **Norm-referenced assessments** measure student performance in comparison to the performance of similar students. Student scores are compared to those from an initial sample of test takers, or **normative group**. Norm-referenced assessments are used to rank students and differentiate between high and low achievers across a broad spectrum of skills, measuring individual performance within the context of a group. These types of assessments are subject to debate due to issues related to the initial group defined as normative: if the normative group is not reflective of the language, culture, and socioeconomic status of the test takers, bias can occur and adversely impact scores. Thus, when selecting norm-referenced assessments to use with English learner populations, educators must carefully review the test publisher's description of the groups initially tested. More variability between members of the initial group often translates into higher reliability in the assessment of diverse learning populations.

SAMPLE QUESTION

12) **How might the outcomes of a norm-referenced assessment be unreliable due to bias?**

   A. The scores of the population sample do not confirm that the test items measure specific criteria.

   B. The scores of the original population sample do not go up after participation in an instructional program.

   C. The population sample tested initially is not representative of the students being assessed.

   D. The initial group of people tested demonstrates a high level of variability between members.

Answers:

   A. Incorrect. This relates to the establishment of criterion-related validity, but it is not evidence of bias.

   B. Incorrect. This relates to the establishment of construct validity, but it is not evidence of bias.

   C. **Correct.** In order for a norm-referenced test to produce reliable outcomes, the normative group must reflect the language, culture, and socioeconomic status of the test takers.

   D. Incorrect. This would translate into higher reliability, not less, because the group has a higher probability of being representative of diverse learners.

INTERPRETING AND APPLYING ASSESSMENT RESULTS

USING TEST RESULTS TO PLAN AND DIFFERENTIATE INSTRUCTION

In order to positively and effectively impact learning, assessment results must ultimately inform and serve English learners' authentic academic and language needs. After initial placement in an instructional program, the performance of an English learner must be consistently observed and monitored to ensure that proper placement was made. In addition, a variety of assessment methods in both the primary and secondary languages should be provided to ensure that the breadth of an English learner's abilities is allowed to become evident.

Teachers can use test results from a variety of assessment methods to plan and differentiate instruction for the particular student populations in their classrooms. Assessment results can allow teachers to identify gaps in learning, select content for reteaching, and celebrate mastery of material; results can also illuminate the ways that individual students differ in learning styles so that instructional strategies can be modified to meet the needs of individual learners. In this way, teachers **differentiate** instruction for diverse populations by identifying the conditions and materials that contribute meaningfully to the achievement of individual students. Some examples of differentiated instruction include using visuals, providing learning centers, assigning individual tasks, providing manipulatives, allowing for more thinking time before accepting responses, offering one-on-one instruction, providing background information, defining relevant vocabulary, simplifying text, and adjusting assignments for manageability. Teachers best engage diverse classroom populations by implementing instruction that approaches concepts from many different pathways and through a variety of access points; assessment results clarify the best approaches and methods for providing these pathways and access points.

> **HELPFUL HINT**
>
> Due to the challenges associated with learning a new language, all teachers—regardless of the subject they teach—should be prepared to differentiate instruction for English language learners.

SAMPLE QUESTION

13) While reviewing the science logs of her students, Ms. Green notices that some of the LEP students in her class are not describing science labs in detail, which makes it difficult for her to determine if the related science concepts are fully understood.

How can Ms. Green differentiate learning for these students so she can better assess how well they understand the science labs?

Go on →

A.   She can ask students to illustrate the science lab processes.

B.   She can assign low scores to science logs with insufficient detail.

C.   She can administer multiple-choice science lab unit tests.

D.   She can make science logs optional for LEP students.

Answers:

A.   **Correct.** By asking students to illustrate science lab processes in their science journals, Ms. Green adds a non-language-based (visual) method of response and broadens the means by which students can express their understanding.

B.   Incorrect. Assigning low scores is not a means of differentiating assessment. It penalizes students who may understand the content but do not yet have the second-language skills to express their understanding in written detail.

C.   Incorrect. This approach does not address the key issue, which is how to make science logs a more meaningful assessment and instructional tool for LEP students.

D.   Incorrect. This is not an appropriate way to differentiate learning as it reduces LEP student participation in classroom tasks and limits the learning that can take place through active reflection.

Using Test Results to Inform Decisions

Assessment is the means by which English learners are assigned to instructional programs, advanced within those programs, and redesignated from Limited English Proficient to Fluent English Proficient. Depending on how instruction for English learners is approached on both a state and district level, English learners are placed in instructional programs based on English **language proficiency** levels derived from assessment. These levels are defined by states using different vocabulary, but they typically range from beginning to advanced and categorize English learners along a trajectory of English proficiency in the domains of speaking, listening, reading, and writing.

DID YOU KNOW?

Schools and school systems offer varying levels of support for teachers whose students are English language learners. Thus, prior to the beginning of the school year, teachers should be sure to inquire about the resources available to them and their students.

Instructional programs for English learners vary depending on the school of enrollment, with different programs applying different theoretical models to their classrooms. For example, ESL and bilingual programs use a **one-language** approach while dual language programs use a **mixed-language** approach. In each type of program, the **grade-level placement** of English learners must be age appropriate, as language development needs are most effectively addressed in the context of an age-similar peer group.

English as a Second Language: In an ESL instructional model, English learners are placed at the appropriate grade level in English-speaking classrooms in which the teacher differentiates instruction in order to meet the instructional needs of students who have a primary language other than English.

Bilingual: In a bilingual instructional model, English learners are placed at the appropriate grade level in classrooms in which most instruction is delivered in the primary language with supplemental instruction in English taking place at a designated time and place during the school day.

DID YOU KNOW?

It is a violation of the Civil Rights Act of 1964 to retain students on the basis of limited English proficiency.

Dual language: In a dual language instructional model, a common grade-level curriculum is taught in two languages which may either (a) represent the primary and secondary languages of one group or (b) represent the primary and secondary languages of two groups. A one-way dual language program for students whose primary language is Spanish would provide a common grade-level curriculum in both English and Spanish. A two-way dual language program would similarly provide a common grade-level curriculum in both English and Spanish, but the classroom population would include students with a primary language of either English or Spanish. In the two-way dual language model, some students would be learning English as their secondary language, while other students would be learning Spanish as their secondary language.

SAMPLE QUESTION

14) A classroom includes students whose primary languages include both English and Spanish and instruction in all content areas is delivered in both languages.

   Which approach to second-language instruction is being implemented in the classroom?

   A.   a bilingual instructional model

   B.   a two-way dual language instructional model

   C.   an ESL instructional model

   D.   a one-way dual language instructional model

   Answers:

   A.   Incorrect. In a bilingual instructional model, students with a primary language other than English receive content area instruction in their primary language and supplemental instruction in English.

   B.   Correct. In a two-way dual language instructional model, curriculum is taught in two languages that represent the primary and secondary languages of two student groups.

C.   Incorrect. In an ESL instructional model, English learners receive differentiated instruction in a classroom where English is the primary language of use.

D.   Incorrect. In a one-way dual language instructional model, curriculum is taught in two languages that represent the primary language and the secondary language of the entire group of students.

INTERPRETING AND COMMUNICATING TEST RESULTS

Assessment results obtained via a variety of formal and informal means have the benefit of presenting a clear picture of an English learner's unique abilities, areas of challenge, and goals for learning. When presented together, these results can be used by a teacher to effectively illustrate and communicate a student's progress to both the student and his or her parents or guardians. Formal scores from standardized assessments can be balanced with qualitative feedback from performance-based tasks and explained in the context of concrete work examples from student portfolios. In addition, student progress in language proficiency can be articulated independently from student progress in the domains of academic knowledge. Teachers can use the results of assessments to provide a holistic view of the concepts a student has mastered, the instructional strategies being used to help the student master new content, and any accommodations being made to meet the student's educational needs. When communicating assessment results to parents or guardians about assessments, a teacher should be sure to explain the assessment's purpose, how the measures from a variety of assessments differ, and how demonstrated student strengths and weaknesses can be addressed both at school and at home.

SAMPLE QUESTION

15) **Which of the following choices states the most significant purpose of assessment for English learners?**

A.   to identify students as high or low achievers in instructional content areas

B.   to keep a record of student scores on state-mandated assessments

C.   to determine the appropriate grade levels for student placement

D.   to ensure student instructional needs are being met and learning is taking place

Answers:

A.   Incorrect. While assessment can demonstrate low and high levels of achievement, this is not its main purpose. The main purpose of identifying learning gaps in content knowledge or comprehension is to inform educators so that those areas of need can be addressed via curriculum and instructional strategies.

B. Incorrect. While assessment can provide a record of student performance, this is not its main purpose. The main purpose of assessment is to ensure that the instructional needs of students are identified and addressed in instructional programs.

C. Incorrect. Age, not assessment, is used to determine the grade-level placement of English learners.

D. **Correct.** The main purpose of assessment is to identify the instructional needs of a student and take steps to meet those instructional needs in the classroom.

5

Cultural Aspects

Simply put, **culture** is defined as the beliefs, customs, values, and attitudes that distinguish one group of people from another. Culture is transmitted through many means including arts, education, literature, and—perhaps most fundamentally—language. At its heart, language is central to what it means to be human.

CULTURAL UNDERSTANDING

RELATIONSHIPS BETWEEN LANGUAGE AND CULTURE

Although there has been debate over many years about the extent to which language directly affects how people think and view the world, there is widespread agreement now that language does directly affect peoples' thoughts and world views. In linguistics, the **Sapir-Whorf Hypothesis,** named after linguists Edward Sapir and Benjamin Whorf, states that a human's thoughts and actions are determined by the language(s) which that person speaks. By extension, a person's culture is strongly related to the language(s) spoken, since culture is transmitted through language. The debate about the extent of language's influence on thought has led to the establishment of two versions of the Sapir-Whorf Hypothesis: a stronger one and a weaker one. The stronger one, called **linguistic determinism**, states that all human thought and action is totally controlled by language. The weaker version, known as **linguistic relativism**, says that language only partially influences human thought and action. Currently, researchers from many disciplines are working to examine language and its influence on human thought, so the debate continues.

> **HELPFUL HINT**
>
> linguistic determinism = language *determines* culture; linguistic relativism = language *relates* to culture

Anthropologists point to the words, vocabulary, and terminology a culture uses as a way to understand what is important in that culture. In some languages, there may be only one word for a concept, while in others there are many. For example, in the languages of some indigenous Arctic cultures, there might be up to fifty words for snow, each describing different types, uses, etc. In northern Australia some Aborigines speak of direction using only *north*, *south*, *east*, and *west* rather than *forward*, *backward*, *right*, and *left*. It is likely that they have a stronger ability to orient themselves and navigate than people who do not speak of direction using such terms. The landscape in which these Aborigines live, and their lifestyle, encourages and values the ability to specifically articulate direction.

Moreover, there are some words in languages that simply are not translatable to words in other languages, usually because of a strong cultural connection. For example, the Norwegian word *utepils* literally translates as *outside pilsner*, but actually refers to the first beer enjoyed outside in the spring, hopefully in the sunshine, after a long, cold, Norwegian winter. In Chinese, the word *yuánfèn* describes a relationship predetermined by fate, reflecting the importance of building relationships in Chinese culture. The Arabic word *ya'aburnee*, meaning *you bury me*, describes the desire by the speaker to die before the other because of the difficulty of living without him or her. This is a reflection of the importance of love and romanticism in Arabic cultures. In German, *torschlusspanik* translates as *gate-shut panic* and describes, among other situations, the feeling a woman who wants children experiences as she approaches middle age and becomes less fertile. In a country where people marry later and have children later, the cultural connection is clear.

SAMPLE QUESTION

1) **The Sapir-Whorf Hypothesis of language and culture is widely acknowledged as true, but some view it as containing two versions. What are they and what do they mean?**

   A. semantics, which says language controls human thought and action; linguistic transcription, which says language partially influences thought and action

   B. linguistic transcription, which says language controls human thought and action; semantics, which says language partially influences thought and action

   C. linguistic relativism, which says language controls human thought and action; linguistic determinism, which says language partially influences thought and action

   D. linguistic determinism, which says language controls human thought and action; linguistic relativism, which says language partially influences thought and action

   Answers:

   A. Incorrect. These are not the meanings of semantics or transcription.

   B. Incorrect. These are not the meanings of semantics or transcription.

C.   Incorrect. The opposite is true.

D.   **Correct.** This is true.

CULTURAL ASPECTS THAT AFFECT SECOND-LANGUAGE ACQUISITION, ENGLISH-LANGUAGE LEARNERS, AND TEACHING

CULTURAL VARIABLES THAT AFFECT SECOND-LANGUAGE ACQUISITION, TEACHING, AND STUDENT IDENTITY

As an ESOL teacher, it is important to have an understanding of cultural variables that affect SLA, ELL identity, and even one's approach to teaching. Two of the most important cultural aspects are the concepts of **individualism** and **collectivism**. An **individualist** culture is characterized by value placed on the individual and individual accomplishments, rather than on the family or group to which the individual belongs. Individualist cultures value competitive behavior and the belief in equality, with personal goals and ambitions taking precedence over group goals. At the same time, people in individualist cultures form strong family and social bonds; they value the success of the group, and many would state that furthering oneself serves to benefit the family, group, or society at large. On the other hand, a **collectivist** culture prioritizes the needs and outcomes of groups such as the greater community, society, or nation. Identity is based on belonging to a group, and behavior that contributes to group harmony is valued over personal goals or wishes.

> **QUICK REVIEW**
>
> Did you grow up in an individualist or collectivist culture? How do you think that influenced your school experience?

These values can dictate how people communicate with one another and use language. In **high-context** (collectivist) cultures, the context and relationships among speakers figure importantly in communication. There are rules and traditions that dictate interactions, which are often quite formal, and much is understood without having to be stated. These cultures rely heavily on **non-verbal communication**, or the use of gestures, facial expressions, body language, and even distance between speakers. High-context cultures include Japan and China, most of the Middle East and Africa, and South America.

Conversely, communication in **low-context** (individualistic) cultures often seems loose and informal, and much more is explicitly stated. Facts, evidence, and background information must be communicated outright to avoid misunderstanding. Low-context cultures include the United States, Canada, and most of Western Europe.

Perception of time is another cultural variable. In **monochronic** cultures, time is seen as linear, with one event happening at a time. Monochronic cultures value punctuality and starkly divide work and leisure time. Schedules are important. On the other hand, **polychronic** cultures view time more holistically and are able to conceive of many things happening at once. Flexibility is valued over punctuality and the line between work and play can be comfortably blurred. Strengthening relationships and social activities are more important than finishing tasks. Adhering to a strict schedule is not important. Visitors from a monochronic culture to a polychronic environment may feel frustrated at the lack of punctuality and adherence to a schedule. Likewise, visitors from polychronic to monochronic cultures may be surprised at how upset people are when they are late.

> **DID YOU KNOW?**
>
> **Chronemics** is the study of time in communication.

Needless to say, these are generalizations about culture that do not apply to all people at all times. Indeed, in many cultures there are large groups that do not adhere to the culture of the majority, and individuals often do not fit the mold. Moreover, these characteristics are sometimes dynamic and change depending on circumstances or needs. They serve, however, to illustrate some fundamental traits that guide many people's actions, all because of their culture.

SAMPLE QUESTIONS

2) Mr. Jackson, a content area science teacher, counts classroom participation as part of daily grades for students. Classroom participation includes participating in whole class discussions and asking questions during lectures. Why might this be unfair for ESL students in his classroom?

A. Some ESL students might come from collectivist cultures that expect students to play a more passive role in the classroom.

B. Some ESL students might come from individualist cultures that expect students to play a more passive role in the classroom.

C. Some ESL students might come from individualist cultures that expect students to play a more active role in the classroom.

D. ESL students do not have the English skills necessary to ask questions.

Answers:

A. **Correct.** Talking out loud in class and questioning the teacher are not encouraged in collectivist cultures.

B. Incorrect. Individualist cultures do not expect students to be passive.

C. Incorrect. Such students would have an advantage in this situation.

D. Incorrect. This is not necessarily true.

3) Two ESOL students, Hans and Gabriel, have planned to meet after school at 4:00 to work on a class project. When Gabriel arrives at the meeting place at 4:40, Hans has been waiting and is angry. Hans is most likely from which kind of culture?

    A. polychronic

    B. TPR

    C. monochronic

    D. phonemic

Answers:

    A. Incorrect. In polychronic cultures, adhering to a strict schedule is not usually important.

    B. Incorrect. TPR is *Total Physical Response*, an approach to L2 teaching.

    C. Correct. Monochronic cultures value punctuality.

    D. Incorrect. Phonemic refers to phonemes, not culture.

AWARENESS THAT TEACHING AND LEARNING STYLES VARY ACROSS CULTURES

In the classroom, cultural variables play a large role in student and teacher behavior, as well as the expectations each has of the other and the learning environment. It is helpful to be aware of these variables since these behaviors and expectations are often unquestioned and can lead to misunderstanding, or perhaps more seriously, accusations of misbehavior. Becoming more culturally competent will help ESL and content teachers better support the ESL students in their schools. Following are some common cultural variables that may lead to misunderstanding when working with ESL students.

Eye contact, its duration, and what is considered appropriate vary among cultures throughout the world. In the United States, direct eye contact is a sign of honesty, trustworthiness, and respect. In many Eastern cultures, however, direct eye contact with a teacher is considered a sign of disrespect. Furthermore, extended eye contact can be construed as staring and thought of as rude in some cultures, but not others.

In the United States, most teachers would agree that cooperative learning, or group work, is pedagogically sound and should be used in the classroom. In some cultures, however, group work may be a largely unknown concept. Therefore some students may be totally unfamiliar with the rules and mores of negotiation when working collaboratively in groups. Modeling appropriate behavior for cooperative learning would benefit not only these students, but also others who would profit from knowing culturally appropriate ways to collaborate with their peers in the classroom.

In the United States, it is typical to respond with a nod, and maybe a smile, to answer affirmatively when a teacher asks if everything is clear or if students understand a certain point. However such a response may signify that an ESL student is simply trying to be polite; he or she may not understand the issue.

Another area of significant variation can be found in student participation. Individualist cultures value active and vocal student participation, so students will often speak up without being directly addressed and are expected to ask questions or seek clarification when needed. On the other hand, in collectivist cultures, students assume a more passive role in the classroom and may have difficulty speaking up in class. Also, because well-being of the group as a whole is valued, students may be uncomfortable when singled out even for positive purposes. Students from collectivist cultures are accustomed to viewing the teacher as the expert authority figure whose role is to deliver knowledge to the students, so taking an active role or asking questions would be seen as disrespectful of the teacher's rank and expertise.

Related to this idea is the general atmosphere of the classroom. In the United States, most classrooms operate more informally than in some other cultures. Students may be accustomed to a strict learning environment where what will be taught is prescribed and done in a certain order. Conversely, in the United States, often it is considered good practice to break from the lesson if several students have related questions. However to students accustomed to other learning environments, this might make the teacher appear disorganized and unprofessional. Moreover, a classroom where polite debate takes place is desirable in the United States, but in other cultures it may be considered rude to contradict others in public, especially a teacher.

In the United States, cheating is a very serious academic offense that can result in failure or even dismissal from the school. In individualist cultures such as that of the United States, personal achievement is highly valued and students often approach tests competitively, hoping to do better than classmates. However in some collectivist cultures, helping a member of your group to improve on a test might be considered honorable. For example, letting a fellow student who is struggling in class copy answers during a test might be viewed as a display of kinship and concern for the group as a whole. Because of this difference, students might have a hard time understanding the importance attached to what certain cultures consider to be cheating. When new students arrive, policies should be stated clearly, with explicit examples of what is considered cheating in the United States, and subsequent disciplinary actions should be thoroughly explained. If possible, some class time should be dedicated to role play, modeling of appropriate and inappropriate test-time behavior, and so on. If cheating occurs, a private discussion of the offense with the students involved might be warranted before any major discipline takes place, depending on the circumstances.

> **TEACHING TIP**
>
> Culture dictates classroom behavior of both the students *and* the teacher.

4) During a standardized test given to all students in school, two advanced ESL students from Saudi Arabia, Yusef and Ali, are called to the principal's office because the teacher saw them talking and sharing answers during the test. Yusef and Ali are both well-behaved students who work hard in all their classes, yet they do not seem to understand that they have done something wrong. What is the likely explanation for their lack of understanding?

   A.   They actually understand what they have done, but they are pretending not to.

   B.   They come from a monochronic culture.

   C.   They come from an individualist culture.

   D.   They come from a collectivist culture.

Answers:

   A.   Incorrect. Since they are hard-working, well-behaved students, this is unlikely.

   B.   Incorrect. Monochronic deals with perception of time.

   C.   Incorrect. Individualist cultures value individual achievement and competition, so the students would likely understand what cheating is if they were from an individualist culture.

   D.   Correct. In collectivist cultures, the success of the group is more important than individual achievement, so helping a fellow student do well would be seen as the right thing to do.

CULTURAL IMPACT ON STUDENTS AND SECOND-LANGUAGE ACQUISITION

ESL students bring a rich array of cultural backgrounds to the ESL classroom and school. This cultural diversity brings many opportunities for positive enrichment to the ESL students and the school at large. As ESL students adjust to American culture, however, and all students in the school begin to interact with each other, conflicts that affect student behavior and learning can arise.

Acculturation is the process of adapting to a new culture. It is a process that may take several years, so ESL teachers should be familiar with it because most of their students will likely be passing through one of the phases. There are four widely accepted stages of acculturation: **honeymoon**, **hostility**, **humor**, and **home**.

In the **honeymoon** stage, students are delighted about the novelty of the new culture around them. All of these new things seem interesting and fun. The new culture may seem exotic and stimulating, and students will be excited about the differences.

After a few months, the **hostility** stage sets in. At this stage, students are getting comfortable with getting around and meeting basic needs, but they may feel at odds with the new culture and may be homesick. They will start to make comparisons between the new and old cultures and will view the new culture unfavorably when they do. Students in this second stage may complain a lot and feel moody and depressed. The new culture now seems strange, undesirable, and annoying.

Next, students enter the **humor** stage. In this stage, students start to come to terms with their circumstances and move toward acceptance of their new culture. They now see positive things about the culture around them. In this stage, some have a tendency toward extremes. These students may be openly critical about their home countries and cultures. However, for many, this stage can sometimes be difficult and often prolonged as students struggle with the feeling that they are rejecting their home culture for the new culture.

Finally, usually after several years, students arrive at the **home** stage and are comfortable within their new culture. They now embrace it as home and are at ease with their identity within the culture. They feel comfortable with their heritage and can be themselves within the new culture. At this point, they have **assimilated** and become part of a new country or culture.

Unfortunately, some newcomers never make it to this stage and may experience difficulties stuck in the second or third phases, which often encompass much negativity. Teachers should remain aware of the different stages of acculturation so that they can be sensitive to the needs of their students as they pass through them, and/or be able to refer these students to outside support if needed.

In addition to the process of acculturation, other cultural factors can affect students' dispositions and academic lives. ESL students, especially refugees, may come from countries or regions in the midst of war and/or chaos. What they are experiencing as a result could be as severe as post-traumatic stress disorder (PTSD) and clearly could have negative implications for learning.

In a classroom with students from many cultures, there is also a good possibility that there may be students from two or more countries with histories of tension due to war, genocide, or other extreme causes. Examples would be Japan and China, Turkey and Armenia, and the countries and peoples involved in the Bosnian War. Teachers need to be aware of the potential for conflict between students when assigning pair or group work. Becoming informed about students' home countries and cultures, and their histories, may help teachers avoid a potentially tense situation. Keeping activities and interactions structured rather than open-ended is one strategy for minimizing tension. Additionally, games are helpful tools for allowing students to work together, as long as they revolve around neutral or structured topics such as grammar rules, classroom vocabulary, and so on. Until a teacher gets to know his or her students and can better gauge

HELPFUL HINT

Join the 4-H culture club! **HO**neymoon, **HO**stility, **HU**mor, **HO**me.

how they will react, it is wise to stay away from controversial topics during classroom discussions and activities.

Additionally, there are taboos in every culture that can cause great offense. The list is extensive, but some well-known examples are the taboos against pointing the bottom of your foot or shoe at another person in Islamic cultures, writing a person's name in red in Korea, pointing with one finger in Brazil or Vietnam, or using the left hand to eat or pass something in Nigeria, among other countries. As an ESL teacher, recognizing the potential for cultural conflict and being able to diffuse it when it occurs is an important component of classroom management. Many teachers take a proactive approach using modeling and role-play to demonstrate desirable classroom behavior.

SAMPLE QUESTION

5) During the spring semester a Chinese student named Fen, who began school in the fall, starts having difficulty in class and often seems depressed. Moreover, she complains a lot to other students about life in the United States and feeling homesick. What phase of acculturation is she probably experiencing?

A. home

B. honeymoon

C. humor

D. hostility

Answers:

A. Incorrect. Students in the *home*, or final phase, embrace their new culture and feel comfortable in it.

B. Incorrect. Students in the *honeymoon* phase are excited about their new culture.

C. Incorrect. Students in the *humor*, or third phase, have begun to accept their new culture and see positive aspects in it.

D. Correct. Students in the *hostility*, or second phase, see negative aspects in their new culture and are homesick and depressed.

CULTURAL FACTORS THAT COULD IMPACT READINESS AND LEARNING

Other important factors that could impact school readiness and learning include gender, educational attainment of parents, and the extent of a student's previous experience with formal learning. Gender roles and expectations in students' home cultures may affect their level of preparation as they start school and language study. In some cultures and situations, gender may also determine how many years a student has already spent in school. Moreover, gender roles may determine students' level of participation in the classroom, which could affect grading. For example, if female students are expected to assume a passive role in the classroom in their home culture, some teachers may mistakenly view this as laziness or lack of interest. If, however, women have a lower status in their home country, female students may become eager language learners because they readily embrace the elevated status of women in their newly-adopted country.

Some ESL students might have limited or interrupted formal education. These students are referred to with the acronym **SIFE: S**tudents with **I**nterrupted **F**ormal **E**ducation. Researcher and Professor Margarita Calderón has done extensive research in effective instruction for SIFEs. She states that SIFEs may have experienced, among other scenarios, inconsistent or disrupted education in their own country or the United States (as the children of migrant workers may experience). This could include periods of schooling in the United States—then a return to their home country—then a return to school in the United States, or even deficiencies due to inadequate schooling in the United States. Such students will not only face the challenge of learning English, but may also be struggling with basic literacy skills in both their native language and English; moreover, they may be performing at an academic level well below that of others of their age. Additionally, the entire formal classroom structure may be unfamiliar; a SIFE may not understand normal and expected classroom behavior and may engage in behavior such as talking to friends while the teacher is speaking, roaming around the classroom at will, and so on. Many SIFEs will have learning experiences in informal, non-academic situations. Furthermore, the events that interrupted a student's education may have been traumatic, so students may face the additional challenges of coping with post-traumatic stress disorder.

QUICK REVIEW

How does the education level of parents affect children?

The education levels of students' parents are also important in determining readiness and learning. Much research has revealed that there are direct links between the level of parental education and the success of their children in school. Parents who have attained more education are likely to have higher expectations of their children and to engage in behaviors which are conducive to learning, such as going to the library. Regardless of their education levels, there are strategies for engaging parents to help their children succeed in school, some of which are discussed in chapter six.

SAMPLE QUESTION

6)   SIFE is an acronym most relative to which of the following?

A.   culture and student preparedness

B.   phonetics

C.   expository writing

D.   ELP (English Language Proficiency) standards

Answers:

A. **Correct.** Students with Interrupted Formal Education, or SIFE, is most related to concepts of culture and student preparedness.

B. Incorrect. SIFE is less related to phonetics.

C. Incorrect. SIFE is less related to expository writing.

D. Incorrect. SIFE is less related to ELP standards.

TEACHER'S CULTURE AND INFLUENCES ON TEACHING STYLES

A teacher's culture and cultural assumptions can have a significant effect on classroom pedagogy and approach. Cultural assumptions are beliefs people hold due to their culture. These beliefs are unquestioned because most of the people in the culture believe them; thus, it is assumed they are right. This is important to any classroom, but it takes on special significance in an ESL classroom where there are many cultures represented. ESL teachers must be sensitive to ESL students' beliefs, circumstances, and the challenges they face when entering a new culture. Moreover, ESL teachers must strive for constant awareness and periodic check-in of their own cultural assumptions and bias. **Bias** means favoring something over others, often unreasonably, whether it is a group of people, ideas, or even practices.

One danger comes in the belief that Western models of teaching and learning are superior to non-Western models, thus undervaluing the knowledge and approach that students bring to the classroom and risking alienation and low student participation.

> **QUICK REVIEW**
>
> Bias = partiality.

Teachers also bring cultural assumptions about what is pedagogically sound, such as the use of technology in the classroom and the importance of group and pair work to language practice. Being aware of these assumptions does not mean teachers have to refrain from using such practices or that such practices are necessarily wrong. Rather, teachers must be aware of their own bias and remain open to other approaches when students are not progressing as expected or are having difficulties with the activities themselves.

SAMPLE QUESTION

7) In an ESL classroom, a group of students from the same country approaches the teacher with an idea for a classroom activity to help them learn idioms. The teacher is polite and thanks them, but dismisses their idea immediately. In doing so, the teacher is exhibiting cultural

A. sensitivity.

B. acculturation.

C. bias.

D. chronemics.

Answers:

A.   Incorrect. In this example, the teacher would actually be culturally *in*sensitive.

B.   Incorrect. The teacher is not going through cultural acculturation.

C.   **Correct.** The teacher is biased toward his or her culture's way of teaching and learning.

D.   Incorrect. This behavior is not related to chronemics.

Cultural Awareness, Sensitivity, and Inclusion

Incorporating the Diverse Cultures of Students in the Classroom

Cultural **awareness** is the development of sensitivity to and understanding of other cultures and the ways culture influences individuals. After becoming aware of cultural variables and bias, there are specific techniques teachers can use to incorporate the diverse cultures of students in the classroom. The goal is to create a **multicultural** classroom: one which includes, incorporates, and represents many cultures. Teachers can keep this in mind when doing something as basic as choosing classroom materials. Including materials that use important or common symbols and pictures from other cultures, as well as languages, will help students feel at ease in their new surroundings and with their classmates. This is especially important when building a classroom library. Books representing different cultures and languages should be included; this sends a message that all of the class cultures are valued. Teachers can also make a point of learning at least a few words of the native languages spoken by their students.

HELPFUL HINT

Cultural awareness has *two* components: 1) knowledge of and sensitivity to other cultures; and 2) understanding of how culture influences everyone.

Allowing students to share their own cultures is also effective in creating a multicultural classroom. There are many ways this can be organized and guided. At the beginning of the year, or when new students arrive, students can get to know one another and each other's culture by sharing names and their meanings. One popular event is a class or school food fair in which students bring and share traditional or common foods from their countries. Students can also be encouraged to share important holidays with the class by hosting an event in the classroom or sharing stories related to the holiday. The classroom can have a multicultural calendar that highlights holidays and important dates. Sharing folktales is also beneficial and may be especially important for those students from cultures with a strong tradition of oral storytelling. Allowing students to present information about historical events and figures from their home countries enriches all students' global awareness. Planning a day for show and tell of contemporary pop culture—including music, games, and film—also promotes awareness and is especially important for young people.

SAMPLE QUESTION

8) **Which of the following is characteristic of a multicultural classroom?**

   A.   a classroom that includes, incorporates, and represents many cultures

   B.   a classroom that allows students to participate in sharing their own cultures

   C.   a classroom with a focus on CALP needed for universities in the United States

   D.   both A and B

Answers:

   A.   Incorrect. This is true, but so is option B.

   B.   Incorrect. This is true, but so is option A.

   C.   Incorrect. University academic language is not characteristic of a multicultural classroom.

   D.   Correct. Both A and B are true.

IMPLICATIONS OF CULTURAL STEREOTYPING IN THE SCHOOL SETTING

While promoting cultural awareness and tolerance in the school setting, ESL teachers must also guard against cultural stereotyping. To **stereotype** is to hold an oversimplified belief that all people from a certain group or with certain characteristics are the same. Of course, stereotyping can occur with any student belonging to any group, be it ethnic, racial, socioeconomic, or even groups of skill or hobby such as athletes, scholars, and so on. The potential for stereotyping is perhaps stronger with ESL students who come from cultures that may be unfamiliar to many students and teachers in the school. In trying to relate to the new student, faculty and students may rely—intentionally or not—on preconceived notions about that student's cultural group. It is also dangerous to assume that new students are similar to previous students who share the same cultural background.

Why does it matter? Viewing a student through the lens of a stereotype means failing to see him or her as a fully unique person with unlimited potential. Needless to say, this is detrimental in a school setting. Students may try to conform into the stereotyped role without realizing their full potential. Teachers must strive to continually perceive students based on their individual potential and challenges and adjust teaching approaches accordingly. Even a supposed

HELPFUL HINT

Remember, not all stereotypes are negative, but even a positive stereotype can have negative consequences.

positive stereotype can have negative implications. For instance, an Asian American student who struggles with math may hear the stereotype that "Asian students are good at math." This student may become reluctant to seek the help he needs with the subject.

To counter the negative effects of stereotyping, ESL teachers can employ several tactics. Teachers can encourage students to acknowledge their own self-worth with activities that prompt them to identify skills, values, or personal traits that they find worthy or important. Teachers can also ensure that students have opportunities to identify with role models who defy stereotypes, either in person or through study and research. It is also important to allow ESL students to contribute to school culture and activities; this will thwart some people's prejudice and stereotypical impression of ESL students as immigrants who are not interested in participating in or contributing to their new culture.

SAMPLE QUESTION

9) **During a social studies discussion in an ESL classroom, a non-Muslim female student makes a comment saying that all Muslims discriminate against women. This upsets some of the Muslim students in the class. What would be the most appropriate way for the teacher to address the situation?**

A. punish the student who made the offensive comment by banning her from the class

B. hold a moderated classroom discussion in which all students present information about the status of women in their culture

C. privately apologize to the Muslim students after class

D. change the topic and let the students work it out among themselves outside of class

Answers:

A. Incorrect. This would not effectively address the stereotype held by the student and would discourage open communication in the classroom.

B. **Correct.** This would allow students to get factual information about the status of women in many cultures, including Islamic cultures.

C. Incorrect. Doing this may make the Muslim students feel better, but it avoids addressing the negative stereotype voiced by the student.

D. Incorrect. This avoids the issue and may even allow it to develop into a larger problem.

Modeling Positive Attitudes toward English–Language Learners

At times, communities and school districts may receive a sudden influx of ELLs or new groups of ELLs. This may be due to refugee resettlement programs or a spike in immigration to an area because of growing economic opportunity, among other reasons. Staff, teachers, and students are often not prepared for this influx, and negative attitudes may develop as people struggle with the new change. Moreover, many small, rural districts lack resources and professional development opportunities for staff and teachers. ESL teachers have a primary role to play in modeling positive attitudes toward ELLs not only in the entire school, but in the community as well.

Modeling a positive attitude can be as basic as learning how to correctly pronounce a student's name and doing so when addressing students. Because students will not likely correct a teacher, asking how a student's family pronounces a name may be effective. Projecting a welcoming attitude in and out of the classroom is also effective: teachers can greet students in their native language, include them in out-of-class activities, and generally take an interest in their hobbies and lives. Paying close attention to details and student behavior may reveal areas of need or conflict that students are not likely to vocalize. For example, if a student is not eating at lunchtime, a religious dietary restriction might be the issue. Or, if a student is not participating in athletics, related behavior may be prohibited in the student's culture. Noticing and assisting students with these issues promotes an environment of concern and openness.

SAMPLE QUESTION

10) **Which of the following is false?**

   A. Singling out new ESL students to present interesting information about their cultures in school assemblies is the best way to display a positive attitude toward ESL students.

   B. Rural school districts often have the twofold challenge of a sudden influx of ESL students and a lack of resources for professional development, so ESL teachers in rural districts may have a leading role in promoting positive attitudes toward ESL students.

   C. Learning a few words of a student's native language, such as greetings, and using them with the student, is an effective way to model positive behavior toward him or her.

   D. Fostering an atmosphere of concern by noticing ESL students' needs, especially those they might not vocalize, is one way to promote positive attitudes toward all ESL students.

Answers:

   A. **Correct.** This has high potential to embarrass new ESL students, causing them to further withdraw from school culture.

   B. Incorrect. Rural school districts often lack professional development resources, so ESL teachers often have to make up for the lack of professional development with positive modeling for teachers and staff to observe.

C.   Incorrect. Simple actions such as these are indeed good ways to model positive attitudes toward ESL students as they are highly visible and easily replicated.

D.   Incorrect. Aiding ESL students with needs other than academic ones helps other teachers and staff see students as whole people with contributions of their own rather than as stereotypes or as problems that need to be solved.

Helping English Language Learners Understand the Culture of the United States

Teaching ESL involves much more than language teaching. Indeed, one of the most important roles of the ESL teacher is that of cultural liaison, guiding students through the culture of the United States. Many teachers, especially content area teachers, may mistakenly assume that ESL students share the background knowledge and experience that native-born students have. It is important to remember that sharing culture will be an ongoing part of teaching. While it is true that the United States is a big country with a large population and incredible diversity, there are some cultural norms that will help ESL students understand American culture. (Note that the term *American* is used for *United States* because of brevity and ease, with the caveat that South Americans might consider themselves *Americans* as well.) The examples below serve as general indicators; they do not necessarily hold true for all Americans, as individuals or groups, and should not be viewed as always correct or incorrect.

Cultural norms are the rules and standards a group uses to determine what are appropriate or inappropriate, expected, and accepted behaviors. All cultures have them, and many of them vary from culture to culture, sometimes subtly and other times greatly. It is useful for ESL teachers to have a good understanding and awareness of cultural norms in the United States and how these norms might appear to those from different cultures. Bear in mind that people often assume that what is *normal* to them and their culture must be *normal* to others.

One aspect of culture in the United States that visitors find striking is informality. Newcomers often remark on how informal, open, and friendly Americans are. For example, introductions are not needed with strangers before striking up a conversation in a line or with people sitting next to each other, engaging in what is known as *small talk*. Furthermore, such conversations will also cover ground that many would find too private for casual conversation with strangers or superiors: marital status, profession, etc. That said, seeking details about these facts and asking too many questions would make Americans uncomfortable.

In the United States, especially in business dealings, the adage that "time is money" dictates behavior. Punctuality is expected and communication is more direct than in many other cultures. Even in social situations, people are expected to get right to the point in conversation or risk being seen as wasting others' time.

Americans are also not hesitant to voice opinions. This is in stark contrast to many other cultures where dealings and conversations are more circular and require elements of ritual. To people from such cultures, Americans may seem rude or aggressive.

Personal space is very important to Americans. In general, Americans maintain a wide area of personal space—usually about an arm's length—between individuals, even when speaking. This distance may be even greater when speaking with strangers. Many cultures do not require as much space between individuals, so students need to be aware of cues that they may be too close to others. For example, if someone steps back during a conversation, a student should be taught that there is no need to be offended; it probably means that he or she is standing too close. Of course, this wide distance decreases among loved ones in many public situations and with strangers in locations such as buses or subways.

DID YOU KNOW?

Proxemics is the study of the spatial requirements individuals have in relation to each other.

In general, Americans live in very small family units (e.g. a parent or parents and young children). Parents and grown children rarely live in the same house but may do so if a parent becomes severely ill and/or needs constant care. Normally, children are expected to move out of their parents' house by the time they are eighteen to twenty years old, either by moving off to college or working and living on their own. It is quite normal for grown children to live far away from their parents and/or siblings, often across the country, and this does not mean that there is discord in the family. Even when grown children and parents live in the same city or town, they usually live in separate homes. These arrangements might seem odd to others who are accustomed to living with three or more generations in one household.

Americans place an emphasis on the idea of equality. Although much can be said about whether or not—or to what degree—equality exists in America, most Americans believe that everyone should have equal opportunities for success. Therefore, most interactions do not follow rules or guidelines based on status. In contrast, many other cultures have rigid levels of status and expectations of behavior when interacting with others of a different status. They may be shocked, offended, or confused when they are not treated in accord with their social status.

Personal hygiene is very important to Americans and may seem quite excessive to those from other cultures. In general, Americans usually bathe or fully shower once a day. Those involved in sports may shower twice a day. Americans are offended by body odor and take preventive measures in this regard, including the regular use of underarm deodorant. After bathing, clean clothes—especially socks and underwear—are put on. Americans are also very sensitive about breath odors and may brush their teeth two or three times a day. Many chew gum or eat mints to freshen their breath throughout the day.

American sexuality can be confusing for many people. On the one hand, sexualized images and celebrities are widely and frequently seen. Movies and TV are often sexually explicit. On the other hand, many Americans have more conservative views about sexuality, especially concerning birth control and sex education. To some people Americans will seem open about sexuality, while to others Americans will seem uptight. For example, a visitor from Northern Europe may find many Americans to be private and modest about sexuality, since prostitution is legal and regulated in many Northern European countries, and parents in these countries may encourage teenagers to use birth control from an early age. For a person from the Middle East, however, Americans may seem sexually loose and free, since many Middle Eastern countries rarely permit the portrayal of sex and sexuality in the media; moreover, people are commonly discouraged or forbidden to have sex outside of marriage. It should also be noted that many American women and girls routinely dress in a way that might be highly provocative in some cultures; this should not be viewed as an invitation for sex or attention.

> **QUICK REVIEW**
>
> What are two cultural norms related to the school environment in the United States that might be unusual for ESL students?

Even something as seemingly innocuous as giving gifts is bound by cultural norms. For example, in the United States, it is common to open the gift immediately and in the presence of the gift-giver, but in many cultures, this would be rude; gifts would never be opened in the presence of the gift-giver. Also, in many cultures, gifts are elaborate and expensive whereas Americans exchange casual, inexpensive gifts regularly.

Americans' close relationships with pets is an increasingly important cultural norm. To those from other cultures, the idea of having an animal, especially a large dog, in the house—and even on the bed—may be unheard of. Americans treat their pets like family members in many cases, and this will be unusual to many.

These are just a few of the cultural norms that newcomers may find striking, but there are many more. Again, these serve as general indicators and do not necessarily hold true for all Americans as individuals or groups; furthermore, they should not be viewed as being right or wrong.

SAMPLE QUESTION

11) **Maintaining more or less distance between or among people is an example of**

   A.   an ethical issue.

   B.   an IEP.

   C.   a cultural norm.

   D.   realia.

Answers:

A.   Incorrect. Personal space is not an ethical issue.

B.   Incorrect. Personal space is not an example of an individualized education plan.

C.   Correct. Personal space is an example of a cultural norm.

D.   Incorrect. Personal space is not a kind of realia.

RELEVANCE OF MIGRATION AND IMMIGRATION IN THE UNITED STATES

The United States is and has always been a nation of immigrants. Most ESL students will be immigrants rather than temporary visitors, so an understanding of past and present immigration and migration patterns is important for ESL teachers. **Migration** means movement *from* one place to another, as in birds and people, and usually refers to a larger group. **Immigration** means movement *to* one place from another and sometimes refers to individuals and families. So, one might speak of a large migration from Europe to the New World which would result in increased immigration to Brazil or the United States, for example.

The issue is complex; some general trends in immigration to the United States will be addressed here. Native Americans were the first people of any number to come to what is now called the United States, originally migrating from Asia somewhere between 13,000 and 20,000 years ago. This remained mostly unchanged until the late fifteenth and sixteenth centuries when many Europeans began to immigrate to both North and South America. Settlers from Spain colonized parts of what is today the Southwest United States, but the vast numbers of early settlers from Europe to what is now the United States began to arrive in the seventeenth century. Thus began an extended period of migration from Britain and Northern Europe, namely Holland and Germany, that lasted through the mid-nineteenth century. In this time period, the forced migration of hundreds of thousands of Africans as slaves also began.

Immigration in the middle nineteenth century was marked by large numbers of Irish and German immigrants in addition to other immigrants from Britain. This was the time of the well-known Irish Potato Famine and migration out of Ireland. It should also be noted that, though technically not immigrants, many Mexican citizens became citizens of the United States with the end of the United States-Mexican War in 1848. Both countries signed the Treaty of Guadalupe Hidalgo in 1848 which ceded Mexican land to the United States, including all of California and most of what is now the Southwestern United States.

From the late nineteenth century to the early twentieth century, huge numbers of immigrants from Southern and Eastern Europe came, including many Jewish immigrants from Russia. This period was one of growing industrialization in the

United States, and many came seeking economic opportunity as a result. Additionally, many Jews were seeking refuge from religious persecution.

Anti-immigration sentiment began to rise during these periods of early mass immigration. At this time, a new series of laws went into effect that were intended to control immigration, some of which established quotas on the number of immigrants arriving from certain countries. Other such laws prohibited the arrival of immigrants from a number of countries. Perhaps the most well-known such act was the Chinese Exclusion Act, the first major law that restricted immigration of an ethnic group to the United States. Passed in 1882, it limited the numbers of Chinese immigrants allowed to enter the United States. Chinese immigration had swelled during the Gold Rush and the building of the Transcontinental Railroad, and anti-Chinese sentiment began to rise as native-born Americans blamed the Chinese immigrants for unemployment and low wages. In 1924, the Immigration Act, or Johnson-Reed Act, established a quota system based on national origin and completely excluded Asian immigrants. Immigration slowed after this time period, but saw surges at times, including after WWII and after the changes brought by the Hart-Celler Act of 1965. This act replaced quotas with preferences, such as those with family in the United States or certain job skills. More recently, the United States has seen another wave of immigration since the 1970s, mainly from Mexico, but with large numbers also from China and India. In 1986, the Immigration Reform and Control Act was passed which granted amnesty to approximately three million immigrants already living in the United States, mostly from Mexico.

This latest wave of immigration correlates to the tremendous growth and standardization of the ESL field. Bilingualism and the use of many languages was actually quite common in the United States until rising anti-immigrant sentiment made speaking other languages undesirable. It took some decades for the ESL field to emerge as its own entity, separate from the field of linguistics, which is where many of the early developments in second-language acquisition and the instruction of ESL took place. Indeed, most of the growth and innovation in the field has occurred since the 1970s and continues as the United States attempts to meet the needs of millions of immigrants. There is widespread understanding that not speaking English in the United States today will greatly limit educational and economic opportunities. Learning English is a top priority for many immigrants, especially for children and young adults in schools.

SAMPLE QUESTION

12) **When did the United States begin enacting laws that restricted immigration?**

    A.   in the late 1800s

    B.   in the 1970s

    C.   immediately after the United States won independence from Britain in the 1700s

    D.   only very recently, in the twenty-first century

Answers:

    A.   **Correct.** Several laws restricting immigration were first passed during this time period.

    B.   Incorrect. Laws restricting immigration were enacted about 100 years before.

    C.   Incorrect. Restrictive immigration laws were first passed much later, in the late nineteenth century.

    D.   Incorrect. Actually, laws were passed much earlier, in the late nineteenth century.

6

Professional Aspects

Legal and Ethical Issues

Beginning in the second half of the twentieth century, namely in the 1970s, and continuing to the present, there have been legal decisions, both legislative and judicial, that have affected how ESOL is taught in schools. There have been notable mandates around some issues, while the particulars of how best to teach ELLs have been largely left to realization by the growing number of ESOL professionals in the field. Additionally, the ESOL field has found the need to thoughtfully address some of the ethical issues of teaching ELLs because of their unique circumstances and needs.

Laws and Court Decisions Relevant to the Education of English-Language Learners

In the past forty-five years or so, a number of laws and court decisions have had a major impact on the ESOL field and the education of ELLs in schools. One of the earliest such court decisions was **Keyes v. School District No. 1, Denver, Colorado, (1969)**. At issue was the desegregation of schools in a Denver school district. African American and Latino parents sued the school district, claiming that officials were purposefully segregating the schools. This was the first such case involving large numbers of Latino students, and the case was made that Latino and African American students should be grouped in the same category because they suffer the same discrimination when compared to their white Anglo peers. The 1973 Supreme Court decision ruled in favor of the plaintiffs and, in effect, gave Latino students the same rights ascribed to desegregation as had only previously been given to African American students.

On the heels of Keyes, came another relevant Supreme Court case in 1974, **Lau v. Nichols**. In this case, Chinese-speaking students sued the San Francisco Unified School District (SFUSD), saying that the schools in the district had an obligation to provide bilingual and English-learning instruction to non-English speaking students in order for the students to receive adequate education. After both the district and circuit courts ruled in favor of the school, the Supreme Court agreed to hear the case because of its importance to the public in general. Citing the Civil Rights Act of 1964, the Supreme Court ruled that the SFUSD had denied the non-English speaking students' rights to equal educational opportunities, thereby requiring that schools receiving federal funds must provide programs to address the language needs of non-English speaking students. Of particular interest to the ESOL field is that, though the court mandated the requirement to meet the language needs of ELLs, there were no specifics related to program design or implementation and how this requirement should be met. This furthered the debate concerning the nuts and bolts of ELL policy—something that is still being deliberated today.

Although specifics were not addressed, Lau v. Nichols had a substantial impact on federal policy. The Department of Education's Office of Civil Rights instituted the "Lau Remedies" which basically require bilingual education and ESOL instruction for Limited English Proficiency (LEP) students. The **Equal Educational Opportunities Act of 1974** (EEOA) was passed shortly afterward. Of note to the ESOL field is the provision that no state shall deny the access to equal education by "failing to take appropriate action to overcome language barriers that impede equal participation by its students in its educational programs."

Not long after the passage of these laws and court cases, a number of relevant cases were decided that began to undermine the right to bilingual education that had been granted with Lau v. Nichols. Of particular note is the 1981 case of **Castañeda v. Pickard**. In this case, it was decided that ELL programs must meet three different requirements: 1) the program must be based on sound academic theory; 2) it must have adequate resources and personnel to implement it; and 3) the program must conduct evaluation to determine if the language barriers of students are being overcome. Castañeda v. Pickard again left the approach to teaching ELLs open, thereby de-mandating the bilingual education requirement of the decade before it. Since that time, numerous court cases relevant to ELL education have been decided, and the debate continues.

The passage of the **No Child Left Behind (NCLB)** Act of 2001 mandated key actions for schools in regards to ELLs. Title III of NCLB was especially important as it required that LEP students be placed in a *language instruction education program*, and it defined what constitutes a language program as one:

1. "in which a limited English proficient child is placed for the purpose of developing and attaining English proficiency, while meeting challenging State academic content and student academic achievement standards, AND

2. that may make instructional use of both English and a child's native language to enable the child to develop and attain English proficiency, and may include the participation of English proficient children if

such course is designed to enable all participating children to become proficient in English and a second language."

Building on the Castañeda v. Pickard case, NCLB also required that any program receiving Title lll funds must meet the three aspects mandated with that case. The NCLB Act of 2001 also required each state to develop its own set of standards for ELL programs and their assessment. Standards and assessment are addressed in more detail below.

It is important to note that NCLB was a reauthorization of the 1965 **Elementary and Secondary Education Act (ESEA)**. Late in 2015, the ESEA was reauthorized as the **Every Student Succeeds Act (ESSA)**. The ESSA replaces NCLB, which was marked by major emphasis on accountability in the form of high-stakes tests for all students, including ELLs. At the time of writing, it is too early to gauge how ESSA will play out, but supporters are hailing the de-emphasis on high-stakes standardized tests and the inclusion of long-term reporting on ELLs even after exiting ESL classes.

> **HELPFUL HINT**
>
> Castañeda v. Pickard = **3** requisites = Title **3** of NCLB.

SAMPLE QUESTIONS

1) **Which of the following is true of the Lau v. Nichols case?**

   A. It demanded that ELL programs meet three requisites.

   B. It was brought to court by Latino and African American parents.

   C. The Supreme Court ruled that non-English speaking students were being discriminated against by not being offered bilingual and targeted English education.

   D. It defined what constitutes an ELL program.

   Answers:

   A. Incorrect. This was a result of the Castañeda v. Pickard case.

   B. Incorrect. This is true of the Keyes v. School District No. 1, Denver, Colorado case.

   C. Correct. The case was first tried in San Francisco and brought to court by Chinese-speaking students who said that they were being discriminated against by schools that expected them to learn in English-only classes.

   D. Incorrect. This was done under No Child Left Behind (NCLB) Act of 2001.

→ Go on

2) **Which of the following ascribed Hispanic students the same rights as African American students regarding access to equal education?**

  A. Keyes v. School District 1, Denver, Colorado

  B. Lau v. Nichols

  C. Castañeda v. Pickard

  D. Title III

  Answers:

  A. **Correct.** Decided in 1973, this case gave Hispanic students the same rights ascribed to desegregation as had only previously been given to African American students.

  B. Incorrect. Lau v. Nichols was brought to court by Chinese-speaking students.

  C. Incorrect. Castañeda v. Pickard mandated that ELL programs must meet three different requisites but did not single out Hispanic students relative to African American students.

  D. Incorrect. Title III of NCLB requires that LEP students be placed in a "language instruction education program"—and defined what constitutes a language program—but did not single out Hispanic students relative to African American students.

LOCAL, STATE, AND NATIONAL REGULATIONS AFFECTING ESL TEACHERS

As with any publicly funded education matter, ESL programs in public schools must adhere to certain regulations at all levels of government. What may distinguish the ESL field from many others, though, is the fact that there are some aspects that are well-regulated at the federal level, but there are also many that are left up to governmental bodies at the state and/or local levels. This means that there may be great differences from one state or school district to another throughout the United States. However, there are some commonalities that are relevant to most, if not all, public school K–12 ESL programs.

For any school, the first steps that must be taken for an ESL program are the identification of students who need ESL services. Federal regulations do not specify what assessments should be used, but many states have adopted the use of a **Home Language Survey** as an initial screening tool to be given to enrolling students. A Home Language Survey helps to determine what language(s) is/are spoken in a student's home. If a language other than English is spoken in a student's home, then the student will undergo a formal diagnostic assessment to determine his or her proficiency level in reading, writing, listening, and speaking in English. In addition to Home Language Surveys, schools may conduct parent interviews and rely on teacher input, among other methods, to identify ELLs. Federal law also requires schools to notify parents whose children are determined to be ELLs.

With its stress on accountability, NCLB certainly influenced how all ESL teachers nationwide approached their jobs, as teachers felt pressure to assure that their students performed well on tests. Additionally, while NCLB mandated that schools provide ESL services, it also demanded that ELLs meet the same accountability benchmarks in core subjects that non-ELL students did without specifying how this should be accomplished. NCLB required that *all* students take tests in three main content areas: math, science, and reading/language arts. ELLs were not exempt from these tests, though some accommodations were allowed. Additionally, each state was required to annually assess ELL students' proficiency in English, but each state was required to develop or choose its own English Language Proficiency (ELP) standards and assessments. States were also required to develop **Annual Measurable Achievement Objectives (AMAOs)** for districts receiving Title III funds. Three AMAOs were prescribed, but again states had flexibility to determine whether to use percentages or numbers and to determine target goals, among other details. The first AMAO was an increase in the number or percentage of ELLs making progress toward English proficiency. The second was an increase in the number or percentage of ELLs reaching English proficiency. The third AMAO required that ELLs make **Adequate Yearly Progress (AYP)** toward content area knowledge, though there were some exceptions and accommodations allowed such as those exempting new students.

When NCLB was initially put into place, many states did not have established AMAOs or prescribed standardized tests for ELL learners. Additionally, many areas, especially rural ones, were experiencing a sudden influx of ELLs—mostly Hispanic—due to rapidly expanding Hispanic immigration at that time. Faced with the twofold challenge of how to best serve the needs of a growing ELL student population and how to meet the new accountability measures of NCLB, many states formed a consortium. Known as **WIDA**, this consortium initially included the states of Washington, Delaware, and Arkansas, with the acronym reflecting the three pilot states. (Note that when Arkansas later dropped out, the name *World-class Instructional Design and Assessment* was adopted to fit the acronym. The name has since been dropped, and the organization is now simply known as WIDA.)

> **HELPFUL HINT**
>
> **3** AMAOs for Title **3** funding:
> 1) increase *toward* proficiency;
> 2) increase *reaching* proficiency; and 3) AYP toward *content* knowledge.

Currently, a majority of states belong to the WIDA consortium. WIDA promotes research, standards, and professional development to support ELLs in academics and language learning. To further its mission, WIDA partners with several state and national organizations. The two core initiatives of WIDA are the development of ELP standards for member states and the development of a corresponding assessment, known as ACCESS (Assessing Comprehension and Communication in English State-to-State), for English Language Learners. As of this writing, the latest assessment series is known as *ACCESS for ELLs 2.0* and is being premiered during the 2015–2016 school year.

The Every Student Succeeds Act (ESSA), passed in December 2015, maintains and allows for an increase in Title III funding. English proficiency is now built in to the Title I accountability system with accommodations and exceptions for ELLs; many educators have praised changes that take into account the unique needs of these students. ESSA continues support for high-quality ESOL programs as well as language arts and math content instruction for ELLs. Of note is a requirement for states to implement entrance and exit practices that ensure ELLs get the language services they need in between.

Recently, Common Core State Standards (CCSS) have also played a role in the broader discussion about ESL—both for ELLs and ESL instructors. Though the standards were established to address content area skills, it has been recognized that the process of ensuring students have the English language skills needed to master content knowledge should be included as well. Exactly how ELLs and ESL teachers will incorporate CCSS is still uncertain at the time of this writing, but many in the field are positive about taking into account the role of content area teachers in the education of ELLs. Among other groups, WIDA is currently revamping recommendations, policy, and assessments to reflect incorporation of CCSS.

One important and lasting provision of NCLB was the expansion and regulation of the **Migrant Education Program (MEP)**, which currently has programs in every state. The stated goal of the MEP is "to ensure that all migrant students reach challenging academic standards and graduate with a high school diploma (or complete a GED) that prepares them for responsible citizenship, further learning, and productive employment." Migrant children are those who move multiple times throughout the year as their families seek seasonal work in agriculture and fisheries. Needless to say, migrant families face enormous challenges in attempting to provide education to their children in addition to the obvious obstacle of disrupted schooling and frequent and extreme gaps between schooling. Compounding this challenge is the fact that many migrant workers live in some of the most extreme poverty found in the United States and are subject to associated hardship—from lack of healthcare, to low literacy levels, unreliable transportation and in some cases, unsafe and unhealthy living and working conditions. Moreover, migrant children frequently work in the fields while not in school—sometimes even illegally during school hours. Despite these barriers, thanks to the tireless work of educators, many migrant students are experiencing academic success in no short measure due to the innovative practices uniquely suited to the migrant lifestyle.

SAMPLE QUESTION

3) **What is WIDA?**

   A. a group created by the federal government in NCLB

   B. a teaching approach that uses real-life objects; realia

   C. an assessment that the federal government requires schools to use with ELLs under NCLB

   D. a consortium of states that strives to advance quality programs for ELLs

Answers:

A. Incorrect. WIDA was not created by the federal government.

B. Incorrect. WIDA is not a teaching approach.

C. Incorrect. WIDA is not an assessment, and the federal government does not mandate which assessment tools schools use.

D. **Correct.** WIDA is a consortium of states created after the passage of NCLB; it is currently focused on the development of ELP standards for member states and the development of a corresponding assessment.

LEGAL AND ETHICAL ISSUES RELATED TO THE ASSESSMENT OF ENGLISH-LANGUAGE LEARNERS

While it is not yet clear how the ESSA will affect ELL education and assessment what is already known is that the law is seen as giving more control of accountability measures back to states. ESSA provides states with two options to delay ELL participation in accountability measures. The first is that testing ELLs in English language arts can be delayed by one year, and either math or reading or both scores can be excluded. The second option is a three-phase process: report on, but not factoring into accountability ELL students' first-year scores in math and English language arts, then report on improvement on both tests in the second year, and in the third year, include English language arts and math scores in accountability systems.

Prior to ESSA NCLB had required students to take assessments to measure their English skills. These were known as **English Language Proficiency (ELP) exams**. However, states had to identify or create their own ELP exams as mentioned previously. Additionally states were required to develop their own **Annual Measurable Achievement Objectives (AMAOs)**, or performance goals, for ELLs.

NCLB further required ELL students to take the same accountability assessments as non-ELL students, as described above. For many educators, this was a problematic ethical issue related to NCLB and ELLs. While educators welcomed the inclusion of ELLs and provisions for their education, many educators felt it was unfair to assess them alongside their non-ELL peers in content subjects since there was a threshold of English skills required in *all* subjects being tested.

Of course, there are other ethical considerations with ELL testing in general. These include ensuring that tests are culturally inclusive and linguistically appropriate and that those giving the assessments are culturally aware and trained appropriately. Material on tests can be made broadly culturally inclusive by including content that test-takers are familiar with or removing culture-bound information so as not to disadvantage a group that might not be familiar with it. Examples would be not including text about a recent box-office smash

> **QUICK REVIEW**
>
> What are two examples of culture-bound information that should not be included on tests for ELLs?

movie on tests that are given to newcomers but rather including familiar images or symbols from their home countries. Employing various modes of assessment, such as portfolio or oral assessments, can also be more culturally sensitive. All of these practices help to ensure that the process meets validity standards as well.

SAMPLE QUESTION

4) **Which of the following is true about NCLB?**

A. States were required to administer ELP exams to ELLs and to develop AMAOs.

B. States were required to administer ELP exams but not to develop AMAOs.

C. States were not required to administer ELP exams but were required to develop AMAOs.

D. States were required to administer federally-developed ELP exams to ELLs and to adopt federally-developed AMAOs.

Answers:

A. **Correct.** NCLB required states to assess ELLs with ELP exams and to develop target AMAOs.

B. Incorrect. States were required to do both.

C. Incorrect. States were required to do both.

D. Incorrect. While NCLB required states to administer ELP exams and adopt AMAOs, the federal government did not mandate which assessment tools or AMAOs should be adopted.

ROLE OF THE ESL TEACHER

By its nature, teaching is a profession whereby obligations and duties extend beyond the daily classroom. This may hold even more true for ESL teachers whose students—and their families—are in unusual positions in communities. This is primarily due to language barriers, but also because many are newcomers and are often living separately from the established community.

CONNECTING ENGLISH-LANGUAGE LEARNERS TO OTHER TEACHERS AND SCHOOL PROFESSIONALS

It is generally agreed that the primary goal for students in any ESL program is English proficiency. Likewise, educators are in agreement that ELL students must also acquire content knowledge to propel them toward graduation. This means that schools and ESL teachers have the dual challenge of ensuring that ELL students are improving in English while also learning content knowledge, especially in math, science, social studies, and language arts. Since no one teacher can be expected to deliver instruction in all of these areas, however, the teaching of ELLs demands great coordination and cooperation among school teachers and staff.

Some ESL teachers have a fixed classroom where ESL classes are held, while others may be itinerant teachers who move around from class to class or school to school. Regardless of the circumstances, ESL teachers are needed to provide instructional support and guidance to content-area teachers concerning best practices for teaching ELLs. Needs may shift as ELL populations grow or change and as policy changes, but some general strategies can be used when collaborating with other teachers and school staff.

Collaboration among ESL teachers and content area teachers can take several different forms and need not be done through a strictly regimented model. In fact, most ESL professionals agree that flexibility in collaboration is vital to success since student needs, teacher skills and preferences, school resources, and so on are dynamic factors. A basic start to collaboration is often **co-planning**, working together to determine language objectives and key vocabulary as well as content objectives in content lessons. Identifying the academic language and skills associated with mastery of the content often proves to be useful for mainstream students in the classroom as well. The information that results from co-planning can then be used in either a pull-out setting or in a sheltered/push-in model, depending on needs and resources. (More information about program design is found in chapter 3.)

Depending on needs and resources, content area and ESL teachers may also engage in co-teaching. **Co-teaching** means that content and ESL teachers share an instructional space with both mainstream and ELL students. It may take different forms, and there are several models in practice. One is **parallel teaching** in which both instructors teach their respective groups at the same time; they may, at times, switch groups in this scenario. Another is **station teaching**, where students move through various stations set up in the classroom and teachers work with them in small groups. Teachers may circulate or stay in fixed stations. Another model, known as **lead and support**, relies on one instructor assuming a lead teaching role with the other providing support as needed, whether through one-on-one instruction or highlighting essential information in some way as the lead teacher delivers it. Finally, the model that demands the most co-planning and collaboration is known as team teaching. In **team teaching**, each teacher takes an equal role in teaching all the students in a content classroom. Regardless of the model or models used while co-teaching, all involved will benefit from clear and detailed guidelines, expectations, and definitions of roles.

In addition to collaborating with content area teachers, ESL teachers often work with ESL paraprofessionals. An **ESL paraprofessional** is an education professional whose role is to assist ESL teachers and ELL students. Many ESL paraprofessionals are bilingual and often serve as interpreters for ELLs, especially

HELPFUL HINT

COllaborate with **CO**ntent teachers in **CO**-planning and **CO**-teaching.

beginning level students. Whether bilingual or not, paraprofessionals may help ESL teachers in many ways, including lesson preparation, one-on-one instruction with individual students, cultural guidance for students, clerical assistance, and assessment. As with collaborating with other teachers, clearly defined roles for ESL teachers and paraprofessionals will promote a smooth and productive working relationship.

SAMPLE QUESTION

5) Co-teaching:

A. should begin with careful co-planning.

B. means that content and ESL teachers share an instructional space with both mainstream and ELL students.

C. may follow a parallel teaching, station teaching, lead and support, or team teaching model.

D. all of the above

Answers:

A. Incorrect. While co-teaching should involve co-planning, this choice is incomplete given the other options.

B. Incorrect. Co-teaching means sharing an instructional space, but this choice is incomplete given the other options.

C. Incorrect. All of these models are co-teaching models, but given the other choices, this answer is incomplete.

D. Correct. Co-planning, shared space, and different models are all true of co-teaching.

RELATING TO PARENTS

Like all students, ELLs greatly benefit when their parents and families are involved in their education. (Note that for brevity, the term *parent* will be used here to encompass birth parents, legal guardians, and other concerned family members.) For ELL parents, there is often a language gap that must be overcome. Also, it is important to bear in mind that there may be cultural differences that inhibit ELL parents from being directly engaged in their children's education. Foremost is the idea that many cultures hold teachers and educators in very high esteem; thus parents would not want to act in a way that they might see as doubting or questioning the teacher's authority. In the US, parental involvement in school is highly valued and expected, but this is not the case in all cultures. To help overcome the language and cultural barriers, it is often helpful to reach out to ELL families; this can be facilitated in several ways.

Perhaps the most fundamental way to engage ELL parents is to reach out to them in their native language. All information and materials for families should be bilingual when at all possible. Many schools find it useful to prepare bilingual **parent toolkits** that contain relevant information that will help parents navigate the school and its culture. Parent toolkits might include information about American school culture, expectations of students and parents, enrollment information, information regarding grading policies, school calendars, information relevant to the specific school such as campus maps, how to get to the school office, and so on. It is worth remembering that school culture in many countries may be quite different than it is in the US, so information that may seem like overkill for mainstream families may be new and thus well received by ELL families. Including some established ELL families in the process of creating a parent toolkit for newer ELL families can help identify what kind of information is necessary. Though an initial time investment, having such **dual-language resources** on hand will be an immense time-saver when new ELL families arrive at a school.

For parent-teacher conferences, bilingual interpreters will be needed for parents who are still learning English. Information shared at these conferences is imperative for parents to know, so all efforts to communicate with parents in their native language should be

> **HELPFUL HINT**
>
> Parent toolkit = cool tools for school awareness.

made. The student should not be used to interpret for his or her teacher and parents as this may create a disruption in the authority structure in families. Ideally, schools should employ paid professional interpreters. This will be a challenge in many school districts—some more than others—but schools have come up with some creative ways to make interpreters available, from enlisting the support of students at local universities, to seeking other community volunteers. Parents can also be encouraged to bring their own interpreters to teacher meetings.

Ahead of meetings, time will be needed to develop reports on student progress, either in the home language or in explicit and clear English. Parents want to know about their children's progress, so detailed information they can take home to study and reflect on after the meeting is needed. Parents will also feel more invested if they are allowed the opportunity to be involved in decisions regarding their children's work and progress. Furthermore, parents know their children best so can offer valuable input to assist teachers with effective lesson planning and targeted instruction for their ELL students. All parents can take steps at home to be involved in their children's education. Many want to take an active role in helping children with homework and find this an effective way to monitor the child's progress. Others are less comfortable with direct help—maybe because of a lack of language skills or formal education—but they can still be involved. Parents can make a dedicated study/ homework area in their home, whether in a separate room or at the kitchen table, to demonstrate the value placed on academic progress. Simply holding daily conversations

> **CONSIDER THIS**
>
> Some schools have a parent group just for ELL parents. What do you think about starting an ELL parent group at school?

about what students learned or what they did in specific classes is another effective way that any parent can be involved.

SAMPLE QUESTION

6) The Sanchez family moves to a new area and visits the local school with their two children. After meeting with school staff, the family is sent home with a folder containing information about American school culture, expectations of students and parents, enrollment information, and a school calendar. This is known as what?

A. a parent toolkit

B. an IEP

C. behaviorism

D. SIOP

Answers:

A. **Correct.** Parent toolkits contain relevant information that will help new ELL families navigate the new school and its culture.

B. Incorrect. An Individual Education Plan outlines instruction, special services, and methods of progress assessment for students with learning disabilities or differences.

C. Incorrect. Behaviorism is a learning model.

D. Incorrect. Sheltered Instruction Observation Protocol is a model for program delivery.

STRATEGIES FOR BROAD ENGAGEMENT

In addition to teaching English language and content skills, the education of ELLs should also prepare them to be active and engaged citizens of their new community. To that end, broad engagement among community organizations, schools, and ELLs and their families must be fostered. ESL teachers play a critical role in fostering this broad engagement and should thus be informed of strategies for doing so. The ultimate goal is creating a system of **integrative services**, a system where all agencies are working in cooperation and the clients, ELLs and their families, have access to a streamlined and connected range of needed assistance. Because of the importance of the ESL teacher in an ELL student's life, and therefore the lives of his or her family members, ESL teachers often take a role as **advocate** supporting ELL families in the wider community.

In some school districts, especially those with large numbers of ELL students, schools may have a parent/family liaison and/or social worker on staff. These staff members can help ELLs and their families connect to their new community. Even so, and especially in districts without such support, ESL teachers are often called upon to serve as a bridge between ELL families and the community at large. In this role, the teacher often serves as a sort of **cultural liaison**, helping groups from different cultures communicate and work with each other. Newcomers to communities, especially those with language barriers, face an array of short-term tasks and long-term adjustments they must make in order to thrive. Often, ELL families are not aware of the various support groups and outlets for help to which they may have access. ESL teachers can assist by linking newcomers to **community-based organizations** that will help them in their integration into the community. One way of doing this is by inviting representatives from organizations to speak at parent meetings and events at the school. Another is by offering space—when available and practical—in the school for use by community organizations. Community organizations can often offer academic support to ELLs in the form of after-school tutoring and to ELL families with adult ESL classes, among other means. **Faith-based organizations**, those associated with a religious group or groups or a particular church, often provide an array of services that newcomers to the community might need. Additionally, government-directed **social services** organizations also provide needed support intended to benefit all community members.

An effective method to get students involved in the local community is to establish a program of community service for ELL students in your school. In **community service**, volunteers participate in a required structured endeavor to lend a hand to organizations and non-profits in their community.

> **HELPFUL HINT**
>
> ESL teacher = teacher, advocate, cultural liaison.

For this method, it is important to keep an open line of communication with organizations in your community and arrange to have periodic conferences with ELLs, families, and organizations to brainstorm ways in which these entities can work together. It is helpful to remember that community organizations are there to provide aid and are often eager to help; they may simply require an awareness of the needs and access to the people who can benefit from their services. Bridging the gap between ELL families and community resources is one key way ESL teachers can further help their ELL students beyond the classroom.

There is growing interest in school-to-career initiatives, which can play an important role in ELL student success and community connectedness, both during schooling years and after graduation. Pedagogical research backs up the benefits of this type of hands-on, experiential learning for academic as well as job-training purposes. Whether students plan to enter a postsecondary institution of study or whether they plan to immediately join the workforce, school-to-career programs can contribute to success. Additionally, these programs promote deep community engagement, allowing ELL students the opportunity to be actively connected to their communities and neighborhoods and fostering community relationships, something that ELL students may not have traditionally experienced/had access to.

School-to-career programs can take many different forms, and there are often great challenges associated with implementing them. However, while not every school district can afford to restructure their school institutions to implement and support a structured ELL school-to-career program, most schools can fairly easily make an effort to lay a foundation for school-to-career readiness. A first step to consider is incorporating project-based learning into the curriculum for ELL students. **Project-based learning** is a teaching method that challenges students with complex real-world projects or problems to solve collaboratively within a group, typically over an extended period of time. Such experiences result in a deep understanding of the processes and issues relevant to the problem. Examples would be assigning students to design, and maybe even implement, a school-wide recycling program or to develop a plan to create a school or community soccer team.

If a school-to-work program is already in place at a school, the ESL teacher must collaborate with the coordinator to be sure ELL students are prepared to participate and to ensure inclusion in the program. Factors to consider include levels of English proficiency needed for different positions and employment needs and goals of ELL students, among others. Two established school-to-career models are school-based enterprises and internship programs. **School-based enterprises** are commercial ventures housed in a school and run by students. School-based enterprises can focus on tangible goods and products such as tee-shirts or beverages or on services such as graphic design or technology support. Most people are familiar with **internships**, temporary positions with a business or organization designed to provide job training to the intern. Internships offer effective school-to-career opportunities for secondary ELL students. Of particular benefit could be businesses in the community that are owned or run by bilingual community members. Internship programs can also tap into established relationships with community-based and faith-based organizations to network for positions for ELL students. Moreover, community-service positions, discussed above, can provide school-to-work experience for students. Regardless of the design or scenario, most successful programs start small and grow in steps. It might be a good idea to first begin with more advanced ESL students so that established community members can ease into getting comfortable working with non-native English speakers.

SAMPLE QUESTIONS

7) Thanh and Duy, two ELL students originally from Vietnam, are working with a teacher to start a bánh mì, or Vietnamese sandwich, truck to serve sandwiches at school sporting events. The teacher is very supportive of this venture as she knows it will give them valuable work and academic experience. This type of venture is known as what?

A. transformation

B. a school-based enterprise

C. a portfolio

D. team teaching

Answers:

A. Incorrect. Transformation, in linguistic study, describes the rules that define how syntax is properly constructed and manipulated.

B. Correct. School-based enterprises are commercial ventures, such as the one Thanh and Duy wish to start, housed in a school and run by students.

C. Incorrect. A portfolio is a collection of student work used as a method of alternative assessment.

D. Incorrect. Team teaching is a teaching approach where ELL and content-area teachers take an equal role in teaching all the students in a content classroom.

8) Oftentimes, ESL teachers are called upon to be a bridge between ELL families and the community at large. In such a role, teachers are acting as

A. cultural liaisons.

B. ESL paraprofessionals.

C. AMAOs.

D. stereotypes.

Answers:

A. Correct. Cultural liaisons help groups from different cultures communicate and work with each other.

B. Incorrect. ESL paraprofessionals are education professionals whose role is to assist ESL teachers and ELL students in the classroom.

C. Incorrect. AMAOs, or Annual Measurable Achievement Objectives, are performance goals identified in assessment.

D. Incorrect. A stereotype is an oversimplified belief that all people from a certain group or with certain characteristics are the same and is not a defined role of ESL teachers.

Professional Development

Relevant Research, Practice, and Issues

As professionals, ESL educators have many resources and opportunities to further their growth in the field. Indeed, the ESOL field is a very dynamic one, so it is a basic duty for teachers and paraprofessionals to stay abreast of the latest research and developments. There are several professional organizations that do work relevant to the ESOL field, and a great number of websites that exist to provide professional support for issues ranging from lesson planning to best practices to networking with others in the field. Of course, the Internet is a useful place to start for information. Up-to-date resources can be discovered through recommendations from fellow ESL teachers as well as teacher meetings and conferences. Following is a list of several well-known and established organizations and resources for ESL professionals. Bear in mind that this is by no means an exhaustive list nor is it meant to be seen as a "best of" list of resources; there are very many great organizations and resources not listed here. Additionally, many states and regions also have chapters of national organizations and/or locally relevant independent organizations.

CAL, Center for Applied Linguistics

CAL works to promote language learning in general and serves as an important resource for research in English-language learning. Indeed, the early pioneers in the ESOL field came from the field of applied linguistics. CAL works primarily in research, materials development, and professional development via online resources and technical assistance. www.cal.org

Dave's ESL Café

ESL teacher Dave Sperling began Dave's ESL Café in 1995 and has been going strong ever since. It has remained a popular online meeting place for both teachers and students, providing interactive activities, job boards, information about lesson planning, quizzes, forums, and more. www.eslcafe.com

NABE, National Association for Bilingual Education

NABE promotes education among bilingual and multilingual students in the context of a globalizing world. It conducts a variety of activities in this regard, including organizing an annual conference, publishing NABE magazines and journals, and bilingual advocacy. www.nabe.org

OELA, Office of English Language Education

OELA, administered by the US Department of Education, "provides national leadership to help ensure that English Learners and immigrant students attain English proficiency and achieve academic success." OELA provides grants for practitioners and supports practical research of ESL teaching and learning. Perhaps most importantly, OELA maintains the National Clearinghouse for English Language Acquisition (NCELA), which provides online data, a resource library, information about grants, and more. www.ncela.ed.gov

TESL-EJ
TESL-EJ is a mediated e-journal for ESL, begun by independent scholars in 1994 and free to all who access it. http://www.tesl-ej.org/wordpress

TESL JOURNAL
TESL Journal is a free online collection of articles, journals, lessons, teaching ideas, and more published between 1995 and 2010. http://iteslj.org

TESOL, TEACHERS OF ENGLISH TO SPEAKERS OF OTHER LANGUAGES
TESOL celebrated its fiftieth anniversary in 2016 and is seen by many as the "grandfather" organization in the field. It is an association of professionals in the field with an international reach and promotes the development of standards, research, professionalism, and advocacy. In addition to hosting the annual international TESOL convention—the largest professional development conference in the field—TESOL provides online courses and seminars, publishes books and journals, maintains an online job board, and participates in various modes of advocacy for ESOL teachers and professionals as well as students. www.tesol.org

SAMPLE QUESTION

9) **Which is a governmental organization?**
   A. TESOL
   B. Dave's ESL Café
   C. NABE
   D. OELA

   Answers:
   A. Incorrect. Teachers of English to Speakers of Other Languages is a non-governmental professional association.
   B. Incorrect. Dave's ESL Café is a website created by Dave Sperling, not a governmental organization.
   C. Incorrect. The National Association for Bilingual Education is not a governmental agency.
   D. **Correct.** The Office of English Language Education is run by the US Department of Education.

Go on →

IMPORTANT ACRONYMS

The ESOL field is an especially acronym-heavy one, and it seems new acronyms are being adopted every year. Furthermore, there is much specialized terminology found frequently in ESOL publications and resources. The following is an alphabetized reference list of acronyms and terminology used in the field. These may include linguistic terms, organizations, instructional methods and theories, legislative terms, and program types, among others.

- ▶ ADA: Americans with Disabilities Act
- ▶ AMAO: Annual Measurable Achievement Objective
- ▶ BICS: Basic Interpersonal Communication Skills
- ▶ CAL: Center for Applied Linguistics
- ▶ CALP: Cognitive Academic Language Proficiency
- ▶ CCSS: Common Core State Standards
- ▶ CLT: Communicative Language Teaching
- ▶ EFL: English as a Foreign Language
- ▶ ELD: English Language Development
- ▶ ELL: English Language Learner
- ▶ ELP: English Language Proficiency
- ▶ ELPA 21: English Language Proficiency Assessment for the 21st Century
- ▶ ESEA: Elementary and Secondary Education Act
- ▶ ESL: English as a Second Language
- ▶ ESOL: English for Speakers of Other Languages
- ▶ ESSA: Every Student Succeeds Act
- ▶ IDEA: Individuals with Disabilities Education Act
- ▶ IEP: Individualized Education Program
- ▶ IPA: International Phonetic Alphabet
- ▶ L1: first language or native language
- ▶ L2: second language or foreign language
- ▶ LEA: Language Experience Approach
- ▶ LEP: Limited English Proficiency
- ▶ MEP: Migrant Education Program
- ▶ NABE: National Association for Bilingual Education
- ▶ NCLB: No Child Left Behind
- ▶ SIOP: Sheltered Instruction Observation Protocol

- ▶ SLA: Second-Language Acquisition
- ▶ TBI: Task-Based Instruction
- ▶ TEFL: Teaching English as a Foreign Language
- ▶ TESL: Teaching English as a Second Language
- ▶ TESOL: Teachers of English to Speakers of Other Languages
- ▶ TOEFL: Test of English as a Foreign Language
- ▶ TPR: Total Physical Response
- ▶ WIDA: This is no longer an acronym, but it began as a grant project involving Wisconsin, Delaware, and Arkansas; it then expanded and became World Class Instructional Design and Assessment.

Part II: Practice

Linguistics

Read each question carefully, and then choose the best answer.

1

In semantics, denotation means

A. the emotional association of a word.

B. how words are formed into phrases or sentences.

C. a speech act of one or more words with silence before and after.

D. a word's actual dictionary definition.

2

While writing a paragraph describing her house, a student mistakenly uses the following terms: *in the porch*, *on the basement*, and *around the ceiling*. She needs extra practice with which point of grammar?

A. prepositions

B. conjunctions

C. pronouns

D. , verbs

3

Which of the following IPA phonetic symbols represents the –a sound in the word *sat*?

A. [ʃ]

B. [ə]

C. [æ]

D. [ɑɪ]

4

Regional and social dialects are important points of study in

A. pragmatics.

B. sociolinguistics.

C. syntax.

D. interference.

5

Which word below uses the sound of the IPA symbol [j]?

A. young

B. jump

C. man

D. boy

6

In _____, the context of the situation and the communication between speaker and listener are important beyond the meaning of the words and phrases.

A.   linguistic competence

B.   pragmatics

C.   Cognitive Academic Language Proficiency (CALP)

D.   phonetics

7

Which definition best describes a pidgin?

A.   a variety of a language that people in a certain region speak

B.   a grayish bird often found in cities

C.   a grammatically simplified mode of communicating that may use elements of two languages

D.   a stage of first-language acquisition

8

In an ESOL classroom, many Spanish-speaking students routinely make mistakes saying sentences such as "Is cold today," or "Alejandra is growing. Is tall now." The teacher could guess that this interference is due to what?

A.   prepositions in Spanish

B.   dropped pronouns in Spanish

C.   using gerunds in Spanish

D.   Spanish not having noncount nouns

9

The area of communicative competence that deals with being able to recognize and repair instances of communication breakdown is _____ competence.

A.   linguistic

B.   discourse

C.   sociolinguistic

D.   strategic

10

In the ESOL classroom, why would the concept of World Englishes be important?

A.   Both native English speakers and those learning English as a second language must be accustomed to speaking to and understanding others with various dialects.

B.   World Englishes means English should be the only language spoken in the world, so students should study very hard to be fluent.

C.   World Englishes are pidgins that students should learn so they can communicate in a global marketplace.

D.   English is the easiest language to learn in the world.

11

A student is having trouble pronouncing the following words: *child, bench,* and *watches.* Which sound is likely the problem?

A.   [ʃ]

B.   [k]

C.   [ŋ]

D.   [tʃ]

12

What are "false friend" cognates?

A. ways of thinking that are not helpful to language learning

B. words that are similar in spelling and meaning in two languages

C. words in two languages that look similar but are actually different

D. two-faced study partners

13

Four students write sentences using apostrophes on the board. Which one is correct?

A. Its medicines are still at the vet's office.

B. It's medicines are still at the vet's office.

C. It's medicine's are still at the vets office.

D. Its medicine's are still at the vets office.

14

During a lesson on commas, four students write sentences using commas on the board. Which sentence has a mistake in comma usage?

A. Mario, Mona, and Ming are in the play.

B. Ahmed is in the play, but Salem did not even try out for it.

C. Inge, a talented singer, is also in the play.

D. Ms. Platt approved the play a little-known work by Ibsen.

15

At mid-semester, an ESOL student is socializing well with both ESOL and non-ESOL students and is excelling in sports after school. However, she is struggling in many of her content area classes. In which area is she lacking proficiency?

A. BICS

B. CALP

C. TPR

D. SIOP

16

A student pronounces *stay* as "suh-tay," *please* as "puh-lease," and *fry* as "fuh-ry." What is his problem?

A. transformation

B. elision

C. epenthesis

D. interlanguage

17

The underlined part of which of the following words is a derivational morpheme?

A. <u>weather</u>ed

B. weather<u>ed</u>

C. weather<u>ize</u>

D. weather<u>s</u>

18

Vowel reduction usually occurs with _____ syllables and often changes vowel sounds to _____.

A. unstressed; consonants.

B. stressed; [ə].

C. unstressed; [ɒ].

D. unstressed; [ə].

19

A teacher transcribes the following from a student's presentation:

"For this, uh, holiday, my mother, uh, my mom, she go to the store and buy many special fruits for family. We prepares the fruits for salad, uh, and for dessert, we makes many things with fruits. My father grill, uh, grills, meat for all the family. My brother play special songs on piano. We all has happy time."

The student could benefit from some practice with which of the following?

A.   object pronouns

B.   adverbs

C.   subject-verb agreement

D.   diagnostic assessment

20

What do the following consonant pairs have in common: p, b; f, v; s, z?

A.   The first is the unvoiced sound, and the second is the voiced.

B.   The first is the voiced sound, and the second is the unvoiced.

C.   The first is the stressed consonant, and the second is the unstressed.

D.   The first is the unstressed consonant, and the second is the stressed.

ANSWER KEY

1)

A.   Incorrect. This is connotation.

B.   Incorrect. This is syntax.

C.   Incorrect. This is an utterance.

D.   **Correct.** Denotation is a word's actual dictionary definition.

2)

A.   **Correct.** Her mistakes are in the use of prepositions.

B.   Incorrect. There are no conjunctions in the terms.

C.   Incorrect. There are no pronouns in the terms.

D.   Incorrect. There are no verbs in the terms.

3)

A.   Incorrect. This represents the /sh/ sound in *ship*.

B.   Incorrect. This represents the schwa sound in *around*.

C.   **Correct.** This represents the /a/ sound heard in *sat*.

D.   Incorrect. This represents the /y/ sound in *guy*.

4)

A.   Incorrect. The field of pragmatics examines meaning in context.

B.   **Correct.** Regional and social dialects and their importance to cultural stereotypes and prejudice are important points of study in sociolinguistics.

C.   Incorrect. Syntax examines how words are formed into phrases or sentences.

D.   Incorrect. Interference occurs when language learners incorrectly apply the rules of their native language to the rules of the language they are learning.

5)

A.   **Correct.** The IPA symbol [j] is the /y/ sound in *young*.

B.   Incorrect. There is no IPA [j] sound in this word. The /j/ sound in this word is actually [dʒ] in IPA transcription.

C.   Incorrect. There is no IPA [j] sound in this word.

D.   Incorrect. There is no IPA [j] sound in this word.

6)

A.   Incorrect. Linguistic competence means knowledge of the linguistic components of a language such as syntax, semantics, and so on.

B.   **Correct.** Pragmatics examines meaning in context.

C.   Incorrect. CALP is the language needed for academic work and study.

D.   Incorrect. Phonetics is the study of the production of sounds in speech.

7)

A.   Incorrect. This is a regional dialect.

B.   Incorrect. This describes a pigeon.

C.   **Correct.** A pidgin is a language of necessity developed to help people with different native languages communicate.

D.   Incorrect. A pidgin is not a stage of language acquisition.

8)

A.   Incorrect. No prepositions are used or needed.

B.   **Correct.** Both mistakes are due to a lack of subject pronouns.

C. Incorrect. No gerunds are used or needed. The word *growing* in the second example is part of a verb phrase, though a student might mistake it for a gerund.

D. Incorrect. Noncount nouns are not used or needed in these sentences.

9)

A. Incorrect. Linguistic competence deals with knowledge of the linguistic components of a language such as syntax and semantics.

B. Incorrect. Discourse competence deals with constructing smaller units of language like phrases and sentences into larger cohesive works.

C. Incorrect. Sociolinguistic competence means using the language in a socially appropriate way.

D. **Correct.** Strategic competence is the ability to recognize and repair instances of communication breakdown.

10)

A. **Correct.** This is relevant to the concept of World Englishes.

B. Incorrect. This judgmental phrase is untrue. While English is widely spoken and fluency a valuable skill, linguistic diversity enriches the world.

C. Incorrect. A pidgin is a language of necessity developed to help people with different native languages communicate.

D. Incorrect. This is not relevant to the concept of World Englishes and is an opinion.

11)

A. Incorrect. This is the /sh/ sound in *short*.

B. Incorrect. This is the /k/ sound in *cut*.

C. Incorrect. This is the /ng/ sound in *thing*.

D. **Correct.** This is the /ch/ sound, which is found in all three words.

12)

A. Incorrect. Cognates are not ways of thinking.

B. Incorrect. This is the definition of cognates.

C. **Correct.** This is the meaning of "false friend" cognates.

D. Incorrect. Cognates are not study partners.

13)

A. **Correct.** This sentence uses apostrophes correctly.

B. Incorrect. *It's* as a possessive does not need an apostrophe.

C. Incorrect. Neither *it's* nor *medicine's* need apostrophes, but *vets* does in this sentence.

D. Incorrect. *Medicine's* does not need an apostrophe, and *vets* needs an apostrophe.

14)

A. Incorrect. Commas are used correctly in this sentence.

B. Incorrect. Commas are used correctly in this sentence.

C. Incorrect. Commas are used correctly in this sentence.

D. **Correct.** A comma is needed between the words *play* and *a*.

15)

A. Incorrect. She obviously has proficiency with BICS, or Basic Interpersonal Communication Skills.

B. **Correct.** She clearly lacks CALP, or Cognitive Academic Language Proficiency.

C. Incorrect. Total Physical Response is an approach to language teaching.

D. Incorrect. Sheltered Instruction Observation Protocol is a program-delivery model.

16)

A. Incorrect. In linguistics, transformations deal with rules of syntax.

B. Incorrect. Elision occurs when sounds are omitted.

C. **Correct.** Epenthesis involves inserting additional sounds in a word.

D. Incorrect. Interlanguage describes a phase of second-language acquisition.

17)

A. Incorrect. This is the root, or stem, of the word.

B. Incorrect. This is an inflectional morpheme, indicating past tense of the verb.

C. **Correct.** The –ize suffix changes the word's meaning from a noun to a verb.

D. Incorrect. The –s is an inflectional morpheme used for subject-verb agreement.

18)

A. Incorrect. While it usually occurs with unstressed syllables, it does *not* change vowel sounds to consonants.

B. Incorrect. While it often changes vowel sounds to [ə], it usually occurs with unstressed syllables.

C. Incorrect. While it usually occurs with unstressed syllables, it doesn't change vowel sounds to [ɒ].

D. **Correct.** Vowel reduction occurs mostly with unstressed syllables and often changes the sounds to the schwa, [ə].

19)

A. Incorrect. There are no mistakes using object pronouns.

B. Incorrect. There are no mistakes with adverbs.

C. **Correct.** The student has multiple errors with subject-verb agreement.

D. Incorrect. Practice with assessment would not help the problem.

20)

A. **Correct.** These pairs of sounds are formed in the same way, but the first in all of them is unvoiced and the second is voiced.

B. Incorrect. The reverse is true.

C. Incorrect. Consonants are neither stressed nor unstressed.

D. Incorrect. Consonants are neither stressed nor unstressed.

Language Learning and Acquisition

Read each question carefully, and then choose the best answer.

1

Why was the audio-lingual method of language instruction created?

A. to help deaf soldiers learn a second language

B. to allow communication between deaf and hearing soldiers

C. to aid American military officers in speaking with foreign prisoners of war

D. to assist American soldiers in communicating with foreign military personnel

2

The connectionist theory of language development evolved in response to the work of which studied theorist?

A. Jean Piaget

B. Noam Chomsky

C. B.F. Skinner

D. Stephen Krashen

3

Which theory of development focuses on the idea that children acquire language through a series of efforts and rewards?

A. behaviorist

B. connectionist

C. social development

D. cognitive development

4

Marlin enjoys participating in class discussions with his peers and even initiates them occasionally. Though he sometimes makes errors in his speech, he is able to self-correct and often repeats the correct phrasing back to himself. What stage of second-language acquisition might Marlin be in?

A. preproduction

B. early production

C. speech emergence

D. intermediate fluency

5

Which of the following characteristics should ESOL teachers avoid when modeling language for students?

A.   speaking in a measured pace

B.   using appropriate vocabulary

C.   speaking in short phrases and sentences

D.   overemphasizing stressed syllables

6

During which universal stage of first language acquisition do children begin to produce sounds based upon friction?

A.   pre-speech stage

B.   babbling stage

C.   one-word stage

D.   early multi-word stage

7

Which of the following classroom activities BEST incorporates Stephen Krashen's input hypothesis?

A.   having students listen to a pre-recorded conversation that incorporates both familiar and unfamiliar vocabulary

B.   having students select poems of their choice to read aloud in their new language

C.   having students use a dictionary to write a report on a topic of interest

D.   having students practice verb conjugations with new vocabulary words before discussing them as a class

8

Which of Stephen Krashen's hypotheses of the monitor model states that the sequence of language acquisition does not rely on the grammatical features of the language and therefore cannot be altered through direct teaching methods?

A.   acquisition-learning hypothesis

B.   input hypothesis

C.   natural order hypothesis

D.   monitor hypothesis

9

An ESL teacher has noticed that one of her new students is very good at recognizing similarities in vocabulary between her first language and the English she is learning. The student is demonstrating which element of second language acquisition?

A.   code-switching

B.   interference

C.   phonemic awareness

D.   positive transfer

10

Which of the following is an appropriate assignment for an ESL student who is in the silent period of second language acquisition?

A.   read a poem aloud to the class

B.   complete a matching activity, pairing words with their illustrations

C.   write a research paper on a topic of interest

D.   listen to and translate a song into the target language

11

Which of the following best summarizes Noam Chomsky's notion of the poverty of stimulus?

A. Poverty is caused by a lack of literacy and learning materials within various communities.

B. Exposing children to literacy materials from birth affords them greater opportunities to develop linguistic skills.

C. Children born in poverty struggle with emergent literacy because of a lack of exposure to literacy materials.

D. Children's capacities for language acquisition cannot be explained by exposure alone.

12

Which of the following describes an English language learner with intrinsic motivation?

A. Elliana wants to get an A on her English test so that she will be permitted to have a sleepover party.

B. Margot likes working in small groups because she understands the work better when she has the opportunity to discuss it with other students.

C. Terrique studies his math facts every night because the teacher hands out candy to students who have correct answers.

D. James writes down notes that the teacher puts on the board so that his parents will see that he is paying attention in school and will be proud.

13

Naveen shows little interest in learning English and regularly tells his classmates that he will move "home" after he graduates. His teacher, Mr. Harris, has been trying to motivate him to participate in class but has had little success so far. What might Mr. Harris do to encourage Naveen to participate in class?

A. allow Naveen to be the classroom assistant for a day

B. ask Naveen to choose a topic that he would like to write about

C. have Naveen design a project that everyone in the class will work on

D. assign Naveen a reading passage that uses vocabulary the class has learned

14

Mr. Muñoz is preparing to deliver the first oral language quiz to his ELL class. Students will be expected to listen to a conversation and answer questions about what they understand. Which of the following would be the most appropriate method of scaffolding for his newest students?

A. give students one week of advance notice of the quiz

B. describe several of the topics that might be covered on the quiz

C. provide students with a copy of the conversation before the quiz begins

D. present students with the specific questions they will be expected to answer

15

Reya is struggling in her honors world history class despite the high marks she received in the class at her previous school, where classes were taught in her native language. She turns in all of her written work and gets good grades on reading and writing assignments, which she completes on her own outside of class. However, she struggles to keep up with the lectures and reading assignments. What might be the cause of Reya's struggles?

A. poor cognate awareness

B. low intrinsic motivation

C. a lack of comprehensible input

D. a lack of phonemic awareness

16

What are the smallest units of language that can convey meaning or play a part in the grammatical structure of a word?

A. digraphs

B. logographs

C. morphemes

D. phonemes

17

Guillermo regularly pronounces the letter *e* with the English long /a/ sound. His ESOL teacher has corrected him on several occasions, but he continues to pronounce the letters the way he does in his first language. What is Guillermo experiencing?

A. code-switching

B. displacement

C. negative transfer

D. cognate awareness

18

Marcus has been instructed to write a story for his psychology class about the time in his life when he felt most afraid and the events that led him to that moment. What kind of paper has he been assigned?

A. descriptive

B. expository

C. narrative

D. procedural

19

Klaus began taking English lessons when he was seventeen. He was able to reach an intermediate fluency level, but since graduating high school has not been able to progress any further. What is Klaus likely experiencing?

A. fossilization

B. interlanguage

C. cognate awareness

D. poverty of stimulus

20

When asked to explain his approach to literacy development, Mr. Gomez explained that he thinks students learn best when given a targeted set of skills in reading, writing, and speaking that they practice and repeat daily. Which approach to literacy development does Mr. Gomez most likely use in his classroom?

A. the Language Experience Approach

B. phonics/skills-based

C. Universal Grammar

D. Whole Language

21

During which stage of literacy development will students focus on the sounds of language and how they combine to form words?

A. emergent

B. early

C. transitional

D. fluency

22

Mr. Worth asked the students in his literature class to analyze why the characters in a novel have decided to rebel against the leader of their tribe and what they believe will be the result of the coup. What kind of rhetorical pattern are students being asked to use in their papers?

A. compare/contrast

B. classification

C. chronological order

D. cause and effect

23

Ms. Wright, an ESL teacher, plans to use the Language Experience Approach to generate new vocabulary for her students. Which of the following is the most logical first step to take in her lesson planning?

A. design an experience for the class to share

B. determine how her students should be grouped for the activity

C. create a universal assessment for her students to work toward

D. read a story about a topic with which all of her students are familiar

24

Mr. Cole wants to assign his speech emergent ELL students a descriptive writing task. Which of the following prompts would be most appropriate?

A. Imagine you are a superhero or a supervillain. What is your power? What kind of suit do you wear?

B. Think about the best day of your life. What was the series of events that occurred that day?

C. Research your favorite animal. What did you discover about your animal?

D. Recall the last lab you completed in science class. What steps did you take to complete the experiment?

25

How does phonological awareness in a first language impact second language acquisition?

A. It helps students recognize and apply cognate awareness.

B. It aids learners in transferring skills from their first language to their second.

C. It inhibits learners' ability to transfer skills from their first language to their second.

D. It indicates that learners would benefit from phonological direct instruction in the second language.

26

Julia is having difficulty structuring her sentences properly in English. With which component of the standard conventions of written English is she struggling?

A. grammar

B. mechanics

C. semiotics

D. usage

27

Which of the following materials would NOT be found in the classroom of a teacher who uses the Whole Language approach to literacy development?

A. displays of students' written work

B. audio recordings of poems and stories

C. anchor charts depicting grammar skills

D. leveled readers in the classroom library

28

How can teachers assess students' phonemic awareness?

A. have students sound out unfamiliar words in a textbook

B. ask students to write down vocabulary words they have studied

C. ask students to make a list of areas they would like to work on further

D. have students create a portfolio demonstrating their best written work

29

Krashen argued that language acquisition only occurs when comprehensible input reaches the processing facilities of the brain without being filtered by mechanisms such as low self-esteem, poor motivation, and anxiety. This idea is also known as

A. the input hypothesis.

B. the natural order hypothesis.

C. the affective-filter hypothesis.

D. the acquisition-learning hypothesis.

ANSWER KEY

1)

A. Incorrect. The audio-lingual method is unrelated to deaf education.

B. Incorrect. The audio-lingual method is unrelated to deaf education.

C. Incorrect. The audio-lingual method was not restricted to use by soldiers communicating with prisoners of war.

D. Correct. The audio-lingual method was developed to teach American military personnel to communicate effectively with personnel of foreign, non-English-speaking nations.

2)

A. Correct. Piaget's theories on linguistic development served as the roots for connectionist theory by introducing the notion that children learn language through experience and experimentation.

B. Incorrect. Chomsky proposed the theory of Universal Grammar, which postulates that people are born with the innate capacity to distinguish parts of language.

C. Incorrect. Skinner's theory of language development was built on the principles of behaviorism.

D. Incorrect. Krashen was most known for his monitor model of second language acquisition, composed of five hypotheses that explored the relationship between acquisition and learning.

3)

A. Correct. Skinner theorized that children's speech efforts are made in response to the positive reinforcement they receive from those around them.

B. Incorrect. Connectionist theory states that language acquisition occurs through exposure to input and is the result of personal experiences.

C. Incorrect. Social development theory focuses on the development of language through the active participation in and construction of the social world.

D. Incorrect. Cognitive development theory focuses on the importance of experimentation in language acquisition but does not address rewards.

4)

A. Incorrect. Preproduction is characterized by little speech and much listening. Students may copy words down and respond to visual cues such as pictures and gestures to communicate their comprehension.

B. Incorrect. Early production is characterized by the building of vocabulary and the production of single word and two- to three-word phrases and responses.

C. Incorrect. Speech emergence is characterized by the ability to create multi-word responses; however, in this stage students do not yet have a working grasp of grammar concepts and thus must model their sentence structures after others' speech.

D. Correct. Marlin's interest in conversation and his ability to self-correct indicate that he is moving toward advanced fluency and has reached the intermediate stage.

5)

A. Incorrect. Using a measured pace allows ELL students to follow along with the speech that they are hearing.

B.   Incorrect. Using appropriate vocabulary allows ELL students the opportunity to understand the material being discussed.

C.   Incorrect. Using short phrases and sentences allows ELL students to better understand what is being said because they are not overwhelmed by complex sentence structures.

D.   Correct. Overemphasizing syllables in words can lead to mispronunciation for ELL students who are acquiring new vocabulary.

6)

A.   Incorrect. This stage is characterized by crying and cooing sounds.

B.   Correct. This stage is characterized by the creation of sequences of consonant-vowel sounds that babies often repeat in lengthier spans as they learn to use their mouths to create phonemes.

C.   Incorrect. This stage is characterized by a child's use of a single word to convey a complete idea.

D.   Incorrect. This stage is characterized by the early use of grammatical elements and the repetition of longer sentences.

7)

A.   Correct. A pre-recorded conversation such as this represents an example of what Krashen called comprehensible input: it introduces new information alongside relevant, existing knowledge so that students are able to access the new information more readily.

B.   Incorrect. Without guidance, students might select poems that are either far below or far above their current mastery.

C.   Incorrect. A writing assignment such as a report represents student output, not the linguistic input on which the theory is centered.

D.   Incorrect. New information can be overwhelming and discouraging for students if it is not made accessible to them via their existing knowledge; in this case, reviewing the words or providing one example of the proper conjugation first might equip students to receive the rest of the information.

8)

A.   Incorrect. This hypothesis states that learning is the conscious process of developing skills through formal lessons in grammar, syntax, and vocabulary.

B.   Incorrect. This hypothesis states that language is only acquired when learners are exposed to written and/ or spoken input that is accessible to them based on their existing knowledge.

C.   Correct. This hypothesis states that learners must be ready to gain new knowledge of language in order for them to do so.

D.   Incorrect. This hypothesis states that students use what they have learned to self-correct their output when speaking in a new language, sometimes to the detriment of clear communication.

9)

A.   Incorrect. Code-switching occurs when a speaker mixes words from his or her language in with the new language.

B.   Incorrect. Interference occurs when language learners incorrectly apply rules from their native language to their new language.

C.   Incorrect. Phonemic awareness is the ability to hear, identify, and control individual sounds in spoken words.

D.   Correct. Positive transfer occurs when students find similarities between their native and second languages and use those similarities to help them learn.

10)

A. Incorrect. Students in the silent period are unwilling or unable to communicate in their new language and should not be forced to speak.

B. **Correct.** Students in the silent period may begin activities that help them pair words they are hearing with familiar objects.

C. Incorrect. Students in the silent period generally have not acquired enough vocabulary to complete a full-length writing assignment.

D. Incorrect. Students in the silent period generally have not acquired enough vocabulary to translate from one language to another.

11)

A. Incorrect. Poverty of stimulus is unrelated to children's access to literacy materials.

B. Incorrect. Poverty of stimulus is unrelated to children's exposure to literacy materials.

C. Incorrect. Poverty of stimulus is unrelated to children's socioeconomic standing.

D. **Correct.** Poverty of stimulus states that children are not born with enough exposure to their native languages to explain their ability to recognize and understand its parts, so exposure alone cannot account for their language capabilities.

12)

A. Incorrect. Elliana's reliance on her parents for a reward demonstrates extrinsic motivation, the reliance on outside rewards for motivation.

B. **Correct.** Margot demonstrates intrinsic motivation because she

relies on her personal drive to succeed in school.

C. Incorrect. Terrique's reliance on his teacher for a reward demonstrates extrinsic motivation.

D. Incorrect. James's reliance on his parents for a reward demonstrates extrinsic motivation.

13)

A. Incorrect. Naveen is showing a lack of motivation, so his behavior should not be rewarded with special privileges.

B. **Correct.** Allowing Naveen to choose an area of interest may spark his motivation by generating personal interest in and ownership of an assignment.

C. Incorrect. Naveen is showing a lack of motivation, so his behavior should not be rewarded with special privileges.

D. Incorrect. Giving Naveen traditional assignments is not likely to encourage him because he has not shown any interest in them before.

14)

A. Incorrect. Giving students advance notice of a quiz can be helpful; however, new ELL students may require additional support in order to be successful on their assessment.

B. Incorrect. Telling students the topics may be helpful; however, new ELL students may require additional support in order to be successful on their assessment.

C. Incorrect. Providing students with a copy of the conversation prior to giving the quiz would allow them to memorize the translation without learning the materials.

D. **Correct.** Providing students with the specific questions that will be asked allows them to focus their studies on the information most pertinent to their success, while still challenging them to know the material.

15)

A. Incorrect. Cognate awareness refers to the ability to recognize similarities between words in first and second languages.

B. Incorrect. Intrinsic motivation is one's personal drive to succeed, which Reya displays in the assignments she completes outside of class.

C. **Correct.** Comprehensible input is information that students are able to understand. Reya may be struggling to keep up with her class because the input she is receiving is not delivered at an appropriate level for her limited English proficiency.

D. Incorrect. Phonemic awareness is the ability to hear, identify, and control individual sounds in spoken words.

16)

A. Incorrect. Digraphs are groups of two consecutive letters whose phonetic product is a single sound.

B. Incorrect. Logographs are systems of writing in which each spoken word in the language is represented by a symbol.

C. **Correct.** Morphemes are the smallest units of language that can convey meaning or play a part in the grammatical structure of a word.

D. Incorrect. Phonemes are the smallest units of sound that can be heard within a word.

17)

A. Incorrect. Code-switching occurs when a speaker mixes words from a first language in with their second language production.

B. Incorrect. Displacement is the capacity of language to communicate about things that are not immediately present.

C. **Correct.** Negative transfer occurs when language learners incorrectly apply the rules of their native language to their new language. Guillermo is incorrectly applying pronunciation rules of his first language, Spanish, to his English practice.

D. Incorrect. Cognate awareness is the ability to recognize similarities between words in first and second languages.

18)

A. Incorrect. This assignment does not ask students to complete a descriptive writing task because they do not have to describe anything with specific, definitive details.

B. Incorrect. This assignment does not ask students to complete an expository task because they do not have to provide readers with information on a topic.

C. **Correct.** This assignment asks students to complete a narrative task by telling a story.

D. Incorrect. This assignment does not ask students to complete a procedural task because they do not have to explain the steps taken to do something.

19)

A. **Correct.** Fossilization occurs when a language learner's growth freezes in place, and further linguistic development becomes highly unlikely.

B. Incorrect. Interlanguage is a rule-based system that language learners develop over time that blends elements of their first language with their second.

C. Incorrect. Cognate awareness is the ability to recognize similarities between words in first and second languages.

D.   Incorrect. Poverty of stimulus states that children are not born with enough exposure to their native languages to explain their ability to understand language, so exposure cannot account for their capacities.

20)

A.   Incorrect. The Language Experience Approach uses prior knowledge and experiences to generate specific lessons that are designed to enhance the learning of each individual student.

B.   Correct. The phonics/skills-based approach focuses on specific skills in reading, writing, and speaking, which are targeted and practiced each day.

C.   Incorrect. Universal Grammar is a language development theory which postulates that people are born with the innate capacity to distinguish parts of language.

D.   Incorrect. The Whole Language approach focuses on language as a social process. It should be considered in its complete form prior to being broken down into smaller pieces.

21)

A.   Correct. Students in the emergent stage are generally focused on the sounds of language and how they combine to form words.

B.   Incorrect. Students in the early stage are beginning to make meaning of what they are reading and benefit from discussing it with others.

C.   Incorrect. Students in the transitional phase are able to explain what they have read and to discuss their interpretations of the material.

D.   Incorrect. Students in the fluency stage are able to discuss what they have read in detail, to provide evaluations of the material, and to offer explanations for their opinions.

22)

A.   Incorrect. Compare/contrast patterns are used to show similarities and differences between two or more things.

B.   Incorrect. Classifications are used to group or categorize information into predetermined topics. They are then explained in order to support a writer's main idea.

C.   Incorrect. Chronological patterns describe or explain events in the order in which they occur.

D.   Correct. Cause and effect patterns explain why something happened and what its result was.

23)

A.   Correct. In order for students to develop vocabulary through the Language Experience Approach, they must share a common experience to begin discussion.

B.   Incorrect. The Language Experience Approach is based upon students' recreation of an experience; however, they must have a common ground (a shared experience) on which to build their discussions.

C.   Incorrect. An assessment cannot be created until there is an established vocabulary that is generated by the students' shared experience.

D.   Incorrect. The Language Experience Approach is based upon a shared experience from which classroom material is drawn.

24)

A.   Correct. This assignment asks students to complete a descriptive writing task by describing something they are imagining in detail.

B.   Incorrect. This assignment asks students to complete a narrative task by telling a story.

C.   Incorrect. This assignment asks students to complete an expository task by providing readers with information.

D.   Incorrect. This assignment asks students to complete a procedural writing task by explaining the steps taken in a process.

25)

A.   Incorrect. Cognates are words that are visually similar between languages and are not impacted by learners' phonological awareness.

B.   Correct. Students who possess phonological awareness understand that language is made up of sounds, syllables, rhythms, words, and patterns. They are able to apply this knowledge from their first language to the language they are learning.

C.   Incorrect. Students who possess phonological awareness understand that language is made up of sounds, syllables, rhythms, words, and patterns. This awareness can be transferred from the learner's native language and applied to his or her target language.

D.   Incorrect. Students who possess phonological awareness usually do not require direct instruction in phonics.

26)

A.   Correct. Grammar is the set of rules concerned with the function of words and how they can be combined to create effectively structured sentences.

B.   Incorrect. Mechanics are the rules of print that include spelling, capitalization, punctuation, and proper paragraphing of written work.

C.   Incorrect. Semiotics is the study of symbols and their meanings and interpretations.

D.   Incorrect. Usage refers to the way people use language to communicate, particularly when there are multiple correct ways of stating something.

27)

A.   Incorrect. The Whole Language approach calls for students to bring their own experiences and work into their learning in order to become invested in their own success.

B.   Incorrect. The Whole Language approach calls for students to be exposed to all communicative elements of language, including the spoken word.

C.   Correct. The Whole Language approach calls for students to focus on language acquisition and communication with relatively little emphasis on grammar and convention.

D.   Incorrect. The approach calls for students to be exposed to language as a whole, as in leveled reading books, before moving on to learning the component parts of the language.

28)

A.   Correct. This activity asks students to separate words into sounds, which then helps them transfer those sounds to corresponding printed letters.

B.   Incorrect. This activity asks students to examine words that they already know, which does not allow for assessment of phonemic awareness.

C.   Incorrect. This activity asks students to reflect on areas that they feel need greater focus but does not look at phonemic awareness.

D. Incorrect. This activity asks students to examine works they have written, which calls for reflection but does not relate to phonemic awareness.

29)

A. Incorrect. The input hypothesis states that language is only acquired when learners are exposed to written and/or spoken input that makes sense to them.

B. Incorrect. The natural order hypothesis states that learners must be ready to gain new knowledge of language in order for them to do so.

C. Correct. The affective-filter hypothesis states that comprehensible input must reach the brain without being filtered out by the affective stressors such as low self-esteem, poor motivation, and anxiety.

D. Incorrect. The acquisition-learning hypothesis states that learning is the conscious process of developing skills through formal lessons in grammar and syntax.

Instruction

Read each question carefully, and then choose the best answer.

1

Which of the following is an example of cooperative planning between a content area teacher and an ESOL teacher?

A.   A content area teacher follows plans that are written by ESOL teachers and contain both content and language acquisition objectives.

B.   A content area teacher writes the lesson plans and the ESOL teacher serves as a classroom aide while working with English learners.

C.   An ESOL teacher pulls small groups of students into a separate room to deliver the same content area lesson as the native English speakers are receiving.

D.   An ESOL teacher and a content area teacher create lesson plans together to incorporate content area objectives for all students and language objectives for English learners.

2

According to the direct method of instruction, how will students learn the grammatical rules of new languages?

A.   by receiving direct instruction

B.   by reading various works in class

C.   by writing personal stories and essays

D.   by playing speaking and listening games

3

Why is total physical response (TPR) most useful when working with beginning language learners?

A.   because students must follow commands

B.   because students are not required to speak

C.   because commands are repeated frequently

D.   because instructions are modeled for students

4

The direct method of instruction is based on which of the following principles?

A. Second languages should be acquired through many of the same ways as first languages.

B. Learners must use real communication to engage their natural strategies for language acquisition in order to acquire a new language.

C. Students use repetitive exercises that emphasize grammatical structure and vocabulary, focusing on key phrases and significant dialogue.

D. Teaching students in their native languages and concentrating on grammatical rules allows learners to find similarities between their native and learned languages.

5

Which of the following activities would be used by an ESOL teacher who has implemented the grammar-translation method of instruction?

A. Students read essays aloud in English.

B. Students write poems in English and read them aloud to the class.

C. Students select a short story in their native language and rewrite it in English.

D. Students listen to a famous speech in English and discuss it with a small group.

6

Ms. Jacobs is having students learn new vocabulary by listening to the lyrics of their favorite songs and repeating back the choruses of each one. As students repeat back the new words, Ms. Jacobs reviews the proper pronunciation, applauding students who say the words correctly. What method of instruction is Ms. Jacobs using?

A. audio-lingual method

B. communicative approach

C. direct method

D. grammar-translation method

7

Which of the following is a key component to instruction done the Silent Way?

A. problem solving

B. repetition

C. rote memorization

D. translation

8

What is the purpose of clearly written language objectives for ESOL students?

A. to describe how students will achieve mastery of materials in a given subject area

B. to identify what students should be able to do at the end of a content area lesson

C. to tell how ESOL students will learn or demonstrate their mastery of materials in a given lesson

D. to identify what students are supposed to learn throughout a given time period in a specific subject area

9

A seventh grade ESOL teacher has asked students to write down a description of what it is like to order lunch in the cafeteria, a common experience that all students share. She plans to use the students' accounts to develop their new target language objectives and create a role-playing lesson in which students use the target language to create scripts and act out common occurrences.

Which of the following explains how the activity may be beneficial to the students?

A.   Students are using authentic texts on which to base their lessons.

B.   Students are generating their own target language, thereby creating personal interest.

C.   Students are preparing to work in a context that they will use outside of the classroom.

D.   Students are being provided with a specific task to complete in order to learn new vocabulary.

10

Materials that take into account students' backgrounds, experiences, and interests are said to be

A.   culturally appropriate materials.

B.   content-appropriate materials.

C.   level-appropriate materials.

D.   age-appropriate materials.

11

Which of the following describes a push-in model of classroom instruction?

A.   Mr. Albrecht works individually with ESOL students during their study hall classes.

B.   Mrs. Olsen takes a group of three kindergarten students to her classroom for two hours of reading instruction on Tuesdays and Thursdays.

C.   Ms. Garcia travels to Ana's eleventh-grade English class each day and provides services in that classroom through small-group and one-on-one instruction.

D.   Mr. Forrester teaches nine middle school ESOL students in his own classroom where they study the same curriculum as native English speakers in other classes for the full day.

12

What is the primary emphasis in pull-out ESOL programs?

A.   making students aware of the importance of translation abilities

B.   developing English skills that prepare learners for their content area classes

C.   fostering a sense of community between all English learners within the classroom

D.   creating an environment where students feel free to speak in their native languages

13

Which of the following materials are likely to be found in a classroom in which the ESOL teacher uses Communicative Language Teaching (CLT)?

A.   a shelf of usage and syntax manuals

B.   charts displaying various verb conjugations

C.   audio recordings of famous speeches made in English

D.   a box of magazines and take-out menus written in English

14

A game of *Simon Says* in which students must point to body parts as the teacher calls them out would best aid what kind of learner in gaining new vocabulary?

A.   analytic

B.   kinesthetic

C.   tactile

D.   visual

15

Which of the following criteria is NOT considered essential in a language objective?

A.   using active verbs to name targeted functions

B.   determining language objectives prior to developing content area objectives

C.   specifying the targeted language skills that students must use in completing the task

D.   emphasizing speaking and writing skills without neglecting listening and reading

16

Which of the following is considered a key component to the natural method?

A.   providing students with learning materials using the target language

B.   focusing on grammar and syntax in order to build linguistic understanding

C.   requiring that students respond to questions with single- and multi-word answers

D.   acclimating students to the target language by providing them with materials in their native languages

17

How can ESOL teachers best assist Students with Interrupted Formal Education?

A.   by focusing on academic linguistic skills first

B.   by providing students with individual attention on a regular basis

C.   by encouraging students to keep pace with other learners in their classes

D.   by planning content area and linguistic objectives separately to avoid confusion

18

Which skill set refers to the elements of language that are governed by rules?

A.   discrete language skills

B.   integrated language skills

C.   productive skills

D.   receptive skills

19

Mr. Juarez is working on cognitive strategies to help his students remember and organize information. He has decided to split the class into two teams to research information on a selected topic and then hold a class debate. After they have completed their research, students will be permitted to choose which side of the argument they would like to debate. What kind of cognitive strategy is he looking to develop with his students?

A.   comprehension strategies

B.   problem-solving strategies

C.   reasoning strategies

D.   self-regulation strategies

20

Which of the following activities results in the rehearsal of receptive skills?

A.   writing a song

B.   telling a story

C.   reading a poem

D.   giving a speech

21

Which of the following activities would be most helpful in activating students' prior knowledge before reading a new text?

A.   writing letters to an author of their choice

B.   holding a discussion about the students' favorite books

C.   examining vocabulary words students will find in the text

D.   completing an activity in which students define types of texts

22

Which of the following activities demonstrates the use of task-based instruction (TBI)?

A.   Students read the play *Romeo and Juliet* from their English textbook, taking on parts.

B.   Students complete a science lab report describing the steps they took to conduct an experiment.

C.   Students organize and then advertise a clean-up for the local playground and recruit volunteers to help.

D.   Students create personal portfolios of their written works and display them at a parent-teacher conference day.

23

Which of the following is NOT a use for Cuisenaire rods in a classroom that uses the Silent Way for ESL instruction?

A.   make comparisons

B.   represent other objects

C.   demonstrate prepositions

D.   track students' translation successes

24

Children who have not yet undergone puberty have more success at acquiring new languages because their brains have not undergone

A.   realia.

B.   lateralization.

C.   affective domain.

D.   communicative competence.

25

Which of the following is an example of constructive feedback?

A. "I loved reading your paper."

B. "Your pronunciation is incorrect."

C. "I think you misunderstood the directions."

D. "You need to include more examples to illustrate your point."

26

Maya, a second year ELL, is able to easily converse with her friend Jamie about what she plans to do for her birthday. What is Maya likely to be experienced in?

A. ALM

B. BICS

C. CALP

D. CLT

27

Which of the following classroom activities uses authentic materials?

A. Students create take-out menus with descriptions of their favorite foods.

B. Students write biographies of their favorite actors for an imaginary website.

C. Students use maps of the city to write directions from the school to their homes.

D. Students watch a version of *Romeo and Juliet* that has been adapted for ESOL classrooms.

28

Which of the following activities would be considered a metacognitive learning activity?

A. Students keep a log of book titles they have read throughout the school year.

B. Students write down an evaluation of the role they played in a group project.

C. Students create illustrations of their vocabulary words as part of their homework.

D. Students take notes on information presented in a slide show and review them for an exam.

29

Which of the following would be considered both content- and task-based instruction?

A. having students complete presentations on an experiment that the class has done

B. having students translate and diagram poems from their native language into English

C. having students create a game that includes instructions, rules, and the necessary play pieces and board

D. having students hold an election in which candidates must write and deliver speeches on their goals for office

30

Which of the following methods would an ESOL teacher implementing the direct method use to teach students grammatical and syntactical skills?

A.   oral verb conjugation drills

B.   worksheets on subject/verb agreement

C.   written assignments on sentence structure

D.   participation in a class discussion about a story

ANSWER KEY

1)

A.   Incorrect. Though the plans were developed by one teacher and implemented by another, the plans were not written together and therefore have not been developed cooperatively.

B.   Incorrect. The plans have been developed by the content area teacher, so the ESOL teacher cannot fully exercise his or her expertise in shaping the language objectives.

C.   Incorrect. Though the plans were developed by one teacher and implemented by another, the plans were not written together and therefore have not been developed cooperatively.

D.   **Correct.** When content and ESOL teachers work together on plans, they are working cooperatively.

2)

A.   Incorrect. The direct method avoids direct instruction because students are believed to acquire understanding of grammatical skills through induction.

B.   Incorrect. The direct method of instruction focuses on speaking and listening, not reading, in order for students to inductively learn grammatical rules.

C.   Incorrect. The direct method of instruction emphasizes speaking and listening, not writing, to help students inductively learn grammatical rules.

D.   **Correct.** With the direct method of instruction, students inductively learn grammatical rules by speaking and listening.

3)

A.   Incorrect. Students will need to interpret commands as they move toward proficiency and fluency, not only in the early stages, but in later stages as well.

B.   **Correct.** Students who are beginning language learners often start the acquisition process with a silent period. Activities that require only physical responses allow them to participate while they acclimate to the classroom and begin to acquire their new language.

C.   Incorrect. Students may need commands to be repeated frequently even in later stages of language acquisition.

D.   Incorrect. Students will require modeling throughout their language learning.

4)

A.   **Correct.** The direct method follows the principle that all languages learned subsequent to the first can be acquired in the same ways.

B.   Incorrect. This principle is part of the communicative approach to instruction.

C.   Incorrect. This principle is part of the audio-lingual method of instruction.

D.   Incorrect. This principle is part of the grammar-translation method of instruction.

5)

A.   Incorrect. The grammar-translation method does not emphasize the speaking skills necessary for this activity.

B.   Incorrect. While students are encouraged to write in the grammar-translation method, activities that emphasize the speaking skills are avoided.

C.   Correct. The grammar-translation method focuses on students' reading and writing in their new languages by working through translations.

D.   Incorrect. The grammar-translation method does not emphasize the listening skills necessary for this activity.

6)

A.   Correct. Praising correct reproductions of words and implementing oral practice indicate that Ms. Jacobs is using the audio-lingual method.

B.   Incorrect. The communicative approach emphasizes authentic interactions in which students seek to communicate meaning.

C.   Incorrect. The direct method assumes that students learn second languages as they did their first languages— through induction; Ms. Jacob's direct instruction in pronunciation and her use of rewards indicate that this is not direct method instruction.

D.   Incorrect. The grammar-translation method focuses on reading and writing as communication, with no emphasis placed on students' speaking and listening skills.

7)

A.   Correct. The Silent Way calls for students to solve problems and learn through discovery in order to create real learning.

B.   Incorrect. The Silent Way avoids repetition so that language practice mimics encounters that students are likely to have outside of the classroom.

C.   Incorrect. The Silent Way avoids rote memorization in order to allow students to practice language in an authentic way.

D.   Incorrect. The Silent Way avoids translation for students in order to teach them problem-solving skills and to immerse them in English.

8)

A.   Incorrect. Content area objectives indicate how students will achieve mastery of content area material.

B.   Incorrect. Content area objectives identify what students will be able to do at the end of a given lesson.

C.   Correct. Language objectives are intended to explain how students will demonstrate their learning of language in a given lesson.

D.   Incorrect. Content area standards identify what students are supposed to learn in a given content area throughout a predetermined time period.

9)

A.   Incorrect. Authentic materials in language learning are those that are intended for use by native language speakers, not second-language learners.

B.   Incorrect. While the students are being asked to write about personal experience, the prescribed scenario does not guarantee that students will be interested in the topic.

C.   Correct. The students are likely to use the newly acquired vocabulary and to encounter scenarios like the ones they will role-play.

D.   Incorrect. Students are not being asked to complete a specific, vocabulary-based task.

10)

A.   Correct. Culturally appropriate materials take into account students' backgrounds, experiences, and interests.

B. Incorrect. Content-appropriate materials are those that are considered suitable for teaching given content.

C. Incorrect. Level-appropriate materials are those that are considered appropriate in length and task for student proficiency levels.

D. Incorrect. Age-appropriate materials are those that are considered appropriate in scope for students' ages and levels of proficiency.

11)

A. Incorrect. Taking students from their study hall classes is an example of pull-out instruction because students are removed from their classroom in order to receive ESOL instruction.

B. Incorrect. Taking students from their kindergarten classes is an example of pull-out instruction because students are removed from their classroom in order to receive ESOL instruction.

C. Correct. An ESOL teacher who works within a subject classroom to provide additional support and instruction follows a push-in model.

D. Incorrect. Students who are placed in a separate classroom to learn both English and content area subjects are given sheltered instruction.

12)

A. Incorrect. Depending upon the teacher's method of instruction, students in pull-out programs may learn to translate; however, translation is not the goal of this model.

B. Correct. The goal of pull-out models is to teach ESOL students the skills necessary to succeed in their content area classes without additional language support.

C. Incorrect. While many ESOL teachers place an emphasis on community building in order to increase students'

comfort with their speaking skills, this is not the goal of the pull-out model.

D. Incorrect. While some ESOL teachers allow students to speak in their native languages while learning English, this is not the area of emphasis for a pull-out model.

13)

A. Incorrect. CLT places emphasis on realistic experiences and activities that students are likely to encounter, with little focus on formal acquisition of language systems.

B. Incorrect. CLT focuses on language acquisition through experiences and does not use direct instruction to enhance communicative competence.

C. Incorrect. While speaking and listening are key elements to CLT, these components should be based upon students' personal experiences.

D. Correct. The use of authentic materials is a key component of CLT.

14)

A. Incorrect. Analytic learners learn by focusing on details.

B. Correct. Kinesthetic learners learn through physical movement.

C. Incorrect. Tactile learners learn by touching and manipulating objects.

D. Incorrect. Visual learners learn best by seeing things.

15)

A. Incorrect. Active verbs should be used when writing language objectives in order to provide precise expectations for student performance.

B. Correct. Language and content area objectives should be created together in order to provide students with context and skills that will be useful to them in multiple settings.

C. Incorrect. Specifying targeted language skills provides students with precise expectations.

D. Incorrect. Emphasis is placed on speaking and writing skills in order to provide students with a strong base in communicative skills.

16)

A. **Correct.** The natural method requires that students are provided with learning materials that depict their target language in order to aid them in their vocabulary acquisition.

B. Incorrect. Little focus is placed on grammar and syntax because this method holds that students will learn these skills through induction and practice.

C. Incorrect. Students are never required to speak in natural method instruction because it is believed that they will produce comprehensible output when they are ready to do so.

D. Incorrect. Students are not provided with materials in their native languages when learning through the natural method.

17)

A. Incorrect. Teachers of Students with Interrupted Formal Education should focus on communicative skills before working on academic language.

B. **Correct.** Teachers of Students with Interrupted Formal Education should plan a consistent schedule to keep students progressing in their language acquisition.

C. Incorrect. Students with Interrupted Formal Education should be permitted to learn at their own pace.

D. Incorrect. Linguistic and content area goals should be collaboratively planned in order to allow students

the most significant amount of growth.

18)

A. **Correct.** Discrete language skills refer to the aspects of language which are governed by rules such as those that make up phonics, grammar, and syntax.

B. Incorrect. Integrated language skills refer to the integration of linguistic abilities in reading, writing, speaking, and listening.

C. Incorrect. Productive skills refer to speaking and writing, those activities that result in a product.

D. Incorrect. Receptive skills refer to listening and reading, those activities that require students to receive and interpret messages or ideas.

19)

A. Incorrect. Comprehension strategies help students understand and remember content.

B. Incorrect. Problem-solving strategies help students discern ways to achieve a specific goal.

C. **Correct.** Reasoning strategies help students determine what they believe to be correct or incorrect.

D. Incorrect. Self-regulation strategies help students monitor their behaviors.

20)

A. Incorrect. Speaking and writing activities rehearse productive skills, those which result in the creation of a product.

B. Incorrect. Speaking and writing activities rehearse productive skills, those which result in the creation of a product.

C. **Correct.** Skills that require students to receive and interpret a message or idea, such as reading and listening, are referred to as receptive skills.

D. Incorrect. Speaking and writing activities rehearse productive skills, those which result in the creation of a product.

21)

A. Incorrect. While writing a letter may help students recall elements of stories they have enjoyed, it is not the most effective task to activate prior knowledge for reading a specific new text.

B. Incorrect. While holding discussions may help students recall elements of stories they have enjoyed, it is not the most effective task to activate prior knowledge for reading a specific new text.

C. **Correct.** This activity will be most effective in helping students recall words, themes, or ideas that they have encountered in previous texts, providing a foundation for new learning.

D. Incorrect. While this activity may help students recall components of various types of texts they have read, it is not the most effective task to activate prior knowledge for reading a specific new text.

22)

A. Incorrect. Though this reading requires students to complete a task, it does not generate a real outcome by which students can judge their performance.

B. Incorrect. Though students completed a task in doing the science experiment, writing a lab report does not allow students to evaluate their own performance.

C. **Correct.** This assignment requires students to use their knowledge of language to complete a task and

then to measure their success by the outcome of their efforts.

D. Incorrect. Though students are required to create a portfolio, this assignment does not require them to complete a task that will generate a measureable outcome.

23)

A. Incorrect. Instructors can use Cuisenaire Rods to demonstrate comparisons based on their different colors, lengths, etc.

B. Incorrect. Instructors can use Cuisenaire Rods as props or visual aids to represent other objects.

C. Incorrect. Instructors can use Cuisenaire Rods to demonstrate prepositions to students by placing them in various positions and describing their locations.

D. **Correct.** The Silent Way avoids translation exercises in order to teach students problem-solving skills and immerse them in English.

24)

A. Incorrect. Realia refers to objects and materials from everyday life that can help in creating authentic learning experiences for students.

B. **Correct.** Lateralization refers to the process in which the brain's functions become localized to one hemisphere or the other.

C. Incorrect. The affective domain addresses emotional issues such as feelings, motivations, and attitudes.

D. Incorrect. Communicative competence refers to knowledge of grammar and syntax, and the ability to interpret and execute appropriate social behaviors and conversational elements.

25)

A. Incorrect. Although this feedback is positive, it does not provide students with any areas to aid in their growth. They may be left wondering, "Why?"

B. Incorrect. This feedback does not provide students with specific information that can aid in their growth. They may be left wondering, "What part did I mispronounce?"

C. Incorrect. This feedback does not provide students with specific information that can aid in their growth. They may be left wondering, "What did I do wrong?"

D. **Correct.** This feedback tells students in a polite and appropriate manner precisely what they must do to improve.

26)

A. Incorrect. ALM refers to the audio-lingual method of language instruction in which students learn targeted language through repetition.

B. **Correct.** BICS refers to basic interpersonal communication skills, which develop when students use contextual support to aid in language processing and delivery.

C. Incorrect. CALP refers to cognitive academic language proficiency, learning and understanding academic language not typically used in casual conversation.

D. Incorrect. CLT refers to Communicative Language Teaching. Students communicate through interactions made in the target language and use authentic texts and scenarios to practice skills they would utilize outside of the classroom.

27)

A. Incorrect. Because students are creating their own materials for the assignment, they are not using authentic materials intended for native English speakers.

B. Incorrect. Students are creating their own materials for the assignment, so they are not using authentic materials intended for native English speakers.

C. **Correct.** The use of materials intended for native language speakers, such as maps, constitutes the use of authentic materials.

D. Incorrect. Students are using materials that have been adapted specifically for ESOL use; these materials are not intended for native English speakers and therefore are not authentic.

28)

A. Incorrect. In order for students' reading logs to be considered metacognitive, they would need to reflect on their learning regarding the books they have read.

B. **Correct.** Having students evaluate their participation in a group project requires them to examine their learning.

C. Incorrect. Though this strategy may help students understand and remember their new vocabulary words, it does not require them to reflect on their thinking.

D. Incorrect. Though taking notes and reviewing them for exams is a standard practice in most classrooms, it does not require students to actively reflect on their learning.

29)

A. Incorrect. This is an example of content-based instruction because it does not require students to manipulate the English language.

B. Incorrect. This is an example of content-based instruction because it does not require students to comprehend the language being used, only to translate it.

C.   Incorrect. This is not an example of content-based instruction because it does not require students to use material from a given content area.

D.   Correct. This is an example of both content- and task-based instruction because students are required to produce, manipulate, comprehend, and interact with content-based language.

30)

A.   Incorrect. The use of drills does not allow students to learn through induction as is called for in the direct method.

B.   Incorrect. The use of worksheets does not allow students to learn through induction as is called for in the direct method.

C.   Incorrect. The use of written assignments does not allow students to learn through induction as is called for in the direct method.

D.   Correct. Participation in class discussions allows students to learn about grammar and syntax through induction by listening and speaking in the target language.

Assessment

10

Read each question carefully, and then choose the best answer.

1

Which of the following is the first step in assessing the English learner needs of a new student?

A. placement test

B. instructional program

C. achievement test

D. home survey

2

Which determines when an English learner no longer requires English language programs and services?

A. The student's home survey reports that the primary language is English.

B. The student has been enrolled in an English learner program for two years.

C. The student's scores on state-selected tests meet designated cutoff points.

D. The student has completed an instructional program aligned to ELP standards.

3

Which of the following is one way teachers can eliminate the impact of assessment bias when determining the academic abilities of English learners?

A. use the state-mandated progress-monitoring assessment

B. apply standardized methods of assessment only

C. apply performance-based methods of assessment only

D. use a variety of assessment types and methods

4

An assessment is reasonably priced, well paced, and easy to score.

What quality does the assessment demonstrate?

A. reliability

B. construct validity

C. criterion-referenced validity

D. practicality

5

A video of an English language learner orally presenting a research project is an example of which type of assessment?

A.   standardized

B.   portfolio

C.   diagnostic

D.   receptive

6

Which of the following choices identifies the assessments that can be used to measure oral language proficiency?

A.   BSM II and BSM II

B.   BINL, BSM I, and BSM II

C.   BINL, BSM I, BSM II, and IPT

D.   BINL, BSM I, BSM II, IPT, and LAS

7

With respect to English learners, what stipulation does the Individuals with Disabilities Education Act make?

A.   Low achievement due to second-language acquisition is not an appropriate reason for learning disability designation.

B.   English learners in language instruction programs must meet the same achievement standards as all students.

C.   School districts must administer placement tests to students with primary languages other than English.

D.   Organizations that receive federal money are prohibited from discrimination on the basis of disability.

8

After each lesson involving the reading of a classroom novel, Mrs. Gonzalez has students submit words or phrases from the text that need clarification. Prior to the subsequent lesson, she reviews the submitted words and phrases orally with the whole class.

How is this instructional strategy an example of using assessment to differentiate learning?

A.   Mrs. Gonzalez is collecting words and phrases to use in the vocabulary section of a unit test on the classroom novel.

B.   Mrs. Gonzalez is gathering student feedback on difficult vocabulary to determine student achievement levels in reading.

C.   Mrs. Gonzalez is gathering data from students to ensure that the language in a classroom novel is accessible.

D.   Mrs. Gonzalez is collecting data to determine if the classroom novel is too difficult for students' reading comprehension levels.

9

Which of the following describes an assessment that ranks students according to a predetermined average based on the performance of a peer group?

A.   criterion referenced

B.   norm referenced

C.   diagnostic

D.   rubric

10

Which best describes the teacher's key role with respect to student use of self-assessment tools?

A.   A teacher must ensure that students use self-assessment tools aligned to state standards.

B.   A teacher must provide self-assessment tools to those students who demonstrate an ability to use them.

C.   A teacher must include the use of self-assessment tools as one component of a student's learning goals.

D.   A teacher must show students how to accurately identify and apply assessment criteria to their work.

11

The text used for a classroom reading comprehension assessment describes the process of glycolysis in the body.

Which is the most likely reason that the results of this assessment will not demonstrate content validity?

A.   Student success depends on an ability to use context clues to draw conclusions.

B.   Student success depends on an understanding of the terminology of a specific science domain.

C.   Student success depends on an ability to identify features of an informational text.

D.   Student success depends on an understanding of transition words.

12

Why is it especially important that a thorough and methodical process be implemented to identify a learning disability in an English learner?

A.   to ensure that the English learner is provided with the supports necessary to participate in general education curriculum

B.   to prevent the English learner from being identified as learning disabled when the real problem may be difficulty with the second language

C.   to determine the instructional methods and strategies that best contribute to the English learner's academic progress

D.   to measure the performance of the English learner in broad terms against state and/or national norms

13

What is the purpose of using both standardized and performance-based assessments in the classroom?

A.   to gain an extensive understanding of the abilities and instructional needs of students

B.   to gather as much data as possible with respect to student achievement levels

C.   to gather samples of student work that can be used during parent conferences

D.   to ensure that all students are progressing at the same pace and in similar ways

14

Which of the following is an example of a standardized classroom assessment?

A. a teacher asks a student to paraphrase information from an article

B. a teacher uses a rating scale while a student reads aloud

C. a teacher has students keep science journals to record observations

D. a teacher meets with a student one-on-one to discuss a poem

15

Which of the following best illustrates cultural bias in a math test item?

A. The item references standard shapes.

B. The item includes a chart with tally marks.

C. The item references national sports teams.

D. The item includes a graph with rows of fruit.

16

Standardized assessments measure student ability in relation to criteria that correlates to areas of content knowledge.

Which is another term meaning *areas of content knowledge*?

A. constructs

B. portfolios

C. inferential items

D. criterion referenced

17

Which of the following best describes the WIDA Consortium?

A. The WIDA Consortium identifies standards for student achievement in five content areas.

B. The WIDA Consortium supplies standardized English learner materials to its member states.

C. The WIDA Consortium aligns its goals to the EL proficiency standards developed by the CCSSO.

D. The WIDA Consortium provides a series of English learner assessments for use anywhere in the world.

18

Which of the following documentation is NOT relevant prior to assessing an English learner for special education services?

A. documentation that shows that no progress in learning outcomes has resulted from the use of various instructional strategies

B. documentation that shows a restricted ability to communicate knowledge and ideas in the English language

C. documentation that shows staff agreement that performance differs significantly from that of linguistically similar peers

D. documentation that shows the feedback and input of parents and/or guardians with respect to learning outcomes

19

An assessment claims to measure mathematics ability. However, student outcomes are dependent on their abilities to read complex directions.

Which explains why this assessment does NOT demonstrate content validity?

A. The assessment does not adhere to an underlying construct.

B. The assessment scores are based on abilities other than the one being measured.

C. The assessment does not show consistent outcomes in different settings.

D. The assessment is time-consuming and difficult to score.

20

Mr. Barnes has posed a question to his class. Some students have already raised their hands to answer, but Mr. Barnes waits another minute before selecting a student to respond because he has noticed that some students need more time to formulate their answers before raising their hands.

Which best describes what Mr. Barnes is doing?

A. He is identifying gaps in learning.

B. He is assessing listening skills.

C. He is differentiating learning.

D. He is observing student behavior.

21

A teacher asks a bilingual panel of community poets to provide constructive feedback to students in response to the students' spoken recitations of original poems in their language of choice.

Which best identifies the type of assessment the teacher is using?

A. standardized assessment

B. self-assessment

C. diagnostic assessment

D. performance-based assessment

22

After completing a unit on poetic elements, students are asked to write original poems, which they are told can be written in their language of choice.

Which best explains why a teacher might have students write original poems in their language of choice?

A. The teacher is interested in assessing student understanding of the unit content separate from language proficiency.

B. The teacher is gathering data to find out the language most students prefer for writing assignments.

C. The teacher is not planning on assessing the students' poems because poetry is an enrichment activity.

D. The teacher is planning on having students translate each other's poems during a peer-editing session.

23

A classroom includes students with a primary language other than English. The teacher differentiates learning for these students to ensure that their instructional needs are met.

Which approach to second-language instruction is being implemented in the classroom?

A. a one-way dual language instructional model

B. a bilingual instructional model

C. a two-way dual language instructional model

D. an ESL instructional model

24

A teacher has divided students into groups of three to discuss the internal and external motivations of a character from a story. The teacher takes notes while moving around the room to monitor student discussions.

Which best identifies the type of literary assessment the teacher is using?

A. formal group literacy assessment

B. formal individual literacy assessment

C. informal group literacy assessment

D. informal individual literacy assessment

25

A student is reading aloud to a teacher while the teacher marks boxes on a checklist used to assess reading fluency.

Which of the following choices names the type of literary assessment the teacher is using?

A. formal group literacy assessment

B. formal individual literacy assessment

C. informal group literacy assessment

D. informal individual literacy assessment

26

Which accurately identifies English learner instructional programs that use a one-language approach to content area instruction?

A. bilingual and ESL programs

B. dual language programs

C. ESL and one-way dual language programs

D. two-way dual language and bilingual programs

ANSWER KEY

1)

A. Incorrect. Prior to assessing a student for placement in an English learner program, a home survey needs to be sent home to determine the new student's primary home language.

B. Incorrect. Before an instructional program is determined for a new student, a home survey needs to be sent home to determine the student's primary home language, and if the primary language is not English, a placement test needs to be administered.

C. Incorrect. An achievement test is not appropriate for assessing the English learner needs of a new student. The first step is to send home a survey to determine the student's primary home language. This is followed by a placement test if the home language is not English. Then, the student can be placed in an instructional program. An achievement test would be administered to measure the outcomes of the instruction provided.

D. **Correct.** The first step in assessing the English learner needs of a new student is to send home a survey to determine the student's primary home language.

2)

A. Incorrect. A home survey is an initial screening method for determining if a student should be assessed for English learner placement. A student whose home language is English would not be placed in an English learner program.

B. Incorrect. Scores on state-selected tests provide the criteria for removing an English learner designation from a student, not time spent in an English learner instructional program.

C. **Correct.** Specific scores on state-selected language and achievement tests are designated as cutoff points that determine when English learners no longer require English language programs and services.

D. Incorrect. English learners remain in instructional programs aligned to ELP standards until their scores on state-selected language and achievement tests meet designated cutoff points.

3)

A. Incorrect. One way teachers can eliminate skewed outcomes is to use a variety of assessment types and methods, not just the state-mandated assessment.

B. Incorrect. One way teachers can eliminate skewed outcomes is to use a variety of assessment types and methods so that student ability is not determined by only one type of measurement.

C. Incorrect. One way teachers can eliminate skewed outcomes is to use a variety of assessment types and methods so that student ability is determined by a balance of assessment outcomes.

D. **Correct.** Using a variety of assessment types and methods is one way teachers can eliminate the impact of assessment bias on student outcomes.

4)

A. Incorrect. An assessment demonstrates reliability when it can be shown to produce consistent outcomes in different settings and under different conditions.

B. Incorrect. An assessment demonstrates construct validity when it can be shown to adhere to an underlying construct.

C. Incorrect. An assessment demonstrates criterion-referenced validity when it can be shown to measure specific criteria confirmed by participant outcomes or scores.

D. **Correct.** Practicality is the term used to indicate that an assessment demonstrates relative ease of acquisition, use, and scoring.

5)

A. Incorrect. Video of a student's oral presentation is assessed more broadly and holistically than by standardized means.

B. **Correct.** Appropriate for a portfolio, video of a student's oral presentation is one example of a concrete demonstration of student learning.

C. Incorrect. Diagnostic assessment is used to place students in instructional programs, not to assess the learning that results from instructional programs.

D. Incorrect. The word *receptive* describes a type of language skill, not a type of assessment.

6)

A. Incorrect. The BSM I and II can be used to measure oral language proficiency, but additional answers are correct.

B. Incorrect. The BSM I, BSM II, and BINL can be used to measure oral language proficiency, but additional answers are correct.

C. Incorrect. The BSM I, BSM II, BINL, and IPT can be used to measure oral language proficiency, but additional answers are correct.

D. **Correct.** All of the identified assessments can be used to measure oral language proficiency.

7)

A. **Correct.** IDEA stipulates that children whose educational achievement is low due to challenges associated with learning a second language must not be mislabeled as having a learning disability.

B. Incorrect. This is a stipulation of the No Child Left Behind Act.

C. Incorrect. This is a legal requirement that arose out of the Elementary and Secondary Education Act of 1965, which was reauthorized in 2001 and 2015.

D. Incorrect. This is a broad mandate of the Americans with Disabilities Act, which IDEA elaborates on with respect to the education of children with disabilities.

8)

A. Incorrect. While the teacher may use some of the words and phrases on a final assessment, this would not be an example of differentiated learning. In this instance, the teacher is gathering data from students to ensure that the language in the novel is accessible, even to those students who may not ask questions orally or have the ability to understand vocabulary definitions in the written form.

B. Incorrect. Collecting student feedback as a means of assessing student achievement is not an example of learning differentiation. The teacher is collecting vocabulary feedback from students in order to ensure that the language in the novel is accessible, even to those students who may not ask questions orally or have the ability to understand vocabulary definitions in the written form.

C. **Correct.** The teacher is gathering data from students to ensure that the language in the novel is accessible, even to those students who may not ask questions orally or have the ability to understand vocabulary definitions in the written form.

D. Incorrect. In this example, the teacher is facilitating comprehension by ensuring that the language in the novel is accessible even to those students who may not ask questions orally or have the ability to understand vocabulary definitions in the written form.

9)

A. Incorrect. A criterion-referenced assessment measures student achievement in relation to specific instructional criteria.

B. **Correct.** A norm-referenced assessment measures student performance in comparison to a normative group.

C. Incorrect. A diagnostic assessment measures a student's current level of performance prior to instruction.

D. Incorrect. A rubric is an assessment tool students can use to review their work against expected outcomes and the criteria required to meet each outcome.

10)

A. Incorrect. The key role of a teacher with respect to students' use of self-assessment tools is to make sure that students understand how to accurately identify and apply assessment criteria to their assignments. Otherwise, the exercise loses meaning.

B. Incorrect. Teachers are not required to provide self-assessment tools to students, but if they do, all students should receive the opportunity to use them.

C. Incorrect. Self-assessment is a tool for reaching learning goals, but it is not a learning goal per se. The teacher's main role with respect to students'

use of self-assessment tools is to show students how to accurately identify and apply assessment criteria to their work.

D. **Correct.** A teacher is responsible for ensuring that students know how to assess their work using established criteria that have been explained in developmentally appropriate ways.

11)

A. Incorrect. Using context clues to draw conclusions is appropriate content for a reading comprehension test and would most likely contribute to the content validity of the assessment.

B. **Correct.** If responses to reading comprehension items are inhibited by an insufficient understanding of domain-specific vocabulary from a separate content area, the results will not demonstrate content validity.

C. Incorrect. Identifying features of an informational text is appropriate content for a reading comprehension test and would most likely contribute to the content validity of the assessment.

D. Incorrect. Understanding transition words is appropriate content for a reading comprehension test and would most likely contribute to the content validity of the assessment.

12)

A. Incorrect. This is the underlying purpose of IDEA and relates to students who have already been identified as having a learning disability.

B. **Correct.** English learners have been shown to be both overrepresented and underrepresented in special education populations due to the confusion of second-language acquisition challenges with learning disability challenges and vice versa.

C.   Incorrect. This is the purpose of progress-monitoring assessments, not learning disability identification processes.

D.   Incorrect. This is the purpose of a large-scale standardized assessment, not a learning disability determination.

13)

A.   **Correct.** Using both types of assessment allows educators to obtain a detailed awareness of students' abilities and instructional needs, which vary from student to student.

B.   Incorrect. The purpose of using different types of assessment is not just to gather achievement data, but also to recognize student abilities that data cannot measure and to inform instruction to meet student needs.

C.   Incorrect. A portfolio is one type of performance-based assessment that is used to inform and illustrate student progress and growth over time, not just at parent conferences.

D.   Incorrect. One purpose of using both types of assessment is to facilitate differentiated instruction for diverse learners.

14)

A.   Incorrect. Having a student paraphrase information is an example of performance-based classroom assessment.

B.   **Correct.** A rating scale is an example of a standardized classroom assessment.

C.   Incorrect. Having students keep journals is an example of performance-based assessment.

D.   Incorrect. A student conference is an example of a performance-based assessment.

15)

A.   Incorrect. Standard shapes are appropriate for use in a math item because they relate to the core math curriculum.

B.   Incorrect. A chart with tally marks is appropriate for use in a math item because it an element of the core math curriculum.

C.   **Correct.** Reference to national sports teams can introduce bias to the item in that some students may be penalized due to confusion related to a lack of familiarity with the teams and/or the sports they represent.

D.   Incorrect. A graph illustrated with rows of fruit provides accessible numerical information even if students do not have direct experience with the fruit pictured.

16)

A.   **Correct.** Areas of content knowledge are also referred to as *constructs* in standardized assessment.

B.   Incorrect. Portfolios can be used to demonstrate learning in different content areas, but they are not synonymous with *areas of content knowledge*.

C.   Incorrect. Inferential items are assessment items that require test takers to read between the lines. The term is not synonymous with *areas of content knowledge*.

D.   Incorrect. Many standardized assessments are criterion referenced in that they measure scores according to preestablished criterion; however, the term is not synonymous with *areas of content knowledge*.

17)

A.   Incorrect. While this is true, it is not the best descriptor of the WIDA Consortium, which supplies a broad range of English learner materials to member states, not just standards for student achievement.

B. **Correct.** The WIDA Consortium supplies standardized English learner materials to its member states.

C. Incorrect. This answer choice describes ELPA21, which is a separate consortium of states.

D. Incorrect. The WIDA Consortium primarily provides standardized English learner materials to its member states, although it is true that a few products are available to nonmember states and countries.

18)

A. Incorrect. Progress documentation should precede any special education assessment of an English learner.

B. **Correct.** Special education assessment should not be determined by a restricted ability to communicate in English.

C. Incorrect. This type of documentation should precede any special education assessment of an English learner.

D. Incorrect. This type of documentation should precede any special education assessment of an English learner.

19)

A. Incorrect. This relates to construct validity, not content validity.

B. **Correct.** An assessment that tests skills other than those claimed does not have content validity because it provides skewed results.

C. Incorrect. An assessment that fails to show consistent outcomes in different settings does not demonstrate reliability.

D. Incorrect. An assessment that is time-consuming and difficult to score does not demonstrate practicality.

20)

A. Incorrect. In this example, the teacher is differentiating learning so that all students have opportunities to respond to questions, not just those who can formulate answers in their heads quickly. A teacher would review a variety of assessments to identify gaps in learning.

B. Incorrect. In this example, the teacher is differentiating learning so that all students have opportunities to respond to questions, not just those who can formulate answers in their heads quickly. The teacher is observing processing time, not listening skills.

C. **Correct.** In this example, the teacher is differentiating learning so that all students have opportunities to respond to questions, not just those who can formulate answers in their heads quickly.

D. Incorrect. In this example, the teacher has already observed student behavior and based on those observations, the teacher decided to differentiate learning so that all students have opportunities to respond to questions, not just those who can formulate answers in their heads quickly.

21)

A. Incorrect. A panel of community poets will most likely provide feedback that is open-ended as opposed to standardized due to the integrated skill sets required of spoken poetry performance.

B. Incorrect. In this example, students are being assessed by experts in the field of study, not themselves.

C. Incorrect. Diagnostic assessment is used to place students in instructional programs, not assess performance.

D. **Correct.** The teacher is using an open-ended, performance-based assessment by having experts in the field provide constructive feedback to students.

22)

A.   **Correct.** By allowing students to write original poems in the languages they are most comfortable using, the teacher can best assess their conceptual understanding of poetic devices and elements because language proficiency is not limited.

B.   Incorrect. In this scenario, the teacher is removing language restrictions in order to accurately assess whether students understood the content area concepts introduced in the unit on poetic elements.

C.   Incorrect. Poetry is an integral element of K – 12 language arts curriculum.

D.   Incorrect. Translating poetry written in another language is not an appropriate use of peer-editing sessions. A better approach would be to have students read and discuss their poems in small groups using drawing, movement, and oral language skills to increase comprehension.

23)

A.   Incorrect. In a one-way dual language instructional model, curriculum is taught in two languages that represent the primary language and the secondary language of the entire group of students.

B.   Incorrect. In a bilingual instructional model, students with a primary language other than English receive content area instruction in their primary language and supplemental instruction in English.

C.   Incorrect. In a two-way dual language instructional model, curriculum is taught in two languages that represent the primary and secondary languages of two student groups.

D.   **Correct.** In an ESL instructional model, English learners receive differentiated instruction in a classroom where English is the primary language of use.

24)

A.   Incorrect. The teacher is taking observational notes, which is an informal assessment strategy.

B.   Incorrect. The teacher is assessing several students at a time by circulating and taking observational notes, which is an informal, group assessment strategy.

C.   **Correct.** The teacher is assessing several students at a time by circulating and taking observational notes, which is an informal, group assessment strategy.

D.   Incorrect. The teacher is assessing several students at a time.

25)

A.   Incorrect. The teacher is assessing one student (individual) in this scenario, not the whole group.

B.   **Correct.** The teacher is assessing one student (individual) using a formal assessment tool (checklist).

C.   Incorrect. The teacher is assessing one student (individual) with a formal assessment tool (checklist).

D.   Incorrect. The teacher is using a formal assessment tool (checklist).

26)

A.   **Correct.** Both bilingual and ESL instructional models use a one-language approach to content area instruction.

B.   Incorrect. Dual language instructional models use a mixed-language approach to content area instruction.

C.   Incorrect. The ESL instructional model uses a one-language approach to content area instruction, while the one-way dual language model uses a mixed-language approach.

D.   Incorrect. The bilingual instructional model uses a one-language approach to content area instruction, while the two-way dual language model uses a mixed-language approach.

Cultural Aspects

Read each question carefully, and then choose the best answer.

1

In the four phases of acculturation, the humor phase is often marked by what?

A. a lot of laughter at the cultural norms of the adopted country

B. delight at the newness of the culture of the adopted country

C. comfort and feeling like a part of the new culture

D. difficulty as the person grapples with feelings of rejecting the old culture for the new

2

Cultural factors that could influence ESL students' readiness and learning may include which of the following?

A. parents' education levels

B. gender

C. a student's previous formal education

D. all of the above

3

Cultural awareness

A. can only be achieved by visiting a foreign country.

B. is best achieved by learning a foreign language.

C. is the development of sensitivity and understanding of other cultures and the ways in which culture influences individuals.

D. means a person's culture is determined by the language that person speaks.

4

In _____ cultures, the context and relationships among speakers figure importantly in communication. Interactions are often quite formal, and much is understood without having to be explicitly stated.

A. low-context

B. high-context

C. Western European

D. superior

5

At times, small and rural school districts may receive a sudden influx of students needing ESL services. This can sometimes lead to negative attitudes as both the school and community struggle to meet the needs of the new students. An ESL teacher in that setting should do what?

A. look for jobs elsewhere since people at this school are obviously racist

B. assume a primary role in modeling positive attitudes toward ELLs for both the entire school and the community

C. greet students in their native languages, learn how to correctly pronounce their names, pay careful attention to the needs of students who are not vocal, and assist them as they adjust to their new culture

D. both B and C

6

Informality, living in small family units, and rigorous daily hygiene are examples of American

A. cultural awareness.
B. cultural norms.
C. interlanguage.
D. TPR.

7

Which cultures view time as holistic and value flexibility over punctuality?

A. behaviorist
B. proxemic
C. polychronic
D. monochronic

8

Which of the following is NOT true?

A. Culture is defined as the beliefs, customs, values, and attitudes that distinguish one group of people from another.

B. Culture is transmitted through many means including arts.

C. Culture and language are separate and unrelated.

D. Culture is transmitted through language, among other means.

9

Mohammed is a new ESL student from Egypt. For a few days, the ELL teacher notices that Mohammed does not eat during lunch. How should the teacher address this?

A. The teacher should discreetly talk with Mohammed about eating practices at home. This may lead to an explanation as to why he is not eating lunch.

B. The teacher should get a tray for Mohammed, invite him to eat with some teachers, and ask each teacher to explain each dish on his or her plate so he will understand more about what he is eating.

C. The teacher should ask other students if they have noticed this, and see if they have any ideas as to why he is not eating.

D. The teacher should send a note home explaining to his parents how important it is for him to eat at school.

10

According to the _____ hypothesis, a human's thoughts and actions are determined by the language(s) that person speaks.

A. Acquisition-Learning

B. Natural Order

C. Affective Filter

D. Sapir-Whorf

11

In the order that a person generally passes through them, what are the four stages of acculturation?

A. honeymoon, hostility, humor, and home

B. shock, honeymoon, homesickness, and home

C. hostility, honeymoon, humor, and home

D. shock, humor, hostility, and home

12

Why is it important to be wary of cultural stereotyping in a school setting?

A. It helps ESL teachers group students who are alike.

B. It reminds teachers that Asian students are all good at math and should be placed in advanced math classes regardless of their English skills.

C. Students may attempt to conform to stereotyped roles without trying to realize their full potential.

D. Listening to music while keyboarding is an important component of SLA.

13

A group of Somali refugees are resettled in a community, and several elementary students from the Somali group are placed in an ESL class. The ESL teacher quickly notices that the students misbehave in class by getting up from their seats and walking around during lessons, talking to each other when the teacher is talking, and drawing in their books. What is the most likely cause of their behavior?

A. The teacher has poor classroom management skills.

B. The students are SIFE.

C. The students do not want to be in school.

D. The students already know everything being taught in the class, so they are bored.

14

In the ESL field, what does SIFE stand for?

A. Students with Interrupted Foreign English

B. Say It First in English

C. Students in Foreign Education

D. Students with Interrupted Formal Education

15

During which time period did large numbers of immigrants from Southern and Eastern Europe, including many Jews, come to the United States?

A. during the late nineteenth and early twentieth centuries

B. after World War I

C. during World War II

D. in the 1970s

16

Non-verbal communication is especially important in which of the following cultures?

A.   high-context (individualist) cultures

B.   high-context (collectivist) cultures

C.   low-context (individualist) cultures

D.   low-context (collectivist) cultures

17

Ms. Sanchez teaches a high school elective world history class that includes outside reading. She has prepared a reading list for students to choose from which only includes classical works from Greece, England, and the United States. What cultural phenomenon is she exhibiting?

A.   norms

B.   bias

C.   acculturation

D.   portfolio assessment

18

There is no word in English for the Norwegian word *utepils*, which means *the first beer enjoyed outside after the long winter*. This supports which idea?

A.   the Sapir-Whorf Hypothesis

B.   the Input Hypothesis

C.   advanced fluency

D.   the Grammar-Translation Method

19

Which of the following is NOT a characteristic of an individualist culture?

A.   identifying with a group

B.   value placed on individual accomplishments

C.   competitive behavior

D.   value placed on the idea of equality

20

Mrs. Lee, an ESL teacher, is holding one-on-one conferences with students during class. In order to help students feel more relaxed, she always sits next to them rather than across from them. When she calls up Luis, a new student from Brazil, he sits very close to her, so close that it makes her uncomfortable. What would be the most appropriate way to address the issue?

A.   Mrs. Lee should discuss the notion of proxemics and culture with Luis.

B.   Mrs. Lee should report Luis for inappropriate sexual advances with a teacher.

C.   Mrs. Lee should discuss the honeymoon phase of acculturation with Luis.

D.   Mrs. Lee should discuss language interference with Luis.

21

In an ESL classroom, the class is playing a game and each group is assigned a color. When one of the students from the red team, Miguel, writes his team members' names on the board with a red marker, Ji-hoon, a student from South Korea becomes visibly upset. Later, Ji-hoon explains to the teacher that writing a name in red signifies death in Korean culture. How can the teacher handle this and possibly avoid similar situations in the future?

A. have Miguel apologize to Ji-hoon in front of the class

B. punish Miguel for offending his classmate

C. have Ji-hoon write an essay about Korean taboos

D. have all the students do short presentations about taboos in their home cultures

22

What is chronemics?

A. The study of meaning in language.

B. The study of the role time plays in communication.

C. The science of the study of language.

D. The study of second-language acquisition.

23

Which of the following is characteristic of a collectivist culture?

A. both B and D

B. value placed on individual accomplishment

C. value placed on group harmony

D. value placed on equality

24

Migration means movement _____ a place and usually includes _____ numbers of people, while immigration means movement _____ a place.

A. from; smaller; within

B. to; smaller; from

B. from; larger; to

D. to; larger; from

25

When a person has assimilated to a new culture, he or she

A. enjoys all the new and exciting aspects of living in the new culture.

B. feels at odds with the new culture.

C. has become a part of it.

D. feels homesick.

ANSWER KEY

1)

A.   Incorrect. This is not a phase of acculturation.

B.   Incorrect. This is the honeymoon phase.

C.   Incorrect. This is the home phase.

D.   Correct. As people begin to accept their new culture, they also experience this difficulty.

2)

A.   Incorrect. While parents' education levels influence readiness and learning, this answer choice is incomplete given the other options.

B.   Incorrect. Gender does influence readiness and learning, but this answer choice is incomplete since parents' education levels and previous formal education do as well.

C.   Incorrect. Previous formal education influences readiness and learning, but so do parents' education and gender.

D.   Correct. Parents' education levels, gender, and a student's previous formal education all contribute to ESL students' readiness and learning.

3)

A.   Incorrect. It is not necessary to go to a foreign country to develop cultural awareness.

B.   Incorrect. Learning another language is not necessary to develop cultural awareness.

C.   Correct. This is the meaning of cultural awareness.

D.   Incorrect. This is related to the Sapir-Whorf Hypothesis.

4)

A.   Incorrect. In low-context cultures, interactions are actually informal and much more is explicitly stated.

B.   Correct. Interactions are usually formal, and context and societal relationships provide much unstated background information in high-context cultures.

C.   Incorrect. Western European cultures are generally low-context.

D.   Incorrect. This cultural tendency is neither superior nor inferior.

5)

A.   Incorrect. This is not necessarily the reason for the negative attitudes.

B.   Incorrect. While an ESL teacher in this situation should model positive attitudes, he or she should also do the actions suggested in answer choice C, so this choice is not complete.

C.   Incorrect. All of these actions would help the new students and the school adjust, but so would modeling positive attitudes in general—answer choice B—so this answer is incomplete.

D.   Correct. Doing what is outlined in answers B *and* C would help both the new students, as well as the school and community, adjust to the changing environment.

6)

A.   Incorrect. People can engage in these without cultural awareness.

B.   Correct. These are just three examples of American cultural norms.

C.   Incorrect. Interlanguage is a stage of language acquisition.

D.   Incorrect. Total Physical Response is not related to these.

7)

A.   Incorrect. Behaviorist is an SLA term.

B.   Incorrect. Proxemic is a term related to personal space.

C.   **Correct.** Polychronic cultures view time holistically and value flexibility with schedules.

D.   Incorrect. Monochronic cultures view time as linear and value schedules and punctuality.

8)

A.   Incorrect. This is a widely accepted definition of culture.

B.   Incorrect. This is true since the arts are one means, among others, by which culture is transmitted.

C.   **Correct.** Actually, culture and language are closely related to each other.

D.   Incorrect. Language is one of the means by which culture is transmitted.

9)

A.   **Correct.** This is a culturally sensitive way to learn why he is not eating at school.

B.   Incorrect. This could cause embarrassment for Mohammed because he may not want to refuse food that is being offered to him, and there could be a religious reason as to why he is not eating.

C.   Incorrect. This could lead to embarrassment for Mohammed.

D.   Incorrect. This may not result in understanding why Mohammed is not eating lunch, and may further serve to alienate the parents from school involvement.

10)

A.   Incorrect. This is a component of Stephen Krashen's Monitor Model.

B.   Incorrect. This is also a component of Stephen Krashen's Monitor Model.

C.   Incorrect. This is another component of Stephen Krashen's Monitor Model.

D.   **Correct.** The Sapir-Whorf Hypothesis states that language determines thought and action.

11)

A.   **Correct.** These are the four stages of acculturation in order.

B.   Incorrect. This is not true; *shock* and *homesickness* are not terms used as any of the four main phases.

C.   Incorrect. These four terms are correct, but they are not in order.

D.   Incorrect. This is not true, and *shock* is not a term used as one of the four main phases of acculturation.

12)

A.   Incorrect. Grouping students based on cultural stereotypes is actually an example of a potentially negative effect of stereotyping.

B.   Incorrect. This is not true and is an example of a potentially negative effect of stereotyping.

C.   **Correct.** Helping students realize their full potential is a primary goal of education; thus it is important for educators to recognize cultural stereotyping since it can thwart students from doing so.

D.   Incorrect. Stereotyping is not related to keyboarding.

13)

A.   Incorrect. Unless other students in the class are behaving similarly, this is not likely the cause.

B.   **Correct.** The students have probably been in transit, in refugee camps, and/or in other situations that would make them Students with Interrupted Formal Education.

C.   Incorrect. There is no other evidence to support this idea.

D.   Incorrect. Since they are young and cannot have been in school very long, this is not likely the cause.

14)

A.   Incorrect. This is not a known term in the ESL field.

B.   Incorrect. This is not a known term in the ESL field and is actually in opposition to current beliefs that encourage L1 literacy and language development in ELL students.

C.   Incorrect. This is not a known term in the ESL field.

D.   Correct. SIFE is an acronym for *Students with Interrupted Formal Education.*

15)

A.   Correct. Many Jews were fleeing persecution as well as seeking increased economic opportunity with the rise of industrialization.

B.   Incorrect. Immigration slowed during this time period.

C.   Incorrect. Immigration continued to slow due to quotas that actually limited the numbers of immigrants from these areas.

D.   Incorrect. This time period is characterized by immigration of large numbers of Mexicans, Chinese, and Indians.

16)

A.   Incorrect. High-context cultures are collectivist.

B.   Correct. Non-verbal communication is especially important in high-context (collectivist) cultures.

C.   Incorrect. In low-context (individualist) cultures, non-verbal communication is not especially important.

D.   Incorrect. Low-context cultures are individualist.

17)

A.   Incorrect. Norms are generally accepted behaviors of a culture.

B.   Correct. This is an example of cultural bias since she has only included works of Western literature.

C.   Incorrect. This scenario is not relevant to acculturation or cultural adjustment.

D.   Incorrect. This scenario is not relevant to assessment.

18)

A.   Correct. The Sapir-Whorf Hypothesis states that culture and language are related, and the word reflects the deep importance that enjoying the spring has in Norwegian culture.

B.   Incorrect. The Input Hypothesis is part of Krashen's Monitor Model and is unrelated.

C.   Incorrect. Advanced fluency is a stage of language acquisition.

D.   Incorrect. The Grammar-Translation Method is related to instructional theory.

19)

A.   Correct. Identifying with a group is a characteristic of a collectivist, not an individualist, culture.

B.   Incorrect. Placing value on individual accomplishments is a characteristic of an individualist culture.

C.   Incorrect. Individualist cultures value and encourage competitive behavior.

D.   Incorrect. Valuing equality is a characteristic of an individualist culture.

20)

A. **Correct.** This would help Luis understand the norms for personal space in the United States.

B. Incorrect. This would not help Luis understand the issue. Furthermore, it would cause undue trouble for him in the school.

C. Incorrect. The honeymoon phase of acculturation is not related to the issue of personal space, so this would not help Luis understand the issue.

D. Incorrect. This is not relative to the issue of personal space.

21)

A. Incorrect. This would not help anyone understand the problem.

B. Incorrect. This would not help anyone understand the problem; it is also unfair to Miguel.

C. Incorrect. This might help the teacher understand Korean taboos, but it does not help students understand taboos in other cultures, nor does it allow the students to learn about each other's cultures.

D. **Correct.** This would help the whole class to better understand each other's taboos while also encouraging a multicultural classroom.

22)

A. Incorrect. This is the meaning of semantics.

B. **Correct.** This is the correct definition.

C. Incorrect. This is the meaning of linguistics.

D. Incorrect. This is not true.

23)

A. Incorrect. These answers are both characteristic of individualist cultures.

B. Incorrect. Valuing individual accomplishment is characteristic of individualist cultures.

C. **Correct.** Valuing group harmony is characteristic of collectivist cultures.

D. Incorrect. Valuing equality is characteristic of individualist cultures.

24)

A. Incorrect. While migration means movement **from** a place, it usually includes **larger**—not smaller—numbers of people, and it does not mean movement within a place, but rather **to** a place.

B. Incorrect. These prepositions do not fit since migration means movement **from**, not to, a place, usually including **larger**—not smaller—numbers of people; moreover immigration means movement **to,** not from, a place.

C. **Correct.** These are the correct prepositions in the correct order.

D. Incorrect. While migration does usually include **larger** numbers of people, it means movement **from**, not to, a place; furthermore immigration means movement **to**, not from, a place.

25)

A. Incorrect. This describes the first phase of acculturation.

B. Incorrect. This describes the second phase of acculturation.

C. **Correct.** Assimilation to a new culture means that a person has become a part of it rather than an outsider or someone who feels at odds with it.

D. Incorrect. This also describes the second phase of acculturation.

Professional Aspects

Read each question carefully, and then choose the best answer.

1

Which of the following is true about the Migrant Education Program (MEP)?

A. It currently has programs in every state.

B. It only serves students in California.

C. It only serves students in California and Florida.

D. It only serves students in California, Florida, and New York.

2

Funding for Title III programs in the No Child Left Behind Act (NCLB) is directly related to outcomes from which of the following court case(s)?

A. Lau v. Nichols

B. Castañeda v. Pickard

C. Keyes v. School District No. 1, Denver, Colorado

D. all of the above

3

ESL paraprofessionals may provide support to ESL teachers by doing which of the following?

A. interpreting for low-level ELLs

B. providing clerical assistance with recordkeeping

C. neither A nor B

D. both A and B

4

An ESL teacher, Mr. Li, and a science teacher, Ms. Huerta, are co-teaching a science lesson on the water cycle. They decide to divide the room into sections representing each stage of the cycle and have the students move through the sections to learn about the stages. What model of co-teaching are they utilizing?

A. parallel teaching

B. co-planning

C. natural order hypothesis

D. station teaching

5

ESL teachers at a school in Colorado have developed a diagnostic placement test for ESL students. After a few years of using it, they compare results and notice that most Central American students consistently miss one of the test items. It is a question featuring a photo of a man snow skiing that tests a low-level grammar skill. There are other test items with photos of people fishing and cooking that are not as problematic for students. What is the best explanation as to why most students miss the skiing question?

A. All of the entering students have poor grammar skills.

B. The image of a man snow-skiing is culture-bound and is one many students from Central America may not be familiar with.

C. The students do not like photos on tests.

D. The students are culturally predisposed to dislike snow skiing and do not want to answer the question.

6

In December 2015, a new version of the Elementary and Secondary Education Act (ESEA) was passed. What is it called?

A. NCLB, No Child Left Behind

B. ESSA, Every School Should Achieve

C. ESSA, the Every Student Succeeds Act

D. STEM, Science, Technology, Engineering, and Mathematics

7

The Equal Educational Opportunities Act (EEOA) of 1974, passed soon after Lau v. Nichols, included a provision that no state shall deny the access to equal education by

A. denying Hispanic students the same rights ascribed to desegregation as had only previously been given to African-American students.

B. not conducting evaluations to determine if the language barriers of students are being overcome.

C. failing to take appropriate action to overcome language barriers that impede equal participation by its students in its educational programs.

D. failing to provide adequate access to transportation in the form of school bus routes.

8

Which two of the following assignments would be considered project-based learning (PBL)?

A. reading a biography about Abraham Lincoln in history class and writing a book report about it with a class partner

B. in a history class, developing questions, conducting interviews, and compiling oral histories of local Vietnam veterans for a show to be aired on a local public radio station

C. working in groups in science class to create posters illustrating the human digestive tract

D. both A and B

9

A new eighth-grade student named Mona Suleiman is enrolling at Elm Street Middle School. School administrators immediately inform the ESL teacher that she will receive a new student. Mona does not speak much in any of her classes, but her first writing assignment reveals that she can write better than most of the students in her class. As it turns out, her family had moved from another state and are all native English speakers. What mistake did the school administrators make?

A. They should have issued a Home Language Survey for Mona's family to complete before assuming she should be enrolled in ESL classes.

B. They should have simply asked her if she needed ESL classes.

C. They should have enrolled her in regular classes, then tested her a few weeks later to determine whether she needed ESL.

D. They should have immediately given her an oral assessment by asking her questions about her home culture.

10

NCLB and ESSA are both versions of the_____
_____, which was originally signed into law in 1965.

A. AMAO

B. ESEA

C. ADA

D. MEP

11

The Sung family is enrolling their daughter Hae in the local elementary school. The family recently moved from Seoul, Korea, and both parents are working as medical doctors in the local hospital. Hae is well-prepared for school and has a strong foundation in Korean language skills. At the first parent-teacher meeting, Hae's parents are very quiet and seem uninterested in participating in Hae's education. The teacher is very confused by this and speaks to the ESL teacher about it. What is the most likely explanation?

A. The Sungs may not have much experience in an educational setting and are uncomfortable meeting with the teacher.

B. The Sungs come from a culture where teachers are held in high esteem, and they do not want to be disrespectful by asking questions.

C. The Sungs are not interested in Hae's classwork.

D. There could be a language barrier, so the teacher should get a bilingual interpreter to assist at the next meeting.

12

Which is the acronym for both a professional association and an umbrella term for ESOL teachers?

A. ESL

B. TESL

C. TEFL

D. TESOL

13

Which of the following would be appropriate to include in a bilingual parent toolkit for ELL parents?

A.   information about American school culture

B.   a map of the school campus with directions to the office

C.   information about expectations of parents and students

D.   all of the above

14

While ESL students are learning English, they also need to learn content information in science, social studies, math, and other subjects. If two teachers work together to determine language objectives, key vocabulary, and content objectives in a social studies lesson about France, this is known as what?

A.   co-planning

B.   AMAOs

C.   fossilization

D.   portfolio assessment

15

Sharon, a young ESL teacher, is beginning her first year of teaching ELLs at an elementary school. Which of the following would be the best web resource for her to find lesson plans and ideas for icebreakers for her first class?

A.   iteslj.org

B.   www.tesol.org

C.   www.cal.org

D.   www.nabe.org

16

With the implementation of the No Child Left Behind Act (NCLB), states were required to use Annual Measurable Achievement Objectives (AMAOs) and English Language Proficiency (ELP) assessments. Because many states did not already have these in place, a consortium of states was created to assist states in developing them. What was this organization called?

A.   TESOL

B.   CAL

C.   CALP

D.   WIDA

17

Why is it particularly important to stay abreast of the latest information in the ESOL field?

A.   ESOL research is especially lucrative.

B.   The ESOL field is very dynamic and new information is constantly being put forth in journals, online, at conferences, and so on.

C.   The legal arena surrounding ESL is ever-changing and teachers need to be aware of changing legal requirements.

D.   both B and C

18

At Oak Street High School, mainstream students have participated for years in a program volunteering with several different community organizations. Mrs. Fournier, the ESL teacher, would like to include her ELL students in the program and thinks that they could readily participate in an ongoing bilingual reading program for children at the local library. This kind of initiative is known as

A. a school-based enterprise.

B. lead and support.

C. community service.

D. group literacy assessment.

19

Which of the following is NOT a requirement of ELL programs as a result of the 1981 Castañeda v. Pickard case?

A. The program must be based on sound academic theory.

B. The program must have adequate resources and personnel to implement it.

C. The program must offer bilingual instruction for the first year of enrollment.

D. Evaluations must be conducted to determine if the language barriers of students are being overcome.

20

ESL teachers are often called upon to advocate for ELLs and their families outside of the school setting. In doing so, ESL teachers often have to act as cultural liaisons by doing what?

A. helping ELL families and established community members communicate and work with each other

B. interpreting

C. giving ELL families tickets to the local art museum

D. teaching art lessons to ELL families

ANSWER KEY

1)

A. **Correct.** The MEP currently serves migrant students in every state.

B. Incorrect. While it is true that there are many migrant workers in California, this answer is not complete.

C. Incorrect. Florida and California are both large agricultural states with high numbers of migrant workers, but they are not the only states that the MEP serves.

D. Incorrect. These are all states with high numbers of immigrants as well as migrants, but the MEP does not exclusively serve students in these states.

2)

A. Incorrect. Title III funding is not directly related to the Lau v. Nichols case.

B. **Correct.** NCLB required that any program receiving Title III funds implement the three requisites of ELL programs as decided in the Castañeda v. Pickard case.

C. Incorrect. The Keyes v. School District No. 1 case is not directly related to Title III funding.

D. Incorrect. Only B is true, so this answer choice is not correct.

3)

A. Incorrect. This is true, but choice B is also true, so this choice is incomplete.

B. Incorrect. While this is true, choice A is true as well, which makes this answer incomplete given the answer choices.

C. Incorrect. Interpreting and clerical assistance are both support activities that ESL paraprofessionals may provide, so this is not true.

D. **Correct.** ESL paraprofessionals may provide support by interpreting and assisting with clerical work, among other activities.

4)

A. Incorrect. Parallel teaching divides the class into ESL students and mainstream students with each teacher working with his/her group.

B. Incorrect. Co-planning is a method of collaborating in lesson planning, not a model of co-teaching.

C. Incorrect. The natural order hypothesis is a component of Krashen's Monitor Model and not a co-teaching model.

D. **Correct.** Station teaching involves students moving through various stations set up in the classroom with teachers circulating or staying in fixed stations.

5)

A. Incorrect. This is not likely as there is probably a range of grammar skills among incoming students.

B. **Correct.** Students may have the grammar knowledge that is being tested but may be unfamiliar with the vocabulary needed to describe skiing since they come from countries where they most likely have never seen snow.

C. Incorrect. This would mean all test items with photos should be problematic so this is not a likely explanation.

D. Incorrect. Being culturally predisposed to dislike skiing is a questionable assumption and not a likely explanation.

6)

A. Incorrect. NCLB was passed in 2001.

B. Incorrect. While this is the correct acronym, this is not the correct meaning.

C. Correct. This is the correct acronym and title.

D. Incorrect. STEM is a curriculum approach and not a version of the ESEA.

7)

A. Incorrect. This is related to the Keyes v. School District No. 1, Denver, Colorado case, not the EEOA.

B. Incorrect. Conducting evaluation to determine if the language barriers of students are being overcome was a provision of the Castañeda v. Pickard case.

C. Correct. This is an outcome of EEOA that is of particular note to the ESOL field.

D. Incorrect. Providing public transportation to school is not a provision of the EEOA.

8)

A. Incorrect. This project does not provide a complex real-world problem for students to solve.

B. Correct. This project typifies PBL by providing a real-world task that students must collaborate on over an extended period of time.

C. Incorrect. This project does not provide a complex long-term problem for students to solve.

D. Incorrect. Since choice A is not a PBL assignment, this answer cannot be correct.

9)

A. Correct. A Home Language Survey is an effective initial screening tool to determine whether a student may need ESL classes.

B. Incorrect. Asking a child directly about his or her needs is not an effective method of gaining accurate information.

C. Incorrect. This is not an effective way to gauge proficiency skills and could actually hinder a student who needs ESL and might lose valuable time participating in classes he or she might not understand.

D. Incorrect. Since many students may be uncomfortable speaking directly to adults, this would not be an effective way to learn about a student's English proficiency.

10)

A. Incorrect. An Annual Measurable Achievement Objective is a requirement of NCLB, but not a version of NCLB and ESSA.

B. Correct. No Child Left Behind and the Every Student Succeeds Act are both reauthorizations of the Elementary and Secondary Education Act.

C. Incorrect. No Child Left Behind and the Every Student Succeeds Act are not versions of the Americans with Disabilities Act.

D. Incorrect. The Migrant Education Program is currently active and is not a precursor to NCLB and ESSA.

11)

A. Incorrect. Since they are both doctors, they are highly educated, so this is not a likely explanation.

B. Correct. In a culture where teachers are held in high esteem, parents would not want to ask questions which could be seen as doubting the teacher's authority.

C. Incorrect. Since Hae is well-prepared for school, this is not a likely choice.

D.   Incorrect. Both parents are working as doctors at their local hospital, so it is unlikely that they do not speak English.

12)

A.   Incorrect. English as a Second Language refers to learning or teaching English in an English-speaking country.

B.   Incorrect. Teaching English as a Second Language refers to teaching English in an English-speaking country.

C.   Incorrect. Teaching English as a Foreign Language means teaching English in a non-English-speaking country.

D.   Correct. TESOL stands for Teachers of English to Speakers of Other Languages, a professional association, and Teaching English to Speakers of Other Languages, an umbrella term for TESL and TEFL.

13)

A.   Incorrect. This would be appropriate, but given the other choices is not the complete answer.

B.   Incorrect. A map would be useful, but since A and C would be as well, this choice is incomplete.

C.   Incorrect. This is true, but since A and B are as well, this answer choice is incomplete.

D.   Correct. Since all of the choices list items appropriate for a parent toolkit, this is the best answer.

14)

A.   Correct. Co-planning lessons is the first step in collaboration between content area and ESL teachers.

B.   Incorrect. AMAOs, or Annual Measurable Achievement Objectives, are performance goals identified

in assessment with NCLB, not a collaboration technique.

C.   Incorrect. Fossilization describes a stage of SLA.

D.   Incorrect. Lesson planning is not a form of assessment.

15)

A.   Correct. The TESL Journal would have a large archive of lesson plans and ideas from other teachers she could look through.

B.   Incorrect. The TESOL website has valuable information and support for teachers but is not a source for lesson plans.

C.   Incorrect. The Center for Applied Linguistics website provides information, research, and support about language learning but not lesson plans.

D.   Incorrect. The National Association for Bilingual Education website provides valuable information about advocacy and research but does not offer lesson plans.

16)

A.   Incorrect. Teachers of English for Speakers of Other Languages (TESOL) is an organization of English-teaching professionals, not a consortium of states.

B.   Incorrect. The Center for Applied Linguistics (CAL) is not a consortium of states.

C.   Incorrect. Cognitive Academic Language Proficiency (CALP) describes a range of academic language functions.

D.   Correct. WIDA was borne out of the need for states to implement AMAOs and ELP assessments according to NCLB.

17)

A. Incorrect. Most ESOL professionals would agree that the ESOL field is not a particularly lucrative one, though it can be very rewarding.

B. Incorrect. This is true, but so is answer C, making this choice incomplete.

C. Incorrect. While this is true, answer B is also true, so this is not the best choice.

D. Correct. Both B and C are true and provide good reasons for ESOL teachers to stay well-informed.

18)

A. Incorrect. A school-based enterprise is a for-profit venture, not a volunteer program.

B. Incorrect. Lead and support is a co-teaching model used by ESL and content teachers who share a classroom.

C. Correct. Structured volunteering in a local reading program to lend a hand to an organization in the community is a good example of community service.

D. Incorrect. There is nothing in the description that indicates that students will be participating in literacy assessment.

19)

A. Incorrect. Having programs based on sound academic theory is a requisite borne out of the Castañeda v. Pickard case.

B. Incorrect. Adequate resources and personnel are required as a result of the Castañeda v. Pickard case.

C. Correct. The Castañeda v. Pickard case actually de-mandates bilingual education requirements by leaving the teaching approach open.

D. Incorrect. Program evaluation was the third requirement to come out of the Castañeda v. Pickard case.

20)

A. Correct. Helping members of different cultures communicate is the role of a cultural liaison.

B. Incorrect. ESL teachers may or may not act as interpreters, so this is not the best choice.

C. Incorrect. While involving ELLs in local art organizations could be a good way to help bridge cultural gaps, this is not the sole purpose of a cultural liaison.

D. Incorrect. Teaching art lessons may be helpful but is not the definition of a cultural liaison.

CPSIA information can be obtained
at www.ICGtesting.com
Printed in the USA
LVOW09s0059050418
572394LV00006B/45/P